PORTUGUESE RULE
ON THE GOLD COAST
1469–1682

frontispiece: São Jorge da Mina
from Georg Braun, *Beschreibung und Contrafactur
der vornembster Stat der Welt* (1574), I

S. GEORGII *Oppidum* MINA *nuncupatum, quod Lusitania Regis iuſſu D. Joannis II. Anno ſalutis,* 1482. *in Genea ædificatum eſt, quo Mauri mercatores aurum infectum apportant, recipientes à Chriſtianis, rubrum, ac flauum, item lineum pannũ, & ſimiles ipſis gratas, conuenientesque merces.*

Trium Regum

S. Iacobi.

Pagus.

S. Georgÿ

Portuguese Rule

ON THE

Gold Coast

1469–1682

JOHN VOGT

ATHENS

The University of Georgia Press

Copyright © 1979 by the University of Georgia Press
Athens 30602

All rights reserved

Set in 11 on 13 point Caledonia type
Printed in the United States of America

Library of Congress Cataloging in Publication Data
Vogt, John.
  Portuguese rule on the Gold Coast, 1469–1682.
  Bibliography.
  Includes index.
    1. Ghana—History—Portuguese rule, 1469–1637.
2. Elmina, Ghana—History.   I. Title.
DT511.V64   966.7'01   77–18831
         ISBN 0–8203–0443–3

TO SHERYL

Contents

List of Source Abbreviations

AGS	Archivio General de Simancas
AHP	*Archivo histórico portuguez*
AHU	Archivo Histórico Ultramarino, Lisbon .
APF	Archivio della Sacra Congregazione di Propaganda Fide, Rome
AR	Algemeen Rijksarchief, the Hague
ASV	Archivio Segreto Vaticano, Rome
ATT-CC	Archivo Nacional de Tôrre do Tombo, Lisbon-Corpo cronológico
BAL	Biblioteca da Ajuda, Lisbon
BCGP	*Boletim cultural da Guiné portuguesa*
BM	British Museum, London
BNL	Biblioteca Nacional, Lisbon
BNM	Biblioteca Nacional, Madrid
BSGL	*Boletim da Sociedade de Geografia de Lisboa*
MMA	*Monumenta Missionaria Africana*
cx.	*caixa* (box)
m.	*maço* (bundle)

Preface

Research was begun on this history of Portuguese trade in Mina during 1964 in Lisbon on a Fulbright grant. Examination of the current literature in the field convinced me that an analysis of the Portuguese presence along the Gold Coast and the economic importance of the area would be a valuable contribution. The complete history of Portuguese Mina and the major trading station of São Jorge had yet to be written, although for more than half a century—between 1470 and 1520—Portuguese Mina provided the greatest source of gold specie in all of Europe's possessions overseas. It was the prime source of royal revenues for the Portuguese monarchs until the opening of eastern commerce in 1499 and figured significantly in the stabilization of Portugal's monetary system. Also, many of the greatest figures in the annals of Portuguese exploration and discovery—Duarte Pacheco Pereira, Fernão Lopes Correa, Bartolomeu Dias, Vasco da Gama, Diogo Cão, Nicolão Coelho, as well as Christopher Columbus—had direct association with the Mina trade. Cão protected Mina from European competitors in the 1470s; Pacheco Pereira, Dias, da Gama, Coelho, and Columbus, all were sea captains engaged in the provisioning of Portuguese stations there; and Lopes Correa served as Mina's governor for two terms. The fortress of São Jorge da Mina (1482–1637) was the first and foremost Portuguese establishment in all of the South Atlantic empire. John W. Blake, in his work *European Beginnings in West Africa* was one of the earliest scholars to recognize the importance of the trade of the Portuguese in Mina. However, as he noted (p. 104), the study of Mina had thus far been considered an auxiliary study, subordinate to that of the more notable Indian Ocean and Atlantic slave trade. Aside from a series of articles by Jorge Faro, Frazão de Vasconcelos, and António Brásio, there has been no serious effort to compile a complete documentation for the entire period of Portuguese activity in Mina

between 1469 and 1682. Also, heretofore only a small portion of
the available primary sources for Portuguese Mina have been
utilized. For example, the translations of John W. Blake in his
Europeans in West Africa, are important within the narrow chronological limits (1469–1560) he imposes. On the other hand, Blake
reproduces less than one percent of the extant documentation pertaining to Mina for this time period. More recently, Father
António Brásio's *Monumenta Missionaria Africana* has opened
new areas of ecclesiastical history for the Portuguese in Mina;
however, even this massive work gives but a fraction of the
primary sources of Mina history. The bulk of the documentation
remaining in archival collections today is scattered over two
continents with major holdings in the archives of Portugal, Spain,
and the Netherlands. Minor amounts of material may also be
obtained from searching through English, Italian, and American
collections. A further complication to the history of Portuguese
Mina has been the lack of a basic chronology for the area. Even the
most recent works of certain authors have persisted in relying
upon secondary sources for their documentation, and old errors
remain. For instance, the governor lists published by Furley and,
most recently, by Henige (cf. Bibliography) require major correc-
tions.

Unfortunately, even after six years of searching serious gaps
persist. For instance, there is almost a complete absence of primary sources for the period of the fifteenth century. Equally dis-
tressing is the lacuna of economic documentation for the period
from 1570 to 1600. It is therefore largely due to the nature of the
surviving Mina documentation that the present study places
emphasis upon both a typological and chronological approach to
Portuguese rule and trade in Mina. Generally, the study may be
divided into two broad time periods. The first section encompasses
the years from 1469 to about 1540, and includes the discovery,
settlement, and organization of Portugal's trading station of São
Jorge da Mina. In particular, there has been an attempt to empha-
size the vital central role which the post of São Jorge da Mina
played in effecting trade and Portuguese authority within the region of Mina. This first sixty-nine years coincides with the height
of the gold trade between Mina and Portugal. Mina treasure made

significant contributions to the overseas enterprises undertaken by the Portuguese crown elsewhere in the world. It was an age of royal monopoly over the Mina trade.

The second phase of Portuguese Mina's history commences about 1540 and is characterized by the open challenge to Portugal's monopoly by several foreign powers, including France, England, and Holland, in chronological sequence. A series of assaults upon the Portuguese Mina establishment created major economic dislocations in the pattern of trade along the coast. In addition, these attacks made serious inroads into the commercial activities of the Portuguese trade. Portuguese governors inaugurated new measures for defense such as the use of patrol galleys to impede interlopers. Portuguese land defenses were extended until at their height the Portuguese maintained four separate garrisons at fortress stations along Mina. In the end, however, the pressure of the Dutch was too great and the Portuguese posts, including São Jorge itself, succumbed. São Jorge fell into Dutch hands in 1637. Of the other three satellite stations, one was destroyed in the 1570s (at Accra); a provisioning station at Shama was abandoned in 1637; and the tiny redoubt of Axem did not finally surrender until 1642.

The present work is admittedly European and imperialist in its scope and organization. It was not my intent to attempt a complete account of the history and development of the structure of African society and life on the Gold Coast during the period under discussion. Rather the relationships between African and Portuguese are limited to the trading affiliations between these two groups and the various political and military alliances by which the competing European powers sought to counter one another's activities.

I want to express my appreciation for the generous assistance rendered me by the director and staff of the many archives which were visited in 1964–65 and again in 1971 and 1973. This list includes the British Museum and the Public Record Office in London; the Algemeen Rijksarchief at the Hague; the Vatican Library, Vatican Secret Archives, and the Congregazione di Propaganda Fide in Rome; the Biblioteca Nacional of Madrid and the Simancas Archives in Spain; and finally, the many fine facilities in Lisbon, including the National Archives of Torre do Tombo, Arquivo Histórico Ultramarino, Biblioteca Nacional, Biblioteca da Ajuda, and the Filmoteca Ultramarina. In the United States, the staffs of Harvard, Columbia, and Newberry libraries greatly facilitated my bibliographical research. A portion of the present study was funded by a subsidy from the American Philosophical Society, without whose aid much of the traveling to the various sources of my material would not have been possible. The editorial comments of Professor Zygmunt Gasiorowski, who spent long hours imparting valuable insights and criticisms, were of inestimable value in completing this work. It should scarcely be necessary to add that I remain solely responsible for any shortcomings in interpretation or style for this study.

PORTUGUESE RULE
ON THE GOLD COAST
1469–1682

1
Auri Sacra Fames:
The Long Search

Portugal's interest in the gold-producing regions of Guinea began long before permanent sea contacts with the lands below the Sahara were attained in the fifteenth century. Throughout recorded history there had been a golden thread linking the Iberian Peninsula through the western Maghrib with the sub-Saharan regions of Africa. Gold and slaves in varying proportions provided the main elements of the northern-bound trade from the Sudan.[1] During the fourteenth century Europeans had already begun to obtain scattered bits of information regarding the source of this wealth. An atlas drawn by Abraham Cresques in 1375 identifies a number of cities including Timbuktu, Taghazi, and Sijilmasa, on the caravan trail from the Sudan to the northern terminus at Ceuta. Not far from the latter town a pass in the Atlas range is drawn to indicate the route of Maghribine merchants penetrating to the Sahara and beyond. This design on the map bears the remark: "Through this place pass the merchants who travel to the land of the negroes of Guinea, which place they call the valley of the Dra'a."[2]

Evidence is more than adequate that strong commercial motivations led Portugal into African affairs. War and trade went hand in hand during the later medieval period. By 1415 Portugal had acquired a powerful, independent, commercial class. Growing mercantile interests in Lisbon cast their support behind the new Avis dynasty and John I could ill afford to neglect their welfare. The crown had to find a solution to the monetary ills of the nation, and the entry into Africa offered hope of securing a respite from chronic bullion shortages. Many Portuguese shippers and merchants desired to move from the Atlantic commodities trade to the promising venture in African slaves and gold. Aside from providing a base for further advances into Morocco, the operations against the prosperous Muslim entrepôt of Ceuta in 1415 secured for Portugal a terminus of the fabled Saharan gold trade.[3] Unfortunately, the hoped-for wealth to be obtained in Ceuta gold never materialized, as Muslim merchants shunned Ceuta after the Portuguese seizure of the city. Until Tangier and other ports in the western Maghrib were securely in Portuguese hands, the conquerors could not be complete masters of the trade coming from the south. Without this monopoly, posts like Ceuta constituted a serious drain upon the already extended Portuguese royal exchequer.

Yet there was not as complete a hiatus of information on this part of Africa as might be supposed. Christian geographical knowledge had advanced from the mythical representations given to Africa south of the Sahara in the late thirteenth century to relatively accurate data depicted in maps such as the work of Abraham Cresques cited previously. In addition, new Muslim sources had filtered into Christian Spain and Portugal. In 1355 Ibn Battuta, an inveterate Muslim traveler, related his adventures in Africa and elsewhere in a series of lectures delivered in Granada. In the mid-fourteenth century an anonymous Spanish Franciscan added a compendium of geographical lore entitled *Libro del conoscimiento* ("The Book of Knowledge").[4] Written in the format of a travelogue, the priest related his fantastic voyages throughout the world, including coastal stretches of west Africa. Despite occasional flights of fancy, scholars like Charles de la Roncière, Jimenez de la Espada, and Clements Markham all recognize that at the base of these stories lies an element of fact about the geography of all north Africa, the trans-Saharan trade routes, and the Guinea Gulf.[5] One might also note that among the supposed voyages of this Franciscan traveler there were two made by sea down the west African coast in search of the gold source, and another journey by land across the Sahara in a quest for the kingdom of Prester John.[6] These same two projects were to be undertaken little more than half a century later by Prince Henry.

Following Ceuta's fall, the Portuguese became engaged in three separate enterprises in Africa—the conquest of the coastal reaches of Morocco, begun at Ceuta; the settlement of the Atlantic islands; and the tentative exploration south along the west African coast beyond the current limits of investigation. By 1420, Prince Henry had contracted the services of the Mallorcan cartographer, Jaffuda Cresques.[7] Subsequent southern journeys cast new light on what lay beyond the fringe of the Maghrib controlled by the Muslims. In 1424, when Henry sent a flotilla of 2500 men and 120 ships to occupy the Canaries, the Portuguese found people in those islands who were not Muslims. This discovery strengthened the Christian prince's hope that Islam's southern limits did not extend far behind the Mediterranean and Atlantic coasts, perhaps only to the Atlas mountain chain.

At this time during the early fifteenth century, new ship designs were evolving to meet the requirements of this renewed interest in Atlantic-African coastal exploration and trade. The older *barca* used in Portugal's northern trade with Europe was a heavy cargo vessel difficult to handle on the shoal-bound coasts of west Africa. Mediterranean galleys with their combination of sails and oars were also unseaworthy for extended passages in open expanses of ocean. What was needed for African exploration was a vessel small enough to be handled easily for coastal sailing, yet one which would stand up under long periods at sea and which required only a minimal crew. While northern Europeans were experimenting with huge carracks of 600 to 1000 tons displacement, the Portuguese and Spanish were working at the other end of the scale to develop a vessel which met their own requirements. The caravel, a name which came to denote an entire class of ships, was the product of this Iberian experimentation. It was a small, lateen-rigged craft, not exceeding sixty to seventy tons and not much longer than seventy to eighty feet overall. Small caravels began to appear among Portuguese merchant squadrons of Prince Henry in the first three decades of the fifteenth century. Their rigging was convenient for normal coastal sailing and for easing in and out of shallow estuaries and rivers. Running before the northeast trades on longer passages south, one mast could be crossed with square sails and mizzen furled. Portuguese caravels quickly came to be considered the handiest and best vessels afloat. They could be worked by a small crew and were not weighted down with provisions.[8] Using this new caravel, Prince Henry commenced to explore systematically beyond the limits of known Africa. About this time, Portuguese ships began visiting the Azores which lay uninhabited and unclaimed a thousand miles west of Portugal, and by 1445 the colonization of these islands had begun.

In the summer of 1434 Prince Henry recommenced his exploration of the African coast and succeeded in rounding Cape Bojador. In 1435 the conqueror of Bojador, Gil Eanes, sailed south again, accompanied by an oared galley under the command of Afonso Gonçalves Baldaia. About eighty miles south of Bojador, the two vessels anchored in a small bay seemingly devoid of any signs of life. But here they soon discovered tracks in the sand indicating that camels and men had passed only a short time before. The bay in which Eanes and Baldaia had anchored was also a rich fishing ground. Thus fishing was to be the first economic benefit of significance for all the years of patient exploration by the Portuguese. This in itself seemed scant compensation for a decade and a half of exploration. Henry could not be expected to continue sending ships down the coast indefinitely. Yet now there was hope. Footprints meant that the region below the Muslim lands in the Maghrib was inhabited. On a subsequent expedition, Baldaia made a fleeting contact with Berber tribesmen of the Sahara about three hundred miles below Bojador in a large inlet which he judged to be the mouth of a great river. The name which he gave to his imagined river, *Rio do Ouro,* is perhaps indicative of what hopes must have been behind his continued exploration. Baldaia hoped that he had at last reached the fabled lands where spices and precious metals were as common as salt was in Portugal. He imagined that this bay could be the very River of Gold of which the Spanish Franciscan had spoken in the "Book of Knowledge" when the latter had written: "Know that from this Cape of Buyder [Bojador] to the river *Del Oro* there are 370 miles, all uninhabited land."[9] Since the late thirteenth century, Arab and Christian geographers alike had been careful to mark the "River of Gold" on their planispheres. Occasionally they accompanied the name with a description of the wealth to be had there. Modern geographers have sought to identify this legendary stream with the Senegal or perhaps the Niger. Both do, in fact, drain the goldbearing regions of the western Sudan. It had been at the mouth of this golden river that Hannibal, during his fabled journey in ancient times, had supposedly traded with gold-rich natives.

In fact, Baldaia's mission was still far short of attaining either the Senegal, the Niger, or the land of the Negroes. Almost a thousand miles of coastal exploration lay before the Portuguese. Yet the adventurers were heartened by the new discoveries. In 1441, after several years' pause in African explorations due to the unsuccessful Tangier campaign, Prince Henry resumed the southward dispatch of caravels. On the first expedition, two of his captains, Nuno Tristão and Antão Gonçalves, returned with the first captives. Henry learned that these Azenegues tribesmen were familiar with the caravan route of the western Sudan and the Saharan routes along the west coast. The following year another expedition, this time under Antão Gonçalves, returned to the "River of Gold" which Baldaia had named and ransomed two of the tribesmen taken captive earlier. For their freedom Gonçalves received a buckler, several ostrich eggs, and a small quantity of gold dust. Gold! This was the first any of the Portuguese African expeditions had seen and the tiny amount obtained by the 1442 expedition was but a temptation to search for more.

From 1443 until Henry's death in 1460 exploratory and trading expeditions to west Africa became more numerous with each passing year as gradually the geographic limits of knowledge were extended south. In 1444 one of Henry's captains passed Cape Verde and brought Portugal its first direct contacts with the Guinea Negro peoples. A decade later a journey as far south as the Gambia was commonplace. Still, the hoped-for wealth in gold had not been forthcoming, and the Portuguese temporarily had to content themselves with exploiting the rich fishing waters off the coast and with trading in slaves. Alvise da Cà da Mosto, a Venetian who traveled in two of the expeditions beyond Cape Verde in 1455 and 1456, related the volume of trade already established between Portugal and this area. He noted that a small trading station erected on the island of Arguim below Cape Blanco was supplying more than a thousand slaves per year to Portuguese vessels sent there for cargoes.[10] Cà da Mosto also described in detail the flourishing Saharan caravan trade in gold and salt between Taghaza and the Sudan. But as yet the Portuguese had been unable to tap this interior gold trade except in a peripheral manner from their coastal stations. Only an occasional caravan journeyed to the coast to obtain salt or other commodities and in return gave a small amount of gold to the Portuguese.

Shortly after Cà da Mosto's commentary was written Prince Henry died, and a pall of silence fell over the west African voyages. No more eyewitness accounts exist for several decades. It is clear, however, that explorations beyond Cape Verde were continuing apace. The rights of the prince to African trade had reverted to the Portuguese crown and to the supervision of Afonso V. Afonso, embroiled in the problem of his personal claim to the throne of Castile, chose to discontinue the systematic African explorations of his late uncle. Portuguese merchants now participated with the coastal trade as far as Sierra Leone and also with the project of colonizing the Cape Verde Islands as a base for this African trade. In 1461 or 1462, one small squadron did succeed in pushing slightly beyond Sierra Leone. One of Henry's captains who had already organized plans for a voyage before his prince died, sailed south and passed along what was becoming known as the Negro Coast *(costa dos negros)* to a point slightly south of Cape Mesurado.

During the early 1460s, other than the expedition described above, there were no more voyages of a purely exploratory nature. Instead of rendering a profit to the crown, west African expeditions had proven to be a serious financial liability. Prince Henry himself had gone heavily into debt attempting to subsidize his expeditions. Only with the financial assistance of his position as Grand Master of the Order of Christ had the prince been able to accomplish as much exploration as he had done. Money was to be made from fishing and slaving ventures along the known portions of the Saharan coast. But even here ship sailings in uncertain seas made these enterprises at best a serious gamble. The crown could not count on a consistent revenue flowing into the royal coffers at a time—during the 1460s and 1470s—when a steady income was sorely needed by Afonso V to finance his Moroccan and Castilian military campaigns.

To remedy the situation, in November 1469 the king responded to a petition from a wealthy Lisbon merchant, Fernão Gomes. Gomes, who had already become quite active in trading with this region, now sought to obtain a monopolistic contract to continue in the Guinea trade. Voyages by one of his captains, Pero da Cintra, had discovered the low-lying portion of the coast of present-day Liberia, which Portuguese seamen called the "Grain Coast." Here quantities of Guinea grains or "grains of paradise" (*Afromomium melegueta*) abounded; this commodity was found to be a cheap but satisfactory substitute for higher-priced Indian pepper shipped through the Levant. The contract which Afonso V granted Gomes in 1469 was a monopoly over the Guinea trade from Sierra Leone southward for a period of five years in return for a payment of 200,000 *réis* annually to the crown. In this way Afonso V assured himself of a steady income, and he was spared the expense of supporting expeditions for continuing the explorations. Gomes's contract further stipulated that the lessee would proceed with explorations by sending out vessels to chart a minimum of one hundred leagues of new coast annually. Gomes could trade only in the land of Guinea. The fort at Arguim, the trade in the Cape Verdes, and all other parts of the west African coast to the north were not included within the scope of this Guinea lease.[11]

In 1470 the new contractor sent his first expedition under the sea captain Soeiro da Costa, considered one of the most experienced navigators of the day. Costa's squadron advanced along the coast which had slowly begun to turn eastward, but they found no major landfalls. The Portuguese were now sailing along a portion of the Guinea coast designated as the "Ivory Coast" (*Costa do marfim*) after the abundance of that commodity which was acquired there in trade. The coastline consisted of a series of swamps and lagoons, with swift and dangerous eastward trending currents which impeded progress and often made landings impossible.

In January 1471 Gomes dispatched two more vessels to continue where Soeiro da Costa had stopped. Martim Fernandes and Alvaro Esteves, both expert pilots, directed their ships past the Ivory Coast and began to encounter a series of pronounced headlands, red cliffs, and bays farther east. In each of these inlets were small fishing villages eager to conduct trade with ivory, foodstuffs, and extraordinary quantities of gold. The Portuguese were astounded by the amounts of gold worn by these villagers and they reported that somewhere in the vicinity there must exist a mine of undreamed wealth. Surely it must surpass all the gold mines which the Portuguese knew in Europe. Both ships returned from their expedition and their commanders reported the news of their discoveries to Gomes. Word quickly reached Lisbon that the ships of Gomes finally had attained the fabled Gold Coast. Soon the region was being called *Mina,* which means simply "the Mine," in honor of the supposed source of this wealth. Portugal's adventure with the Mina coast had finally been born after more than a half century of searching.

Fernão Gomes reported to Afonso V that in the course of explorations, his sea captains had come upon a village of about eight hundred inhabitants on the Mina coast called *Shama.* There, huge quantities of the purest gold could be exchanged for cheap trade-goods of cloth and metal. This discovery immediately spurred Gomes to send new ships to investigate the area. These were not exploratory missions but regular trading expeditions to tap the new gold trade. Additional squadrons were sent beyond Mina during 1472 and 1473 to chart the African coast as far south as the Niger River.[12] Gomes's captains discovered and explored the Guinea Gulf islands of São Tomé and Príncipe and reported the new findings to their master. In 1472 the latter's contract had only two more years to run and Gomes speeded up the exploration of the Guinea Gulf in hopes profiting from any new discovery of riches. As Portuguese ships passed each new headland along the eastward-turning coast, they encountered numerous fishing villages and coastal settlements, all of which possessed gold. At the same time the toponomy of the Mina region was being carefully charted. An anonymous nautical chart of about 1471 demonstrates a detailed knowledge of the numerous important trading villages which the Portuguese frequented along the Mina coast in search of gold. To the east beyond Shama, which the chart calls *A Mina douro,* lay villages with names like *aldea de duas partes, cabo corso,* and *aldea de altro,* to cite only three examples.[13]

The Portuguese found that the Africans were eager to exchange their gold for more useful items such as brass, copper, and cloth. The blacks in the region possessed a high degree of skill in smithing techniques, but lacked metal ores which had to be imported from other adjoining areas. The Portuguese now offered brass bracelets, or *manilhas* as they were termed, in quantities unheard of by black merchants up to that time; also there were brass basins of all shapes and weights, along with pure brass ingots which could be melted down and recast. Cloth was another leading item in the trade. Animal skins and vegetable fibers with which to produce large quantities of cloth were seriously lacking. Some cotton cloth had been imported into the region from areas of the Sudan and from the kingdom of Benin to the east, but the quantities of these imports were very limited.[14] Thus the Portuguese found themselves in command of a ready market for all types of woolens, cotton, linen, carpets, and even secondhand clothing shipped from Lisbon. In a few years the Portuguese also learned that there was an almost inexhaustible market in Mina for north African cloth with wide stripes of red, green, blue, and white. African merchants ventured from far upcountry behind the Mina coast to traffic with Portuguese vessels.

The gold trade between Portugal and the Mina coast became an exceedingly lucrative venture for the lucky contractor Fernão Gomes. He successfully negotiated an extension of his lease until the end of 1474, but at that time the crown decided to reassert royal control over the conduct of the Mina gold trade; therefore in 1474 Afonso V refused to renew Gomes's contract. Gomes himself was compensated by an ennobling coat of arms which Afonso granted him depicting three heads of negro slaves with the inscription "Mina" below.[15] The former contractor became a member of the Royal Privy Council and the responsibility for the Mina trade now became a royal monopoly. The crown had watched as the trickle of gold coming from Mina in 1471 turned into a fortune three years later. By 1474 the royal share of the gold (one-fifth) provided a major source of revenue for the state which assisted measurably in restoring the depleted bullion supply of the nation. Because of the financial importance of the trade, Afonso placed the control of Mina under the immediate supervision of his son and heir, young Prince John, noting that such responsibility would be excellent training in administration for the young crown prince.[16]

Afonso's decision to exercise a firm royal monopoly over trade with Mina was not based solely upon economic considerations. In fact, he had gone counter to the wishes of the Lisbon merchant class, who desired that the trade be opened to all who wished to participate. Aside from the obvious economic advantage, Afonso V was motivated to resume control over the region by the growing competition both from Portuguese and foreign interlopers in the region of Mina. A real danger existed that royal authority over Mina might be supplanted by foreign domination. By 1475 the smoldering rivalry between Portugal and Castile had begun to spill overseas to include the coastal waters of northern and western Africa. On 12 December 1474 Henry IV of Castile died, and Isabella declared herself his rightful heir. The following year Afonso V put forth his own claims to the Castilian throne by invading the Spanish kingdom and marrying Juana, the surviving daughter of Henry IV. However, Portuguese forces suffered a serious setback inflicted by Isabella's army on the battlefield of Toro. Seeing his hopes for the Castilian throne waning, Afonso accepted what appeared to be a proffer of French military assistance and in 1476 he journeyed to France where he remained for almost a year. In Afonso's absence, the conduct of the war and affairs in Portugal and overseas were in the charge of Prince John.

Ferdinand and Isabella took advantage of the absence of the Portuguese monarch to step up their campaigns in the peninsula and to undertake new projects abroad. Partly because of the military struggle in Castile and equally because of the fame of the riches of Mina, the Catholic monarchs dispatched a series of Castilian fleets to Guinea waters with the intent of mercantile exploitation. The Spanish chronicler Alonso de Palencia mentions more than once in his accounts that the extraordinary profits of this African commerce had given a great prosperity to the enemy. More specifically, Palencia states that "the [Portuguese] crown was able to gather an invasion army to march into Castile in 1475 and pay for the soldiers with 600,000 *cruzados*, each equal to a Venetian florin."[17]

The Portuguese crown looked upon its trade with West Africa and Mina as a monopoly, and they based their priority there upon a bull from Pope Nicholas V in 1454 which recognized sole Portuguese rights to the region.[18] When the crown recovered its monopoly from Fernão Gomes in 1474, it immediately set to close the way to all interlopers. Largely through the efforts of Prince John, several new laws were issued prohibiting open trade in Mina. An ordinance dated 31 August 1474 prohibited foreigners from engaging in the trade and reasserted claims to the area as a royal monopoly. Anyone caught sailing to Mina without the necessary licenses would suffer the death penalty.[19]

Notwithstanding Portuguese prohibitions, the Castilian crown and Spanish merchants did not abandon their claims to the commerce of Mina. While the war of succession dragged on interminably in Castile, Isabella granted authorizations to Andalusian merchants to outfit trading expeditions to sail to "*their* Guinea lands." The increased revenues which had accrued to the Portuguese crown since Mina's discovery had quickly aroused the envy of Castile. The Spanish were well advised of the abundance of treasure to be had through trade along the Mina coast. Alonso de Palencia mentions that it was Ferdinand of Aragon who urged his spouse to authorize ships to engage in this traffic. Perhaps Ferdinand was looking beyond interloping to carving out a Spanish claim to Guinea.

In May 1475 Afonso V crossed the Spanish frontier and entered Castile, leaving Prince John behind in command of the kingdom. While the king was campaigning militarily for the Castilian throne, the Catholic monarchs activated a naval campaign against Portugal's overseas empire whence the Portuguese state drew so much of its economic strength. Young Prince John had to parry this new threat. Between 1475 and 1480 a series of expeditions and individual sailings left Spanish ports bound to trade for gold, slaves, ivory, and malagueta pepper along the Guinea coast. The active and open challenge to Portugal's claims to Mina as well as all of the Guinea coast had begun.

In the *Esmeraldo de situ orbis*, the Portuguese cosmographer and pilot Duarte Pacheco Pereira reports that one of the earliest non-Portuguese interloping expeditions was made to Mina in 1475. This interloper was a Flemish ship, but it carried a Spanish pilot. The vessel reached Mina and was able to take on a cargo of gold valued at between 5000 and 6000 *dobras*. Most of this gold was secured in trade with one particular village on the coast named the "Village of Two Parts" (*aldea de duas partes*), situated at the mouth of a small river and on the boundary between two large tribal territories. Pacheco Pereira reports that on the return voyage the interloping vessel shipwrecked on the Malagueta Coast to the west of Mina and all hands were lost. Little else is known of this early expedition, but documentation becomes more abundant for the following year when three well-organized Castilian fleets sailed to west Africa to trade in lands claimed by the Portuguese. Two small squadrons, altogether consisting of five ships, did not proceed beyond the region of Senegal. There several hundred Africans were taken captive and returned to Castile and sold.[20] A larger Castilian expedition of twenty-eight ships, under the command of Admiral Carlos de Valera, sailed into African waters in May 1476, in search of Portuguese shipping. Shortly before this, the same squadron had been gathered to defend Andalusian cities against a possible attack from Portuguese vessels which never materialized. When news reached Seville in the spring of the year that the Portuguese had stepped up their trade with Mina, Queen Isabella chose to utilize her fleet to defend Castile's renewed claims to the Mina region. More specifically, de Valera was ordered to attack a large Portuguese merchant fleet then operating along the Mina coast. Earlier in 1476 Prince John had dispatched the former contractor, Fernão Gomes, to Mina with twenty caravels under orders to secure as much of the gold along the coast as was available, to keep it from falling into Spanish hands. Meanwhile Lisbon mercantile interests continued to press the prince to permit trade with Mina under royal license. Furthermore, the treasury of the crown was being drained rapidly by Afonso's abortive Castilian venture. Although Fernão Gomes no longer held the exclusive right to the Mina trade, his experience clearly warranted John's choosing him to command the fleet.

De Valera departed from Spain in May of 1476 and intended to intercept Gomes and the Portuguese fleet as it returned laden with treasure. In the straits of Gibraltar the Spanish fell upon a Portuguese coastguard squadron, and three Portuguese vessels were captured in the ensuing fight. The Spanish admiral then proceeded to the Portuguese settlement of Santiago in the Cape Verde islands, where he sacked and burned the small settlement to the ground. The officer in command of the colony was not a Portuguese, but rather a Genoese named António de Noli who informed the Spanish that they had arrived too late. The Portuguese gold fleet had already passed Santiago on its way back to Portugal and had thus eluded the Spanish squadron. If the Spanish chronicler Alonso de Palencia may be accepted on this matter, it would appear that the Duke of Medina Sidonia and the Marquis of Cadiz had both been opposed to Isabella's sending the de Valera fleet. One or both of these men had secretly sent agents to Lisbon to warn John of the impending attack. John in turn dispatched a ship which reached Gomes in time for evasive action to be taken.[21] Gomes and his entire fleet reached Portugal safely. It is interesting to note that among the ships of this returning Portuguese squadron were two caravels belonging to the Marquis of Cadiz who participated in the Mina trade under special royal license from Prince John.

De Valera and the Spanish fleet never reached the region of Mina. Instead, following the sack of Santiago, they returned to Seville with António de Noli and other settlers taken captive in the raid. Once in Spain, these persons were imprisoned for violating claimed Spanish territory. However, Noli renounced his Portuguese grant of the captaincy of the island and swore fealty to Ferdinand. The king restored him to his position and ordered that no harm should befall him. Noli was a valuable addition to any Spanish voyage to Mina. He was a skilled merchant, navigator, cartographer, and, most importantly, he was intimately familiar with the Portuguese commercial techniques used in trading in Mina. His former post at Santiago in the Cape Verdes was a prime source for conch shells which were bartered very profitably in Mina.[22]

The first evidence of direct Spanish encroachment in Mina itself dates from April 1477, when Ferdinand of Aragon ordered a trading fleet made ready to sail to the Mina coast. On 6 February 1477, the Catholic monarchs gave the command of this flotilla to Juan Boscan and ordered the two outfitters of the squadron and the merchants traveling on board the ships to obey Boscan's directives. The Spanish rulers had learned much about the Mina trade in the few short years since 1475. The fleet's outfitters, Francisco Bonaguisa (who was a Florentine resident in Spain at the time) and Berenguel Graner of Barcelona, both carried detailed instructions on what stores were to be sent aboard the ships. At least a portion of the tradegoods included conch shells from the Cape Verdes and the Canaries. In May of 1478 the *senhor* of the Canaries, Diego de Herrera, was directed by royal letter to permit Bonaguisa and Graner to secure all the conch shells they needed to carry to Guinea. Aside from this item, the ships carried quantities of cloth, brass basins, *manilhas* or bracelets, glass beads, and a miscellany of other goods.[23]

The fleet of thirty-five ships which departed from several Andalusian ports in the summer of 1478 sailed to Mina without mishap and commenced to trade with several of the coastal villages. However, no sooner had the trading begun than they were surprised by a heavily armed coastguard patrol sent by the Portuguese crown. The Portuguese warships, commanded by Jorge Correia and Mem Palha, arrived on the coast shortly after the Spanish. Prince John had been well informed by his agents in Castile of Spanish preparations to sail to Mina. In 1478 he had assembled this squadron to counter the Spanish designs. The Spanish squadron was scattered and several vessels were taken captive. The Portuguese admirals returned to Portugal with their prizes in tow and arrived in Lisbon in late summer. In the interim, however, the situation in the peninsula had undergone a dramatic change. Peace negotiations between the warring powers were underway and an agreement was imminent.

While Prince John had been actively defending Portugal's African holdings, the war in Castile had reached a point where peace seemed a desirable recourse for both combatants. Afonso V had been thoroughly discredited by 1479 through defeats suffered at Castro Queimado and Toro. The military initiative had passed over to the Catholic monarchs; by early 1479 Portuguese forces had almost been driven from Castilian soil. On the other hand, the Catholic monarchs wished to end the war so they could continue with their policy of unifying the dissident elements within Spain itself. Portugal, or more specifically, Prince John, was motivated by two primary desires: (1) to preserve Portuguese territorial integrity; and equally important, (2) to restore crown authority over the lucrative Mina trade. In the four treaties signed at Alcáçovas in 1479, both Spanish and Portuguese desires were brought into accord with each other and peace was concluded. Among the major settlements, Afonso V renounced all pretensions to the Castilian throne and agreed to the marriage of his heir, John, to Isabella, the eldest daughter of the Catholic sovereigns. Overseas, Portugal confirmed Isabella in her de facto possession of the Canaries in return for Isabella's recognizing Portugal's claim over Madeira, Porto Santo, the Azores, Flores, the Cape Verdes, as well as the west African mainland below Cape Bojador. This included all of Guinea and Mina. Isabella and Ferdinand gave promises they would prohibit all of their subjects from participating in the Mina trade or in any other lands beyond Guinea yet to be discovered by the Portuguese in Africa.[24] In deference to the treaty, Prince John ordered that prisoners captured by the Mina squadron should be released.

Promises to the contrary notwithstanding, Spanish incursions into Mina did not cease. During the early months of 1480 Diogo Cão returned to Portugal with three captive Castilian vessels which he discovered on the Mina coast. The Spanish ships appeared to have constituted the final elements of a trading fleet dispatched by Isabella while peace negotiations at Alcáçovas were underway and the treaties were being signed. Among the prisoners taken captive by Cão was the Fleming Eustache de la Fosse. In a vivid account of the events surrounding his adventure in Mina, de la Fosse throws light upon the jealousy with which the Portuguese guarded their Mina prize. A week before Christmas, on 17 December 1479, the portion of the fleet in which de la Fosse was sailing reached the Mina region and anchored off the small village of Shama. Small craft were sent up and down the coast from this point in search of other trading settlements. This quiet trade by the Spanish was soon shattered by the arrival of the Portuguese coastguard squadron. In the early morning hours of 6 January 1480 the crews on board the Spanish ships were surprised by naval gunfire. Their encounter with the Portuguese and the subsequent activities of the squadron in Mina were captured in de la Fosse's narrative:

On Epiphany, which was a Wednesday, very early in the morning and in a drizzling rain, four Portuguese began to fire at my vessel. We were taken completely by surprise and very quickly were at their mercy. The day before, they had captured our companion ship and on the voyage out they had come upon a third ship which they brought along with them. Everything was lost. Because there were now so many prisoners, they put the crews and the poorer persons in one of the caravels, gave them water, biscuits, a sail, an anchor, and sent them by the grace of God to return to Spain. The Portuguese retained the more important of us to show to their king; and every day we had to assist them in selling our goods which they pillaged from us. We who were still prisoners were divided among the ships, four to one, six to the other. I was placed in the vessel of a kind gentleman by the name of Fernand de les Vaux [*sic*] who treated me with honor. But since he had orders to sail two hundred leagues farther on, I asked to be put on one of the vessels remaining at the Mine. This was granted and I was put on the ship of one Diogo Can [*sic*] who was a knave and consequently did not treat me as well. But I bore this patiently. This Diogo Can claimed my caravel as his prize, and as I have said before, I spent every day selling my tradegoods and each day rendering an account of them. [25]

When trading was concluded and all the goods had been sold, the Portuguese squadron returned to Portugal with gold and prisoners, and arrived in Lisbon in the early spring of 1480. Considering Afonso V's heavy military losses to Castile and the recent treaties of Alcáçovas, the king's response to this flagrant violation of the agreements was swift. Despite the Catholic monarchs' reaffirmation of Portugal's African claims in the treaty of Toledo signed on 6 March 1480, Afonso had little confidence in these pronouncements. He had word that mercantile interests in Seville, Moguer, and Palos were laying plans to intercept and capture the annual Portuguese trading fleet upon its return from Mina. [26] Exactly one month after Diogo Cão's triumphal return to Lisbon, Afonso V instructed all ship commanders that should they encounter interlopers in his Mina dominions, no prisoners were to be taken. Rather, all persons captured were ordered cast into the sea. There is no absolute evidence confirming the strict execution of this royal charge, although clandestine Castilian voyages continued over the next several years. De la Fosse and the other captives returned by Diogo Cão were interrogated, judged guilty, and condemned to death. However, de la Fosse himself and several companions were able to escape from prison through the complicity of a guard and fled to safety in Spain. [27]

On 4 May 1481 Afonso V publicly reaffirmed the authority over Guinea and Mina which he had granted to his son John seven years earlier. Both father and son had changed considerably in the period between 1474 and 1481. John now had a good deal of expertise in administering not only the affairs of Mina, but also heavy matters of state which had fallen into his charge during his father's long absences from Portugal. Afonso V was merely placing the reaffirmation of the Mina control upon his son as part of the process of relinquishing the entire throne. Having resolved to abdicate, the aging king summoned a meeting of the *cortês* at Evora to give its assent to this royal decision. Afonso never lived to see the convocation of the *cortês*. Sick and worn from a long, troublesome reign, he died on 28 August 1481. The assembled *cortês* found itself hailing a new king by right of birth and not by abdication of the old monarch.

John II faced a number of thorny issues at the onset of his reign. The peace with Castile had humiliated the Portuguese crown, and attempts had to be undertaken to remove Castilian influence from Portugal. The Duke of Bragança, who was the new king's brother-in-law, had to be reduced in his political power. Equally important, the continuing threat to Mina by Castilian interlopers had to be halted. Along with these three main issues, each of which was closely related to the others, could be added an immediate fourth problem—what to do about the planned English expedition to Mina. John II learned from secret agents in England that the Duke of Medina Sidonia was now actively enlisting English merchants for a major trading foray into the coastal regions of Mina. The Portuguese sovereign quickly employed all his diplomatic influence to curb the duke's projected plans by sending a special three-man mission, composed of Rui de Sousa, João de Elvas, and Fernão de Pina, to the English court to seek Edward IV's assistance in forestalling the expedition. After considerable discussion, Edward assented to John's request, and for the time being diplomacy rather than force of arms had sufficed to keep Englishmen out of Mina.[28]

No sooner was the English threat parried than John II learned of clandestine negotiations held between his brother-in-law, Fernando de Bragança, and Isabella of Castile. The duke had reached a secret accord with Castile, and the latter had pledged support to assist in unseating John from the throne. One of the clauses of this agreement stipulated that the duke should recognize the right of Castile freely to engage in the Guinea trade.[29] Objections to the

continued presence of interlopers on the Guinea coast were emanating from other sources in mid-1481. In November of that year
the Portuguese *cortês* recognized the importance of the Mina trade
to the economy of the nation when members of the third estate,
particularly the representatives from Lisbon, petitioned the king
to open the Mina trade to all Portuguese merchants under royal
license.

During the years in which young Prince John had directed African affairs under his father, the new monarch had become an enthusiastic imperialist with regard to Portugal's holdings in the Gulf
of Guinea. He and his father had both worked hard to reserve for
the crown the monopoly of importing gold, ivory, slaves, and
spices from Mina. Now, in 1481, John saw this new land slipping
from his grasp. Private, unlicensed trading by Portuguese vessels,
foreign interlopers, and generally ineffective defenses all seemed
to indicate that the gold of Mina was drifting from the royal coffers
into private hands. Drastic and immediate action was required if
the king were to hold his Mina monopoly.

2

Outpost in the Tropics

Shortly after his formal accession to the throne in the fall, John II raised the problem of Mina in a session of the royal council of state, and during this meeting the king broached the possibility of establishing a permanent Portuguese garrison on the Mina coast to replace the current irregular and costly coastguard patrols. Several conflicting opinions were put forth by the councillors.[1] One group felt that John should not commit the nation to a distant Mina fortress. Political issues at home demanded the first considerations of the new reign; moreover, such a venture was at best a chancy undertaking. Other council members argued that the post would be too far removed from Portugal for adequate maintenance. It was common knowledge that the high death rate among ships' crews who had already gone there in the trading reflected the unhealthy airs of the region. It was doubtful whether a permanent garrison could survive for long.

Despite the contrary opinion of some councillors, John II himself was convinced that such a fortress would be the most prudent course of action. One of those supporting him in this decision was Fernão Gomes, former contractor of Mina and now John's councillor. Gomes could well appreciate the king's desire to strengthen Mina defenses, for several years earlier the contractor's fleet had narrowly missed capture by a waiting Spanish squadron. To persist with ineffective policies of the past and dispatch only occasional coastguard patrols to Mina would invite continued interloping and a consequent reduction of the royal share of trade. A fortress at Mina would prevent unlicensed expeditions by foreign merchants as well as Portuguese privateers who sought to circumvent duties imposed by the Royal Guinea House in Lisbon. The erection of a permanent station on the Mina coast would allow for a regular turnover in trade and enable the crown to control the prices of merchandise being sold for gold. Consequently the fortress would allow the Portuguese to tap sources of gold removed from the coast which individual transient trading vessels could not do heretofore.

One of the major hindrances to the barter trade in Mina was the long period of waiting which the ships had to endure while gold and other commodities were being gathered for trading. The method by which all European merchants conducted trade was a time-consuming affair. When a ship anchored off one of the coastal villages, the first step was to secure the cooperation of the local tribal leader so that safe conduct was assured for merchants on both sides. Gifts of trade goods usually sufficed to obtain the chief's approval. Word of the Europeans' arrival then spread among the numerous interior settlements and merchants came to the coastal trading sites from as far away as five days' journey upcountry. Depending upon the merchandise traded and the number of coastal villages visited, a typical sojourn on the Mina coast varied between several weeks and several months. A permanent European station would permit a greater volume of trade by establishing permanent commercial contacts with the hinterland.

John II declared his intent to proceed immediately with the plans for a new post. To command the expedition, the king selected Diogo de Azambuja, an experienced soldier who had already served in Afonso V's African and Castilian campaigns. On 12 December 1481 a squadron of ten caravels, five hundred soldiers and sailors, one hundred skilled stonemasons, carpenters, and assorted workmen embarked for Mina. The captains assigned to the fleet included some of the most notable Portuguese seamen and pilots of the era. Aside from Azambuja himself, who was not a seaman but rather commanded the overall venture with the title of captain-general, the company also included Bartolomé Dias, who was shortly to achieve his fame at the tip of South Africa in 1487–88.

Careful preparations had been laid to ensure the expedition's success. Several weeks prior to departure, two transport ships from the squadron had sailed from Lisbon with orders to await the remainder of the fleet at a prearranged watering point on the African coast. These two vessels, accompanied by a small dispatch boat, were heavily laden and could pass the dangerous west African shore only by standing far out to sea. John II had ordered that many of the materials necessary for the speedy erection of the fort be included among the goods shipped in these transports. Their cargoes included ready-dressed stones for the foundation, gates, windows, and corner rafters of the walls and the tower, all of which had been shaped by Portuguese stonecutters before the departure. Each stone was carefully marked and stowed aboard. Timber for lintels, nails, bricks, tiles, tools, and a great quantity of compounded lime was ready to be disembarked at the site of the fortress.[2] The expedition was further strengthened with a papal dispensation which the Portuguese representative in Rome had secured. On 11 September 1481 the Roman Curia placed the seal of Sixtus IV on the brief *Propter tuam*. It conceded full indulgence for all those "who might perish in the castle of Mina, situated in the African parts."[3]

Prior to the squadron's arrival in 1482 the center of Portuguese trading activity at Mina had been the village of Shama, about forty miles east of Cape Threepoints. To tap the wealth of the surrounding district, the captains of Fernão Gomes had favored this site near the estuary of the Pra River, where African merchants were well supplied with gold transported downstream by canoe or overland from the forest regions. Thus there were trade advantages attendant upon this site. Yet Shama was ill-suited for a permanent European post. Fresh water was scarce there, and the River Pra was over a mile away. This situation would have left any fortress at that point dangerously exposed. An alternative would have been to erect the fort at the river's mouth. But here again, while a guarded water supply would have been secured, harbor facilities were minimal. The Pra was the largest stream on the Mina coast, but the entrance to it was choked with snags and shallows. No transport vessels could remain nearby beyond high tide without the risk of grounding. A further disadvantage was the absence of sufficient native stone in the area. While the Portuguese vessels carried a large amount of the material to be utilized in the erection of the post, the entire fortress was not prefabricated. Only those portions of the structure requiring special tooling and cutting had been brought from Portugal. The bulk of the masonry was to consist of locally-acquired stone.

Azambuja and the fleet sailed beyond Shama for nearly twenty-five miles. Either the captain-general's advance scouts had informed him of a more favorable site, or else previous expeditions trading in this area had noted the advantages of the land. In the late afternoon of 19 January 1482 the Portuguese squadron paused at the mouth of the tiny stream of the Benya and entered the narrow estuary formed by the affluent. The fleet rode at a safe anchorage throughout the night and preparations were made to disembark the following morning. Here Azambuja decided to construct São Jorge da Mina, Portugal's first permanent post in Mina.

An official party consisting of the captain-general, his ship captains, officers, and a guard of soldiers went ashore and sought to negotiate with the local ruler for permission to carry out their sovereign's directives. Coexistence with the villagers was desirable since it would facilitate the gold trade and also greatly simplify the problems of controlling that portion of the coast. However, peaceful negotiations were not absolutely essential to the expedition's success. The five hundred soldiers in the expedition were intended to force submission if African resistance to the erection of a fortress were encountered. For added safety, orders were issued that the landing party carry weapons concealed beneath their clothing so as not to antagonize the blacks. But Azambuja had every reason to expect a friendly reception. Since the first year of the Gomes lease, Portuguese trading vessels had put into the Benya to barter with the villagers for gold. When Azambuja arrived in January 1482, he found a Portuguese vessel already anchored there peacefully engaged in trade. The vessel's captain, João Fernando, had been to Mina several times, knew the African dialect, and was able to act as an interpreter for the official party. Fernando arranged a meeting between the village elders and the Portuguese for the morning of 20 January 1482.

Two Portuguese chroniclers, Ruy de Pina and João de Barros, among others, have left accounts of this famous meeting between Azambuja and his counterpart among the Fante chieftains, Caramansa. Pina never traveled to Mina, but in Lisbon he mingled at court with many of the participants in this expedition. Thus he was privy to the decisions made by the Royal Council when it was first decided to erect the fortress. On the other hand, although João de Barros did not complete his chronicle *Décadas da Asia* until 1552, he was even more closely associated with this African station than Pina. In 1528 Barros was appointed treasurer and factor of the Guinea House, the agency responsible for the supply of this post.[4] Taken together, Pina and Barros's accounts offer rare personal glimpses into the creation of the post known as São Jorge da Mina.

When Azambuja and his party came ashore on that January morning, they gathered around a solitary tree which grew on a rocky peninsula formed by the stream. On this site the Portuguese captain had chosen to erect the station. After Mass was said and the royal banner of John II had been raised on one of the tree's upper branches, the village chief, Caramansa, and his entourage approached the *capitão-mór* through double ranks of Portuguese soldiers. According to Barros, the act of exchanging courtesies was quite extensive. Barros relates how each side was arrayed in finery to impress the other:

He [Azambuja] was seated on a high chair dressed in a jerkin of brocade, with a golden collar of precious stones, and the other captains were all dressed in silk. With the men drawn up in ranks, a long and broad way was made, up which Caramansa who also wished to display his standing, came with many people in war-like manner, with a great hub-bub of kettledrums, trumpets, and other instruments, more deafening than pleasing to the ear. Their dress was their own flesh, anointed and very shining, which made their skins still blacker, a custom which they affected as an elegancy. Their privy parts only were covered with the skins of monkeys or woven palm leaves—the chiefs' with patterned cloth, which they had from our ships. All, in general, were armed after their manner, some with spears and bucklers, others with bows and quivers of arrows; and many, in place of helmets, wore monkey skins studded with the teeth of animals . . . noblemen wore rings and golden jewels on their heads and beards. Their king, Caramansa, came in their midst, his legs and arms covered with golden bracelets and rings, a collar round his neck, from which hung some small bells, and in his plaited beard golden bars, which weighed down its untrimmed hairs, so that instead of being twisted it was smooth.[5]

Following the greeting ceremony Diogo de Azambuja explained why he had come to Caramansa's land. The chief had served his sovereign John very well through the friendly conduct of trade with Portuguese ships which came there over the years. Therefore

King John now sent him, Azambuja, on a two-fold mission—to bring much rich merchandise to trade, and to request that Caramansa accept Christianity and receive baptism in the Holy Faith. But the captain-general also made it clear that in order to safeguard the tradegoods and to teach of the Christian God, it would be necessary for the Portuguese to build a strong house in which priests and merchants coming from over the seas could reside. Therefore, he sought Caramansa's permission to erect such a lodge. As a benefit to the chief for his concession to this request, Azambuja noted how trade would be drawn to this village. Caramansa would become leader of a rich and powerful people, and would also have the military power of the Portuguese in the post to support him.

The arguments put forth by Azambuja were designed to sway the chieftain by dangling before him the prospect of wealth and power through association with the European newcomers. Although the Fante chief replied quite cautiously to his foreign visitors, he finally gave his permission. Whether this relenting was due to further persuasion by Azambuja, as João de Barros would have us believe, is doubtful. Barros relates in his chronicle the reply of Caramansa on his doubts on the feasibility of a Portuguese post:

. . . considering the nature of so important a man as the captain [Azambuja], and also of the gallant people who accompanied him, he [Caramansa] perceived that men of such quality must always require things on a lavish scale; and, because the spirit of such a noble people would scarcely endure the poverty and simplicity of that savage land of Guinea, quarrels and passions might arise between them all; he asked them, therefore, to be pleased to depart, and to allow the ships to come in the future as they had in the past, so that there would always be peace and concord between them. Friends who met occasionally remained better friends than when they were neighbors, on account of the nature of the human heart. . . . To these words and doubts, which seemed to oppose the building of the fortress, Diogo de Azambuja answered. . . . He was neither a son nor a brother of the King, as Caramansa thought, but one of the least of the subjects, and so strictly bound to perform what he had been commanded with regard to peace and concord in the work of that house, that he would prefer to lose his life rather than to disobey. . . . Caramansa replied he would be pleased to permit him to build the house as he wished, warning him that peace and truth must be kept.[6]

Evidently, Caramansa looked forward to the prospect of a permanent foreign garrison there with grave misgivings. Nonetheless, the presence of such a powerful force, with rich presents, would indeed increase the patrimony of this tribe. It was Caramansa's bounden duty as chief to see that none of his people's land was alienated from the village and to hold the wealth of his subjects in trust for future generations yet unborn. What the Portuguese were asking for was not land, but only permission to build upon the tribe's territorial holdings. To have sought to purchase a site for a fortress would not have been possible because of the Africans' lack of a widespread concept of private property ownership. In addition, Caramansa surely recognized the thinly-veiled threat of force which was present at the meeting with the Portuguese. Therefore the chief relented and granted the Portuguese permission to remain there in peace and to build the house they desired; but the newcomers must keep the peace, or else harm would surely befall them. Caramansa purposefully reminded Azambuja that the village could, if necessary, be moved to another site should the relationship between European and African deteriorate.

The day following the formal conference, Portuguese masons and stonecutters began to prepare the foundation for the fortress. The site selected was on the narrow peninsula at the mouth of the Benya River. As the Benya flowed south and neared the ocean, it was diverted by a large outcropping of rock at the coast. The stream turned eastward and ran parallel to the ocean about 150 yards inland from the sea through a narrow valley before emptying into the Guinea Gulf. Thus it created an elongated flat peninsula at the end of which was a rock outcropping. When quarried, this rock could furnish the basic building material for the castle, as well as form a solid foundation for the structure to be built upon. Within the calm waters of the harbor, ships of 300 tons' burden could anchor conveniently near a wide beach upon which goods and supplies could be unloaded.[7] Smaller vessels could sail even farther upstream to a shallow lagoon at the northwestern side of the peninsula. There they could be careened and repaired safe from storm or attack.

The position of the planned fortress was excellent in terms of defense against attack both by land and sea. The river and bay protected it on two sides, while to the south the steady roll of the surf on shore rocks made landings at that point almost impossible. The site was vulnerable by land only from the west, and this approach would require a potential enemy to march over several hundred yards of open ground between the ocean and the tidal flats along a front only two hundred yards in width. Shortly after the fortress's erection, the Portuguese engineers made this approach more secure; they isolated the post from the rest of the peninsula by cutting a double ditch in the rock directly beneath the fortress walls. In the early seventeenth century a stone wall built across the peninsula west of the African town strengthened the landward defenses even further.

On the day the stonecutters set to work leveling a platform in the rock for the placement of the walls, trouble erupted between the villagers and the European workmen. Apparently the Africans were outraged by what they mistook as a violation of one of their deities or spirits which dwelled in the rock. The villagers regarded the great rock at the mouth of the Benya as one of their fetishes, believing it the potential dwelling place of a spirit or spirits. Nearby was a smaller rock among the breakwater which also was honored in an annual ceremony of feasting and worship. Furthermore, the promised gifts from the ships' stores had not been considered sufficient. There were several persons on both sides who suffered wounds in an exchange of fire. Azambuja succeeded in satisfying the Africans' complaints temporarily by giving them a number of additional gifts on the spot. The skirmish was over as quickly as it had begun. But the Portuguese commander recognized that a potentially volatile situation still persisted, and ordered that work on the fortress be hastened. No private quarters were to be built until the inner tower's walls stood at least one story high. Working feverishly, within twenty days Portuguese workmen, under the protective curtain of the soldiers in the fleet, were able to bring the castle's inner structure to the necessary height. The outer shell of the building was completed and it could stand alone as a refuge for the soldiers and workmen in case of sudden attack. Concurrent with the rapid erection of the castle's keep was the building of the circuit walls which projected outward from the central portion of the fortress along an east-west axis and served as the outer line of defense. This protective curtain wall was also brought to a height of fifteen to sixteen feet within several weeks.

Feeling that the garrison would be secure behind their fortifications, Azambuja ordered the extra soldiers and sailors back to Portugal. In this way, provisions could be conserved until a regularized supply system was inaugurated between São Jorge and Portugal. In the ships which returned to Lisbon in the spring of 1482, Azambuja also sent the gold which had been traded since January. The captain-general himself remained in São Jorge to oversee the completion of his assignment, along with the first permanent Portuguese garrison at Mina of sixty-three persons.

Most of the work achieved by Azambuja's workmen in the late fifteenth century has been obliterated by the vicissitudes of time and the many alterations effected by the Dutch and English at São Jorge da Mina after its loss by the Portuguese in 1637. But even before the departure of the Portuguese in the seventeenth century numerous changes had been wrought in the original fortifications of the fort to compensate for rapidly advancing siege and gunnery practices of the period.[8]

After leveling a platform on the rock outcropping close by the Village of Two Parts (Aldea de duas partes), Azambuja had his stonemasons sink a cistern for water catchment. Above this water supply the Portuguese erected a rectangular castle keep eighty-four by ninety feet in its outer dimensions. The dark, brownish-gray stone for this structure came from stone quarried at the site. Bricks and timber for the gates, windows, and lime to bind it all together had already been unloaded from the Portuguese transports at anchor in the harbor. Eventually these two ships were dismantled and their timbers utilized in the construction materials for the fortress. Designed as a two-storied structure, the keep contained a courtyard flanked by round towers projecting from the walls at the north and south corners respectively. To support the great weight of the cannon mounted in the south tower, the floors of these north and south corner rooms were filled solid with stone and rubble to a height of more than twenty feet. Guns at these points stood several feet above all other fortifications and formed a commanding position defending the land approaches to the castle. A similar solid-base battery was made in the north tower which overlooked the bay and watering site for the supply ships using the harbor. Any vessel seeking to enter the bay had to pass along the north wall and under the field of fire commanded by this battery.

A rectangular tower stood at the eastern corner of the castle keep. Unlike the other two round gun mounts, this tower did not project outward from the walls of the keep, nor was it designed to serve as an artillery platform. Instead the tower was built flush with the keep's outer wall and extended almost halfway across the main or eastern side of the structure. The rooms inside this structure served as part of the private quarters for ranking officials at the station. Furthermore, the tower's flat roof made an ideal lookout post.

At the eastern edge of the keep, the level rock platform was extended for another hundred feet toward the beach. This area formed the foundation for a great outer courtyard. Around this open space stood a thick curtain wall between sixteen and twenty feet high. Along its transit was located a number of small projecting towers from which gunners could defend the base of the wall from sappers. To provide a platform of fire for archers and gunners, should the need arise to defend the post from an infantry assault, a narrow catwalk was built around the edge of this curtain wall near the top. This walkway also ran around the keep and further added to the latter's defenses. At the corners of the outer wall farthest from the keep and adjacent to the open sea two three-quarter round towers served as batteries on which a half dozen heavy iron cannon from the transport ships were mounted. Massive low-lying batteries which the Portuguese built in this portion of the fortress in the early seventeenth century have obliterated all evidence of the earlier structures.

The keep and the outer courtyard with its thick curtain wall formed the heart of the early Portuguese defensive system for the fortress. The western side of the fort sloped down from the rock platform toward the beach where numerous sheds and workshops for repairs were situated. The beach area was also enclosed, though probably in the early decades of the Portuguese occupation only a mud wall or wooden palisade protected this portion of the peninsula from the land side. There was no military advantage to be gained in trying to hold the outer defenses since the fortress guns already commanded those areas.

A tiny chapel, dedicated to St. James (Santiago), apparently was the only European-style structure erected beyond the confines of the fortress. Located on the slope of a nearby hill several hundred yards north of the fort and on the other side of the Benya harbor, the chapel was constructed in 1503 on tribal land belonging to the Efutu nation. That year the paramount chief of the Efutu tribe accepted conversion and baptism. The chapel functioned intermittently until 1596, when tribal animosity caused the governor of the fortress, Dom Cristóvão de Melo, to order the building dismantled. At that time, the governor feared that such a building could be utilized by an enemy as the site for a gun battery which would dominate the main post. This did occur later, in August 1637, when the Dutch placed cannon on the hill and precipitated the surrender of São Jorge.

When Diogo de Azambuja had completed the major work of the keep and curtain wall for the fortress in 1482, he set his workmen to the task of providing a second main element in the defense plan. Portuguese stonemasons cut a ditch, or more properly, a double ditch to isolate the fortress from the mainland. An outer ditch forty-two feet deep was sunk into solid rock in a straight line from the river bank to the sea and parallel to the south wall of the fortress. A second, shorter, ditch was quarried between the first fosse and the base of the fortress walls and was separated from the first by a narrow rock ledge. The second ditch began at the southwest corner of the keep and continued along the foot of the walls of the fort and the courtyard until it terminated near the sea. The inner ditch served to heighten the defenses and make the wall at this point invulnerable to portable siege equipment of the late fifteenth century.

Further in keeping with the strongly fortified character of São Jorge da Mina, entry to the post was strictly controlled. A single gate from the landward side was located in the south curtain wall where the latter joined the south round tower of the inner keep. Just above this gate stood a guard platform and a small bronze cannon. Persons approaching the castle from the Fante Village of Two

Parts had to pass over the double-cut ditches by means of a narrow bridge and then they had to clear a small guarded vestibule at the entrance before they reached the main courtyard of the castle. For workmen there were ladders providing quick access to the river-side yard, but this was not the usual means for access to the for-tress. The only other means of ingress and egress was a small watergate, cut in the north curtain wall about 1510 and adjoining the riverside yard. Elevated above the beach and reached only via a ladder or a hoist, this door's main purpose was to facilitate taking merchandise and provisions into the castle from the landing beach where items were unloaded from supply caravels. It was extremely inconvenient to transport all the provisions and trade commodities by way of the ditch ledge and then through the main courtyard to the storage rooms in the inner keep. Thus the small access gate was designed to provide a convenient shortcut.

From any point of inspection, Diogo de Azambuja's work and his successors' improvements to the fortress of São Jorge da Mina were fitted into an interlocking plan. For instance, both the main gate and the watergate opened into the main courtyard which was en-closed by the curtain walls. At the western side of this yard the keep, designed as a self-contained unit, was the final redoubt for defense in the post. Access to the keep's small inner yard was not through the entrance facing the main courtyard, but by way of an L-shaped passage on the north side. To assure a supply of fresh water for the defenders, Azambuja had his stonemasons sink a cistern on the ground level of the inner patio and carefully con-struct drainage pipes from the sloping roof of the keep into this catchment. This admirable inner defensive setup was never tested by an enemy force, for no attacking force ever breached even the outer defenses. Nonetheless, it did serve a useful function by pro-tecting provisions and tradegoods from being pilfered by the garri-son soldiers. The castle keep was the official residence for the governor and his staff, and the lower floor was assigned as a storage area for trade merchandise.

At least one observer of the architectural elements present in the Portuguese post of São Jorge da Mina describes the entire structure as anachronistically medieval in concept and execution. W. J. Varley cites the comparison of the Portuguese post with the

English fortress of Sir John Falstaff at Caister in East Anglia. Construction on the latter was begun in 1432, half a century prior to Azambuja's fortress. Varley characterizes São Jorge as outdated militarily and either as indicative of the lag in Portuguese military architecture or else a concession to the site. Visual inspection of both castles' plans shows that there are only incidental structural similarities between São Jorge da Mina and Falstaff's bailey and keep at Caister. It is true, however, that Portuguese military architecture remained basically medieval in form and execution in its overseas possessions until well into the sixteenth century. As Carlos de Azevedo notes, it was not until the 1540s that the Portuguese began to adopt Italian "modern" schemes for fortifications.[9] Nonetheless, in terms of its multiple lines of defense and the fact that a determined European enemy would be considerably hampered from even approaching the castle, the design for São Jorge was fully adequate for the technology and siege techniques of the period in an area as remote from Europe as Mina. Many decades would pass before naval cannon were improved to the extent that they could successfully threaten the structural integrity of this post.

The garrison at São Jorge was provided with ample weapons for defense. Dotting the walls and towers were thirty cannon, including six large iron pieces capable of hurling a stone ball weighing fourteen kilograms for six hundred yards. These larger cannon were positioned to defend the sea approaches to São Jorge; the remaining two dozen artillery pieces were smaller caliber *falconetes*, each firing an iron ball of .91 kilograms and 7.5 centimeters diameter. The *falconetes* were all forged from bronze to resist corrosion which accompanied exposure in the tropics.[10]

São Jorge's magazine maintained a respectable inventory. In addition to hundreds of cannon shot, molds, and over a ton of powder (along with the raw materials with which to manufacture additional explosive), there were dozens of personal arms. The official entitled the "overseer of provision" *(almoxarife dos mantimentos)* for the fortress was required to have on hand at all times: 24 arcabuses (with serpentine locks and of a caliber of .60 to .80 inch) with their molds and bullet lead; 24 crossbows and their accessories; 100 suits of light armor fashioned from tanned leather; 600 lances; and 100 halberds. In case of attack, these weapons were to be issued to African allies of the Portuguese drawn from the neighboring village.[11]

The administration of Mina and the gold trade was divided into three main areas of operation: (1) a central agency in Portugal which provisioned the post and received the gold shipments from Africa; (2) a regular system of supply by ships sailing between the mother country and this African post; and (3) finally, the close regulation of the persons sent to serve at São Jorge as well as careful supervision of the activities of those garrison members while on duty in Mina.

The first element in the administrative chain of command which joined the king to his royal officials at São Jorge was in Lisbon. When John II instituted direct royal control over Mina in 1481, he placed the management of that region's trade in the hands of the Guinea and Mina House, a royal agency which was already experienced in African trade and its supervision. The Guinea House had only recently been moved to Lisbon from its former headquarters on the Algarve coast. Aside from administrative duties in directing the voluminous correspondence that passed between the Mina House and the post at São Jorge, the royal factor in Lisbon had to meet all incoming ships from Mina. This official also accompanied all treasure shipments arriving from Mina to the Royal Mint where he remained until the Mint's treasurer signed a receipt for the gold cargoes.[12] Similarly, the factor superintended the strict security surrounding the loading and shipment of provisions and trade merchandise to Mina and decided on departure dates for the supply caravels that plied the "Mina Route" (Carreira da Mina). The factor could even dispatch unscheduled supply ships if he deemed it essential to fostering trade.

Another important official in the Mina trade was the treasurer, or recebedor da Mina. This official received all merchandise bound for São Jorge da Mina as well as other feitorias in west Africa. Linen and other cloth came from suppliers in Flanders and Portugal; woolens came primarily from ports in the Maghrib; other commodities were furnished by private contractors working under license from the Mina House. These contractors were required to turn over all their goods to the Mina House to be hauled south in royal vessels. In addition to acquiring the merchandise for the

Mina trade, the *recebedor* aided the factor and the clerks of the house when loading goods for shipment to São Jorge as well as unloading returning caravels and weighing the gold sent from Mina. The *recebedor* also maintained an extensive inventory of goods in his Lisbon headquarters. At the height of the trade during Manuel I's reign, the Mina House's storerooms in Lisbon held tons of metal items, including basins of every sort, bracelets, and ingots of brass and copper. In addition, thousands of items of cloth of every sort were kept on hand so that shortages would not occur at the African trading post.[13]

The process of supplying Mina began about one month in advance of each caravel's departure from Lisbon. The Mina factor set a date for each sailing in advance so that persons who had contracted to supply goods to be shipped on the vessel would have sufficient time to bring these items to the Mina House. Orders were sent from the factor to the head of the Guinea and Mina warehouse (*Armazen da Guiné e Mina*) to secure a caravel and prepare it for the voyage. In addition, all foodstuffs and munitions used by the garrison at São Jorge were provided from the stores of this Lisbon warehouse.[14] If no royal ship was available, the *Armazen* could contract with privately owned vessels for their use. The *almoxarife* of the *Armazen* was usually a skilled captain in his own right and familiar with the requirements of ships bound for the *Carreira da Mina*. For instance, this office was once held by Bartolomé Dias after his momentous voyage around the tip of South Africa in 1487/88, and in the late 1480s and the 1490s, Dias made several voyages as the skipper of one of the supply caravels which provisioned São Jorge.[15] Dias's last voyage there was in 1497, when he accompanied Vasco da Gama's expedition as far as the Azores before turning for the Guinea Gulf.

On the day assigned for loading the caravel, the captain selected to make the voyage arrived at the offices of the Mina House early in the morning, accompanied by his personal clerk, the pilot, and members of the crew who were to assist with the packing and loading of the vessel. In the outer office, where a set of great scales were kept, the captain met with the clerks of the Mina House, and there tradegoods were counted out and handed over. During the 1480s and 1490s tradegoods were carried on board the caravels before being packed and tied into bundles. But in 1507 a new policy was initiated by the Mina factor, Estevão Vaz, who ordered that henceforth all goods were to be packed in the presence of one of the officials of the Mina House. Vaz entertained suspicions from various reports that mariners who carried loose cloth on board sometimes included contraband items in the shipments which they then used for conducting a private trade once in Mina. To end this suspected practice, Vaz ordered all packing operations completed within the Mina House.[16]

To avoid unnecessary confusion, a general list of provisions and clothing allotments permitted for each official sailing to Mina was carefully recorded in the guidelines of the Mina House. Experience gained on Mina sailings established that the foodstuff requirements per crew member were two sacks of biscuits, one *arroba* (about fourteen kilograms) of salted jerky, six liters of vinegar, and two liters of olive oil. These were the minimum provisions allotted to every member in the crew; the captain, pilot, and clerk were assigned slightly increased amounts as their station dictated. The reason behind such circumspection was the fear that any excess foodstuffs might be sold illicitly to Mina blacks who paid in gold for these items, especially for wine. All cloth going to São Jorge was also carefully noted, since this was one of the major trade commodities exchanged there with black merchants. Sale of personal clothing by crew members was permitted on a limited scale and all such transactions had to be made through the intermediary of the factor of the post. Direct bartering between the crews and Africans was strictly forbidden.

When all was in readiness for departure from Lisbon, a muster was made of the crew. The ship's keys were handed to the captain along with letters and dispatches addressed to the officials at São Jorge. The Mina officials then departed, and the caravel set sail. Two guards remained on board and accompanied the vessel while it was still in the Tejo to ensure that no boats came alongside with contraband cargo. They went ashore at Restelo, and the Mina-bound caravel went on its way.[17] Manuel I was greatly concerned by the problem of smuggling, and he required that changes be made in this current guard system. In the new *regimento* issued for the operation of the Guinea, Mina, and India Houses in 1508, the portion pertaining to the guarding of the Mina caravels was among the longest sections of this document. Later, in 1515, Manuel was still concerned with this problem and even suggested that the Mina factor and his entire staff might accompany each caravel until it cleared the river. Mina officials replied that they felt this measure would serve little purpose and it might even facilitate smuggling by delaying the ship beyond the time of the sailing on the tide.[18] Each captain carried specific instructions that he was to make no landfall or stop along the journey to São Jorge. Only the urgent need for repairs could be considered justification for interruption of the voyage. Normal passage from Portugal to the Portuguese post in Mina required about a month's sailing time, according to *Roteiros* of the *Carreira da Mina* which are still extant among archival collections.[19]

When a supply caravel arrived at São Jorge, similar stringent regulations governed the unloading of the vessel. No matter what the provenance of the arriving vessel, whether it was a provision ship from Lisbon or a slave vessel from the nearby island of São Tomé, the regulations were the same. Upon sailing into the harbor at São Jorge da Mina, the ship's commander made a sign to the governor of the fortress by hoisting a flag. If the arrival was effected after sunset, a signal gun was fired from the caravel. In such cases of night arrival, no launch was permitted to land until the following morning. When an answering signal flag was raised in the fortress, the captain and his clerk rowed ashore and presented the dispatches they carried as the first order of business. The captain and the commander of the fortress along with their respective attendants met the ship's officers on the beach. No one from among the ship's crew was permitted within the fortress walls until the loading and unloading was completed.

The officials meeting on the beach were protected from the tropic sun by a small covered shed or *ramada* which was set up near the water's edge. After briefly reading the contents of the dispatches, merchandise and provisions from the vessel were unloaded and brought to the *ramada* and inventoried. In most instances several days were spent unloading all the goods from a supply vessel. Therefore, the captain and clerk returned to the ship at the end of the day and locked the ship's launch in its mountings. Unloading resumed the following morning. In the case of a large *navio* of several hundred tons laden with supplies, upwards of two weeks were necessary to complete the transfer of goods to the beach.[20] During this time, the ship's captain kept a careful watch on board his vessel while it was in port, because it was not unusual for crew members with something of value to trade to light candles at the stern of the ship and secretly barter with Africans who rowed out to the vessel under cover of darkness. The commander of São Jorge similarly kept close watch on the villagers and along the beach to prevent illicit trade.[21]

When the transfer of the cargo to the beach had been completed and the gold shipment was in the hands of the ship captain, the latter was given a packet of dispatches from the officials at the post addressed to their superior in the Mina House and to the crown. The ship then departed on the return leg of its journey to Lisbon. According to the *regimento* drawn up for the Mina trade in 1509, the normal traffic between Lisbon and São Jorge da Mina was set at one ship per month.[22] Superficial accounts of the Mina trade seem to confirm this figure. For example, in 1500 the Cantino map carried the inscription with regard to Mina: ". . . each year twelve caravels carry gold . . . to Dom Manuel. . . ."[23] Two years later, in 1502, Vasco da Gama mentioned that twelve to fifteen ships sailed annually to São Jorge da Mina and back.[24] Notwithstanding these assertions and the *regimento* of 1509 itself, documentary evidence strongly suggests that traffic to and from Mina rarely adhered to such regularity. Both the number of Mina sailings as well as their schedules varied considerably from year to year. For example, in 1501 only six caravels were sent to Mina instead of the prescribed twelve ships.[25] The following year, 1502, was the earliest year in which the simultaneous departure of two or more Mina-bound supply caravels from Lisbon is known to have taken place. Again in 1510 a small flotilla simultaneously provisioned Mina. When regular serial listings of departures started in 1517, the pattern of irregular trade is clearly evident. Several factors explain this deviation from the accepted *regimento*. Whenever a new governor sailed for his post at Mina, it was customary for him to travel in the company of a small flotilla of ships which transported supplies and his new staff. Also, in addition to the small caravels, every few months until about 1530 a large supply transport would be sent to replenish the provisions at Mina. These vessels are not in the records of ship arrivals in Lisbon from Mina because they did not normally carry gold back to Portugal. Therefore the serial listings of arrivals cited by Magalhães from the records of the Casa da Moeda do not include such vessels.[26]

Another element which added to the complexity of the sailing schedule between Lisbon and Mina was climatic conditions. The optimal sailing season ran from September through April to avoid the heavy summer rains. By combining in small flotillas, advantage could be made of favorable winds for voyages to the latitudes of Mina. Also, several caravels sailing in the company of one another provided protection against French corsairs which infested the north Atlantic shipping lanes. It seems clear, therefore, that the adoption of multiple sailings in small squadrons for Mina from Portugal dated from the early years of Portuguese occupation of the region. For instance, in 1497, because of foreign seizures of Portuguese vessels, Bartolomeu Dias was ordered to sail part of the way on a supply run to Mina in the company of da Gama's fleet which was bound for the East.[27] Again in 1517 and in every year of the following decade, at least one pair of caravels sailed together from among the dozen or more annual supply ships sent to Mina. As the threat from privateering increased, maritime contacts between Lisbon and Mina grew more erratic. In 1534 only six vessels sailed for São Jorge da Mina. Four of these went together in the same squadron. In 1543 four or five large supply ships for that year all went in the same fleet. By the 1550s, the supply of São Jorge depended almost entirely on an annual fleet of large transport vessels. All five ships sent to Mina in 1552 sailed in the same squadron for protection from corsairs and again in 1561 all three of the supply ships sent that year went together.[28]

It was a hectic scene on the beach at São Jorge as the factor supervised the black slaves in unloading goods from these large fleets. Literally weeks were spent disembarking, sorting, counting, folding, and storing all the provisions and tradegoods sent by the Mina House. These periods of intense activity would in turn be followed by several months of keen trading with black merchants visiting the station. No more ships would come again from Portugal until the following year. After the reign of John II supply fleets occasionally were not sent to Mina for several years. During these lulls only slave ships carrying captives from São Tomé called at São Jorge.

A Mina caravel returning to Lisbon carried only rock ballast below decks. Aside from the crew, tackle, and unused provisions, the vessel's cargo consisted of two items—an assortment of damaged tradegoods sent back to the Mina House for crediting the accounts of the contractors who had supplied them, and more important, a single locked chest filled with gold kept by the captain in his private quarters. Gold was the major commodity secured by the Portuguese in the trade. Occasionally, small quantities of malagueta pepper and ivory were brought to the Portuguese post and traded by the blacks. However, gold was the only major commodity sent at regular intervals, and it far exceeded all other trade items in value. A single coffer of gold might contain the profits from months of trading at the post. Until the middle of the sixteenth century, the volume of gold carried by each returning caravel averaged 200 to 250 marks or between 46 and 57.5 kilograms of gold of a purity of 22⅛ carats. However, there were wide fluctuations between the recorded receipts of individual gold shipments. The smallest gold cargo from Mina was on 21 July 1521, when the caravel *Santa Maria de Ajuda* returned to Lisbon with only 71 marks, 7 ounces, 1 dram, and 36 grains of treasure. This was a striking contrast to the galleon *São João*, which reached Lisbon in late August 1543 with 753 marks, 5 ounces, 1 dram, and 56 grains.[29] The *São João* was part of a squadron of four ships which carried the former captain-general of São Jorge, Antonio de Miranda, back from his post. Altogether this squadron was transporting 1317 marks of gold, which represented the trade conducted over a nine month period in Mina.

There was no way of forecasting the arrival date of the Mina caravel(s) in Lisbon. When a treasure ship finally reached its anchorage opposite the Mina House and adjacent to the royal palace, the procedures which had accompanied its dispatch were then carried out in reverse. It was mandatory that the factor of the Mina House send a messenger to the official known as the Judge of Guinea and India. This royal official was empowered to ascertain that all regulations stipulated in the ship's sailing orders had been observed during the voyage. He accompanied the official boarding party which met each caravel and he questioned every member of the returning crew and took their depositions. If any infractions of the sailing orders were detected, the offending crew member was arrested and fined for his actions.

The factor, treasurer, and two guards (a different two from those who had overseen the loading) from the Mina House met with the ship's captain on board. No disembarkation was allowed until the judge's enquiries were completed. Sailors sometimes attempted to hide illegally acquired gold between the folds and lining of their clothing or in their personal chests. For example, in 1505 the pilot of a returning caravel was discovered smuggling gold back into Portugal and was promptly taken into custody.[30] Private smuggling remained a continual problem to the crown. While each crew member was interviewed and searched, the pair of guards conducted a search of the ship's chests.

Letters from São Jorge da Mina were turned over to the factor following the search. Normal correspondence from the post included status reports on the condition of the fortress, its garrison, stores, and tradegoods inventories. Likewise, the state of trade with black merchants was relayed to the Mina House, and frequently letters were addressed to the king himself on matters pertaining to the fortress. If any contraband had been discovered in the shipment while it was being unloaded at the *ramada* of São Jorge, the governor informed the Mina factor in Lisbon by a sealed dispatch so that the guilty parties could be taken into custody.

At the Royal Mint the chest's contents were signed over to the treasurer of that agency. The coffer was opened in a room of the mint where the master balances were kept and the dust was carefully weighed. If by chance the chest contained more gold than specified in the accompanying letter from the king's factor at São Jorge, the excess was included in the king's portion. If, on the other hand, a shortage was detected, then the captain of the ship had to make up the difference from his own salary. For it was he who had witnessed the weighing of the same gold at São Jorge when the chest was sealed for transporting. A receipt handed over by Mint officials noted the fineness of the gold received in each shipment. This assay was essential so that the factor of the Mina House could inform his counterparts at São Jorge of the quality of the gold being obtained in the trade, since there was no way in which an accurate assessment could be taken at the Mina station itself. As a rule, gold which merchants brought to trade at the Portuguese post was of a high quality and assayed at 22⅛ carats pure. Gold with a slightly higher assay (23 carats) was reported taken in trade with two particular areas of the Mina coast, at *Cabo das redes,* about sixty miles east of the station of São Jorge, and in the area around Cape Threepoints.[31]

Although the primary functions of the Mina House in Lisbon were devoted to the dispatch of caravels for São Jorge, the provisioning of the fortress, and the enforcement of the crown's security regulations regarding the trade, the Mina House served the African post in another important manner. The Lisbon agency supplied the remote station with a constantly replenished garrison. A royal *alvará* was prepared for each new appointment and the new official, whether he was the governor selected by the king or one of the common soldiers, had to register in the Lisbon Mina House.

In numerical terms the Portuguese crown maintained its position at Mina with a bare minimum of manpower. The São Jorge garrison consisted of three groups classified according to their function within the post. The highest rank consisted of administrative personnel who directed the relations of the post with the Mina House in Lisbon and who maintained contacts with black merchants and local African chiefs. Heading this group was the governor, assisted by a staff of ten men, each personally chosen to accompany him to Mina. Next within this administrative grouping came the factor of the post, his four assistants, and two clerks. The second major element in the garrison included a large maintenance staff which kept the fortress in good repair, saw to the physical needs of the garrison members, and defended the station. This group included the post surgeon, apothecary, overseer of provisions, smith, cooper, stonemasons, carpenters, and other lesser positions as well as an average of eighteen soldiers and gunners assigned to guard duty. Finally, the garrison included two to four priests who were responsible for ministering to the spiritual needs of the garrison and also for converting the black inhabitants of the neighboring settlement to Christianity.

All members of the São Jorge staff, no matter what their individual rank, had to be free men and native Portuguese to be eligible for appointment. Throughout São Jorge's history there is no evidence that convicted exiles (degredados) or native mulatos were ever permitted to serve in an official capacity at the station.[32] However, degredados were sent to São Jorge for galley service from the middle of the sixteenth century until 1637. These exiles served as rowers in the armed galleys which patrolled the coast against foreign privateers. All officials save for degredados received an alvará to their post signed by the king himself and each was sworn into his post in the Lisbon Mina House before departing for his overseas station. On his arrival at São Jorge, the new appointee presented his letter of authorization to the post commander and was registered in the post's ledgers. If by chance the office to which he was assigned was still being occupied by an official whose term had not yet expired, the new arrival had to await the expiration date before being inscribed in the post registry book and drawing his salary.[33]

Judging from the hundreds of petitions filed in the Mina House by persons seeking posts at São Jorge da Mina, it would appear that service at this outpost was considered a prime opportunity to acquire a modest fortune through private trading. In general the important administrative and fiscal offices were carefully regulated. On the other hand, lesser positions at the Mina post were used as a source of royal benefices which were handed out to court favorites and other petitioners. This practice became extremely prevalent after 1550, when the ordinary position of garrison soldier or morador was occasionally given as a dowry to the daughters of deceased crown administrators and captains. These letters of residence (alvarás de moradores) for São Jorge could be transferred by the owner to another person who would serve in the office; or the alvará might be sold. Considerable profit could be had from the sale of offices in São Jorge. For example, in 1552, Cristóvão de Melo, son-in-law to the factor of the India House and relative to the newly appointed captain-general of Mina, used his family connections to secure three positions of moradores at the post. He sold two of these residence licenses for 40,000 to 50,000 *réis* each and sent his manservant to fill the third post. With his servant went a considerable volume of tradegoods destined for illicit trade.[34] Charges and countercharges concerning similar abuses became frequent in post correspondence with the Lisbon Mina House. They increased in frequency particularly during the regency following John III's death in 1557.

Of all the appointees to São Jorge, the most significant was the governor. The governorship of São Jorge was considered to be one of the most important positions in the overseas empire during the early part of the sixteenth century. The authority of the commander of São Jorge was widespread and his duties were manifold. The earliest recorded *regimento* outlining the governor's authority dates from 1529 and the administration of Estevão da Gama. However, this document recognized that most of the procedural techniques and regulations surrounding the headship of São Jorge at that time were adaptations from earlier *regimentos* (now lost) dating back to the original 1482 expedition.

The Portuguese crown obviously felt that the command of São Jorge da Mina was the key to the successful operation of the station and the royal monopoly exercised there. Hence the selection of this official was reserved only for persons who enjoyed the complete trust of the monarch. The actions of the governor set the tone and determined the quality of Portuguese administration in Mina. Thus the commander was provided a high salary to discourage illicit trading on his own part. Unfortunately this policy did not always achieve the desired results. The most famous case of a governor's misuse of authority involved Manuel de Mesquita Perestrello, who assumed command of São Jorge when he arrived in 1562 aboard a supply ship and found the former commander dead. Perestrello remained at the fort for nearly a year before a regular replacement was sent.[35] During that time he divided his energies between composing a narrative of his former experiences on the galleon *São Bento*, sunk off the African coast in 1554, and illicit trading.[36] Other officials at São Jorge accused the new commander of putting his own friends in high offices and disposing of fortress goods to his own profit. Perestrello was supposed to have sold *manilhas* and wine directly to merchants from stockpiles of goods

in the Village of Two Parts. When the fort bailiff sought to inves-
tigate, Perestrello arrested him and condemned him to the galleys.
In 1563 judges from Lisbon took depositions against Perestrello at
São Jorge, arrested the commander, and sent him to stand trial in
Portugal. However, before he could be tried, the disgraced gov-
ernor escaped from prison and fled to Castile.[37]

No clear pattern is discernible in the appointments made to this
position through the end of John III's reign. For example, the
records of most governors of Mina show that they were drawn
both from military service as well as from lower offices in the royal
bureaucracy. However, contrary to accepted belief, São Jorge's
headship was neither a sinecure nor a reward for long years of
faithful service. For instance, one of the earlier commanders,
Diogo Lopes de Sequeira, was given the governorship in 1503
at the young age of thirty-seven.[38] Similarly, a predecessor of
Sequeira, Lopo Soares de Albergaria, was also a young man with
his career ahead of him when he became São Jorge's director in
1495.[39] For Soares de Albergaria, service in Mina was only the
beginning of an overseas administrative career. In 1514 he would
be appointed viceroy of India to succeed Afonso de Albuquerque.[40] According to extant records, the youngest man ever to serve
in the office of governor of Mina was Lopo de Sousa Coutinho,
who was but twenty-eight when he assumed his duties at São Jorge
in 1548.[41] On the other hand, men of advanced age were also
listed in the roster of Mina governors. This included such notables
as Duarte Pacheco Pereira (1519–22) and Rui de Melo (1551–56).
Both of these commanders had a lifetime of overseas service to the
Portuguese crown behind them when they found themselves head
of the Mina station.

In terms of social ranking, the crown selected its commanders of
São Jorge da Mina more from among the ranks of the lower nobility, i.e., fidalgos and escudeiros. Of the twenty-eight appointees to
the office up through John III's reign, only five came from among
the upper nobility, and each of these had already proven his capability as an able administrator. They were: Dom Fernando Pereira
(?–1493), Dom Martinho da Silva (1505–7?), Dom Afonso de Albuquerque (1522–24), Dom Manuel de Albuquerque (1536–39), and
Dom Martim de Castro (1546–48?). Only one governor, Fernão

Lopes Correa, enjoyed the distinction of being sent to Mina as its captain for two separate terms. In 1499, on the basis of his prior performance as steward of the king's private treasure, Manuel I elevated this young administrator to the command of São Jorge da Mina for three years. The king was pleased with his services there, for he dispatched him to São Jorge again as its governor in 1516 for another three years. [42]

In his relations with the other occupants of the fortress, the post commander exercised the role of virtual sovereign. Mina was far removed from Portugal and exemplary conduct on the part of this official was essential as a model for the men under his charge. The commander exercised plenary civil and criminal jurisdiction, including the power to impose the death penalty for serious breaches of conduct. Piecemeal records of São Jorge which were sent to Lisbon and have survived do not cite any instance where this latter action was taken except in the execution of foreign prisoners. The usual punishment for infractions among the garrison involved the commander's ordering that a portion of the offending member's salary be withheld as a fine. Since business acumen was not a prerequisite for the highest office at Mina, it is not so very strange that no merchants appear to have been appointed to that post.

The first duty of each new commander was to assemble the garrison in the great outer courtyard and to assume office by reading to the gathering the full *regimento* which he carried from Portugal. This plenary assembly was repeated at three-month intervals to make certain that officials in the post remained aware of their duties. An up-to-date copy of the fortress regulations was kept by the governor in his private quarters, and in case of a procedural or jurisdictional question, this document was produced and consulted. During each quarterly assembly, the commander also conducted an inspection of arms. Personal weapons and armor for each soldier and official had been issued at the royal armory in Lisbon and sent with appointees to São Jorge. The governor inspected the arms of each new arrival and ensured that everyone was prepared to defend the post in case of attack.

Only the clergy were exempt from military garrison duty within São Jorge. The remainder of the garrison, regardless of their rank or office (except for slaves), were expected to bear arms in defense of their post when necessary. During peacetime this was performed by the twelve to eighteen professional soldiers who formed the nucleus of post defenses. But in a major crisis, such as an open attack by a large black warrior force, this small group was totally inadequate. Therefore each person (excepting clergy) maintained as standard issue the following armament: a metal breastplate, shoulderpieces, a helmet, a lance or a sword, and a crossbow and its accessories. During the sixteenth century, the crossbow was supplemented as the primary weapon at São Jorge by the smoothbore musket. However, sixteenth-century firearms were primitive in design and highly prone to faulty ignition troubles. Because of the tropical climate, powder deteriorated rapidly in Mina. Therefore most Portuguese soldiers there preferred to use more reliable crossbows long after they had been replaced as the primary weapon of war in Europe.

If any part of a soldier's gear was missing or not serviceable at inspection, the commander of the post was empowered to impose stiff penalties. Fines could amount to as much as one-fifth of the offender's yearly salary. Aside from merely ensuring the possession of proper arms, the governor maintained the efficiency of his troops by sponsoring frequent shooting competitions. This was not only beneficial training and a welcome break from the deadly tedium of life at São Jorge, but it also served a useful function in the post's relations with the black population. These contests were held outside the walls of the fortress in nearby open clearings and were frequently attended by villagers. The Portuguese could thus demonstrate their military prowess in a none-too-subtle fashion to merchants and other African visitors.

Beneath the commander's supervision at Mina lay a tiny but varied garrison. Officialdom at São Jorge ranged downward from powerful economic appointees such as the factor of the post to lesser staff positions and finally to the common soldiers, servants, and black chattel laborers. Careful division of labor and the composition of the garrison in this outpost is reflected even in the first such group of sixty-three persons assigned to serve at the station during the command of Diogo de Azambuja between 1482 and 1484. The official size of the garrison as provided for in the *regimentos* remained almost constant over the next century. In 1529 an account of São Jorge's garrison included the following positions, with the respective annual salaries of each staff member:[43]

1	captain-general or governor	800,000 *réis*
10	personal staff of the captain-general, each of whom received 20,000 *réis*	200,000 "
1	vicar	50,000 "
3	chaplains: 1 royal chaplain @ 40,000 and 2 regular chaplains @ 30,000	100,000 "
1	factor	150,000 "
4	personal assistants to factor @ 12,500	50,000 "
2	clerks @ 70,000	140,000 "
1	overseer of provisions	40,000 "
1	physician	70,000 "
1	barber	30,000 "
1	apothecary	20,000 "
1	tender of infirmary	20,000 "
1	overseer of post oven	30,000 "
13	*moradores* or soldiers @ 30–40,000, depending upon rank	390,000– 420,000 "
2	master gunners @ 20,000	40,000 "
1	blacksmith	20,000 "
1	cooper	20,000 "
2	master stonemasons @ 20,000	40,000 "
2	carpenters: 1 shipwright & sailmaker, the other for construction within the post, @ 20,000	40,000 "
1	gatekeeper	40,000 "
1	tailor-mender	20,000 "
4	women to serve in post kitchen & infirmary @ 12,500	50,000 "
55		2,360,000– 2,388,000 *réis*

In addition to the salaried staff listed above, the *regimento* of the post provided for at least sixteen slaves to be kept for duty within the fortress. These captives, brought regularly to São Jorge by slave ships from São Tomé, were under the safekeeping of the post factor and were used as porters and manual laborers. In all, ten males and six female slaves were assigned to assist in construction, repairs, loading and unloading the supply ship's cargoes; female slaves were assigned in a ratio of one slave for each three residents to perform light household duties for the soldiers.[44] Since there was no communal kitchen, these women kept quarters clean and cooked for their owners. An oven operated by Portuguese women provided a daily ration of coarse baked bread for each staff member.

This official list of offices at both São Jorge and Axem continued virtually unchanged throughout the period of Portuguese occupation, well into the seventeenth century. A manuscript dated 1607 in the Biblioteca da Ajuda almost duplicates the earlier list of 1529 regarding the offices at São Jorge da Mina. It shows the garrison numbered about seventy salaried staff and soldiers. At that time, two extra stonemasons were busy strengthening the fortress, four additional gunners manned the batteries, and two extra carpenters were among the minor changes which had been made in the garrison personnel.[45] About a dozen men comprised the garrison at Axem, a small fortified station established just east of Cape Three-points. In addition, there were crews for two coastal armed galleys, each with about thirty-five men. The majority of the latter, however, were drawn from captured interlopers and prisoners or *degredados* condemned to this service.

Despite the seemingly static nature of the positions provided for in Mina, São Jorge at times fell seriously undermanned. Epidemics occasionally swept through the cramped fortress and killed many of its inhabitants. For instance, in July 1499 when Fernão Lopes Correa reached Mina and assumed command of São Jorge, only thirty-two men remained alive to muster for the official reading of the new captain's *regimento*.[46] Lopes Correa arrived just following the rainy season when the greatest number of deaths occurred from malaria and related tropical diseases. Fortunately, reinforcements had come with Correa and the garrison was returned to a respectable size of forty to fifty persons. Eleven years later, in 1510, Manuel de Goios, governor of the station then, reported that he had fifty-five persons under his command. This figure did not include the twenty-eight slaves in the station at that time nor did it count the captain and crew of a small supply caravel which was permanently stationed at São Jorge and used for communication between the main fort and the outlying station.[47]

The Mina *regimento* stipulated that the normal term of office for all officials was to be from two to three years. *Capitães-mores* usually carried a three-year appointment, while the other staff went to Mina for about two years each. In 1541, orders were drawn which forbade anyone from serving in the Mina garrison for a second term without the crown's expressed consent.[48] Such limitation of service to a single term was intended to prevent persons with experience in the mechanics of the Mina trade from using their second terms to conduct illicit trading. In practical application, however, it became increasingly impossible to enforce such a requirement. When a replacement did not arrive upon the termination of an official's tour of duty, that person then in office had to remain at his post until a successor eventually was sent. This sometimes took years, particularly after about 1560. Extended tours were never a problem during the reigns of John II, Manuel I, or even John III. Aside from terms cut short by death, commanders of São Jorge served for periods ranging from about one year (Alvaro Pestana, 1485–86), to a maximum of five years in the case of Rui de Melo (1551–56).[49] Similar terms were served by the factors and other Mina officials. In sharp contrast to this, from the end of John III's reign onward, the tours of service for almost all officials assigned to Mina lengthened significantly. Provisioning the station and replacement of personnel became more and more erratic as the sixteenth century came to a close. For example, commander João Roiz Coutinho remained at São Jorge for eight years (1586–94) before his replacement finally arrived. Coutinho's successor, Dom Cristóvão de Melo, was in command of Mina for twelve years. Melo's letters imploring the king to send a replacement for him went unanswered until 1608, when Duarte de Lima arrived.

One of the factors severely limiting the garrison's size was housing. In keeping with his position of preeminence within São Jorge da Mina, the commander enjoyed the most spacious and comfortable portion of the fortress as his private quarters. Most of the second story of the fortress keep was reserved for his accommodation and the housing of the staff which accompanied him. The governor's personal attendants consisted of ten people, or nearly one-fifth of the entire garrison. Two of this number could be slaves for whom the governor received a regular salary. The remaining eight attendants included servants, friends, and an occasional relative who came with the official from Portugal. It became the custom for the king to issue a letter to each new commander assigning him full privileges to appoint up to ten *moradores*. In general, the new commander was free to select whomever he wished, so long as they were free men and not suspected of heresy. For each of these persons the head of the post received a stipend of 20,000 *réis* per year. From this amount he was free to pay each of his staff at his pleasure or according to a private arrangement between the two men. Usually, each commander's staff included a personal cook who prepared meals for the officers' mess. A private kitchen, complete with fireplace and oven, was located in the fortress keep on the second floor on the western side. To supplement the normal fare of wine and bread, the governor was permitted to bring with him a number of breeding stock, including two sows, a boar, and six lambs. This stock was kept penned in the fortress and it was forbidden to sell or trade them or to use them in any way other than for the governor's personal table. In practice, however, the giving of an occasional lamb as a gift to a visiting merchant became a favorite way to foster trade and commerce, and by the middle of the sixteenth century, these animals were being bred in the Village of Two Parts and elsewhere along the coast. Governor António de Miranda (1540–43) even brought his favorite horse with him; however, there is no record whether other commanders of São Jorge did likewise.

Since the lower echelons of officials and soldiers in the garrison did not dine at the governor's table, other facilities had to be provided. There was no general mess. The only thing shared in common by the entire garrison for food preparation was a communal oven. A *vedor do forno* or superintendent was assigned from the garrison to ensure that the daily ration of bread for each member of the garrison was available when needed. Each person, regardless of rank, received a daily allotment of four loaves of dark, coarse bread made from Portuguese wheat or from millet purchased locally from black farmers. This figure of four loaves represented the product of one-tenth of an *alqueire* (about fourteen liters dry measure) of flour.[50] Two liters of wine were also portioned out daily for all personnel, no matter what their rank. Each month every member received a *canada*, or approximately two liters each, of olive oil and honey, and two *canadas* of vinegar. Each garrison member could and frequently did supplement his minimum rations with fresh fruits and vegetables purchased from the village, as well as chickens and other fowl which could be purchased in the local market.

Of all the officials, the only one enjoying privileges and accommodations similar to those of the governor was the factor of São Jorge. Like his superior, the factor enjoyed private quarters above the ground level of the castle keep and away from the damp rooms assigned to the remainder of the garrison around the walls of the outer courtyard. The factor's quarters were smaller than those of the governor and were situated in the north tower of the inner keep. His staff was also smaller than the one assigned to the governor. The factor was permitted four assistants; for each of these, he received a stipend of 12,500 *réis*.

For the remainder of the garrison, both soldiers and minor officials alike, quarters were quite spartan at best and dismal at worst. For the most part the maintenance and defense personnel were housed in cramped, poorly ventilated rooms adjoining the north and south walls of the outer courtyard. Water percolated upward through the rocky foundation, and the tiled roofs of the rooms afforded only minimal shelter from the downpour that occurred almost daily during the wet season. Considering the scanty daily rations, poor nutrition, and the lack of decent living accommodations for much of the garrison, it was only natural that illness pervaded the daily life of the post. Doubts had been voiced during the royal council meeting with John II in 1481 regarding the salubrity of the region of Mina for permanent garrisons. Even before the fortress of São Jorge had been erected, trading ships suffered high casualty rates from malaria. Life was difficult for the Portuguese garrison soldier or official assigned to Mina. Poor diet led to a general debilitation of many officers. The majority of deaths occurred during the first several months before the new Portuguese arrival could develop a natural immunity to local conditions. Compared with the climate of their native Portugal, the climate in Mina was oppressively hot and humid. Daytime temperature remained in the mid eighties year-round, with only minor variations. Even though São Jorge was usually free from the scourge of mosquitoes, land breezes did occasionally carry them into the fortress. Over a century and a half, many hundred whites died at their post in São Jorge. Scattered reports mention as many as four deaths in less than sixty days, and such occurrences were not considered abnormal. The rainy season from late April to early August was the most unhealthy time on the coast, when torrential downpours, clouds of vapor mists, and cool nights combined to produce sickness among the Europeans. In 1513 one of the officials commenting on the general question of living conditions at Mina remarked that "whoever seeks to serve here ought to be old in wisdom and young in body if he expects to survive."[51]

To meet the heavy medical demands of the post, a well-stocked infirmary in the courtyard adjoined the north curtain wall, staffed by two to three Portuguese female nurses, a male attendant, a physician, a barber-bloodletter, and an apothecary. In fact, one-tenth of the garrison was assigned to this infirmary and its maintenance. A varied medical chest of remedies and herbs was kept to treat those admitted. The regulations in effect in the fortress stipulated that all sick personnel were to be given every care possible to speed their recovery, even to the extent that bread prepared from fine white flour was ordered to be given to all patients. Furthermore, the governor was charged with visiting this facility at regular intervals to ensure that it was being operated properly. The tiny garrison could not afford to lose too many sick or dying members. Almost every man was needed for military duty, both to man the walls and to conduct occasional forays outside the confines of the fortress against interlopers or recalcitrant blacks.

Rounding out the garrison's composition were the ecclesiastical officials residing there. John II was mindful of the spiritual needs of the tiny Mina station when he appointed two clerics to remain at Mina with Diogo de Azambuja to minister to the needs of the other personnel. Like the rest of the garrison, however, their position was not permanent. Each priest served for a specific term of office, usually three years. The service of a priest would occasionally be extended, but they were never permitted to remain at the station permanently. For two decades only two priests at a time were assigned to São Jorge. In 1503, because of increased mission-ary activity conducted among adjoining tribes, an additional priest was assigned to the staff, and in 1520 the number of ecclesiastics rose again to four and stayed at this figure throughout the remain-der of the century.

For nearly a century, until the reign of Sebastian, clerics were selected to serve at São Jorge da Mina from the ranks of the Portu-guese Order of Christ. This order exercised spiritual jurisdiction over all African holdings of the crown by virtue of papal grants issued in 1445 and 1455.[52] Shortly before his death in 1460 Prince Henry, administrator of the Order, transferred spiritual authority to the crown. Appointments of the necessary clergy for São Jorge were made by the chapter-house at Tomar and bore the approval of one of the crown princes who held the administratorship. When the bishopric of Funchal was created in 1514, the São Jorge clergy were included within the jurisdiction of this new see, and before proceeding to the Mina station, each new priest first had to travel to Madeira and present his letter of appointment to his bishop for approval.[53] This scheme proved extremely cumbersome from a logistical point of view, since supply caravels on the *Carreira da Mina* were not authorized to detour from their assigned route to lay over in Madeira. Nonetheless, the sovereignty of the prelate of Funchal continued until 1534, when, after long negotiations with the Holy See, the Portuguese crown secured the erection of a new bishopric located on the island of São Tomé. Mainland areas east of Cape Threepoints all the way to the Cape of Good Hope were put under the charge of the new bishop of São Tomé. Simulta-neously, Funchal was elevated to archepiscopal status.[54]

At São Jorge, the spiritual duties of the clergy encompassed two primary tasks. As members of the Order of Christ, the priests administered the rights and obligations which this Order had undertaken in return for exclusive grants to all African and over-seas churches, i.e., to look after the religious needs of the mem-bers of the garrison. Next there was a broad obligation assigned these clergy as missionaries *ad propagandam fidem* among hea-then Mina blacks.

Regarding the clergy's function as members of the Order of Christ, João de Barros reports that from 1482 onward there was at least one priest assigned to perform a daily mass in the church there in compliance with Prince Henry's will.[55] The chaplain salaried in the name of the deceased navigator prince bore the title of royal chaplain in the *regimento* of the post. Under the terms of Henry's final testament in 1460, a daily mass was to be said for the salvation of his immortal soul. Within a few years of the inauguration of this practice at São Jorge in 1482, this daily requirement was dropped in favor of a weekly special mass for Henry. It was performed each Saturday, and for this service the royal chaplain received an additional 10,000 *réis* salary above that of his colleagues. The royal chaplain also received the equivalent of one mark of fine silver per year as an emolument for his duties. This additional amount was paid from the duty of the *vintena* or twentieth part of the trade which was set aside for the Order from the trade of Mina. Overseeing of the *vintena* and its collection was relegated to the vicar. This exercise supported the enterprises of the Order in their overseas mission work. When the post's accounts were balanced at the end of each three month period, the *vintena* was set aside. A collector was sent periodically to Mina for this portion. He would then receive the money from one of the priests, usually the royal chaplain, who served in the secondary post of treasurer of the church.

In their relationship with the rest of the garrison, it was the duty of the vicar and his staff to perform a daily morning mass within the confines of the fortress. The execution of this duty usually fell upon the shoulders of one of the priests, and only upon high church holidays was the vicar himself expected to officiate at the services. Beyond the saying of the mass, the duties of the clergy were neither onerous nor time-consuming. The vicar maintained the host and baptismal font; he heard confessions, presided over burials, and once a year he composed a list of all parishioners, both Portuguese and Africans, within his church. Of all his duties, perhaps the task which required the most attention was the obligation to minister to sick members of the post. Like the governor, the vicar was charged with ensuring that ill persons placed in the infirmary received special rations of white bread and proper treatment. In case a member of the garrison died from his malady, burial services were held, and a new grave was dug in a small plot in the riverside yard which was consecrated as a cemetery.

There would have been little justification in increasing the number of clergy by the addition of another priest in 1503 and again in 1520 to a total of four within a garrison which rarely exceeded sixty persons, but the additional clerics were needed after 1503 to minister to a growing number of black converts. Apparently little if any preaching was done by the Portuguese clergy among the blacks during the first several decades of the post's life, or else such preaching as was attempted met with little success. The paramount chief of the Village of Two Parts, Caramansa, had refused to accept conversion in 1482, and while he ruled, there was little likelihood of progress in conversions. Also, language difficulties were a major hindrance to missionary activity. Since the São Jorge clergy held only temporary appointments, few priests became sufficiently proficient in the local dialect to preach effectively. Instead, whenever conversions occurred, they were accomplished through the intermediary of Portuguese-speaking blacks. Some of the villagers developed a *patois* form of Portuguese which facilitated contacts between the two cultures. A few curious negroes from the village undoubtedly attended religious services within the fortress, but by 1500 the number of converts from the black population was still extremely small. Throughout the period of Portuguese occupation in Mina, conversion efforts were hindered by the ambivalent attitude of the Portuguese with regard to the blacks of the region. Clearly it was the duty of the Mina clergy to protect their few black converts from heresy and exploitation. The danger of heresy came because of the influence exercised upon the new Christians by unconverted blacks. On the other hand, the danger of exploitation emanated from Portuguese quarters. Conversion efforts received a serious setback in 1522–23, when governor Afonso de Albuquerque impressed Mina blacks from the neighboring village into labor service without compensation. Apparently many of those impressed were recent Christian converts. As a result of his actions, the remaining free villagers began to flee into the bush to escape enslavement. The Mina clergy protested vigorously to John III, and the king officially rebuked Albuquerque for his action.[56]

Dramatic and unexpected conversion occasionally stimulated mission activities among the Mina clergy. For example, in 1503 the first mass conversion of blacks living beyond the territorial confines of the adjoining village occurred. On the 24th and 25th of July 1503 the royal chaplain went in the company of the post factor, and together they crossed the Benya river to meet with the paramount chief of the Efutu nation. This meeting took place within sight of the fortress, on the slopes of the hill called Santiago by the Portuguese. After two days of conversations, the chief, along with his family and more than a thousand of his tribe, decided to receive holy baptism from the Portuguese clergy.[57] A small chapel was built on the conversion site, and for several decades irregular services were conducted.

Following the mass conversions of 1503 at Santiago and subsequent missionary efforts among other neighboring tribes, the Mina clergy took on a new role. Sons of converted chiefs, and sometimes the chiefs' wives, visited São Jorge frequently, and a few black nobles remained for weeks or even months receiving instruction in the faith and learning the ways and language of the Portuguese. Almost immediately after the 1503 conversion, Manuel, son of the baptised Efutu chieftain, came to reside for several months at the Portuguese post. Later, in 1529, provision was made for the initiation of a regular class, supervised by the clerics, to teach the sons and daughters of tribal chiefs and other village children the rudiments of the Catholic faith. Mina clergy were also required to seek conversions among captives used as laborers in the fortress or brought from São Tomé to be sold as slaves. At least one hour each day was set aside for priests to teach these men the catechism and other basics of their new faith. As an inducement to promote conversions, the governor received a small cash reward for each new convert. This practice led to many conversions, but unfortunately, few were of any lasting duration.

The effects of the clergy's mission work at São Jorge may be judged minimal in both effort and success. An illustrative example is the case of a former female slave at Mina named Grace. In 1540 Grace was sent to Lisbon to face charges of heresy before the Portuguese Inquisition. The vicar of São Jorge reported that she had received the Holy Sacraments and had been baptized many years

before. However, she had forsaken her new faith. Grace had received her freedom and in 1540 she was living in the neighboring
Village of Two Parts. She was accused of fetish worship and
brought to the vicar's quarters in the Portuguese fortress for ques-
tioning. Grace could not even repeat the *Ave* when asked to do so.
In a search of her village hut the Portuguese found a dozen fetish
images hidden there, and the black woman freely admitted that she
believed the spirit of her dead father came during the night to eat
small loaves of bread she left for him. When questioned about
Jesus Christ, the Holy Virgin, and her own salvation, Grace replied
that she had little interest in any of these matters. Upon repeating
this affirmation to the inquisitorial judges in Lisbon, Grace was
condemned to perpetual incarceration in the prison of the Holy
Office.[58]

Grace's case was not unique, though few of her Christian neighbors were ever sent before the Inquisition. In the main, conversion
implied the acceptance of the white man's faith as a complement
to the black's own traditional religion. The Mina blacks were heno-
theistic. Oftentimes children born of Christian parents would be
raised in different cultures. The firstborn son might be reared as a
Christian, while the second-born practiced the traditional African
religion. In the face of the haphazard manner in which the Christian doctrine was presented to the blacks, it was virtually impossible to break the new converts completely from their fetishism and
superstitions.

In the realm of secular affairs, the Mina clergy served a vital
function as a check upon the authority of the post commander.
The vicar made regular and frequent political reports to the Lisbon
Mina House regarding the activities of the commander, factor, and
other persons within the fortress. Unlike other letters from sub-
altern officials (save the factor) which the commander could read
prior to forwarding, the vicar's dispatches were strictly confiden-
tial. Therefore, a great deal of personal antagonism between the
vicar and governor was often reflected in these dispatches. For instance, it was largely the result of the attacks of the vicar upon the
policy of Afonso de Albuquerque which prompted his reprimand
from John III in 1523. Decades later, in 1560, accusations of a
pecuniary nature were leveled upon the post commander, Manuel

de Mesquita Perestrello. Eventually Perestrello was arrested and transported to Lisbon where criminal charges were brought against him. He was accused of not having pursued an English interloping vessel, having instead chosen to continue trade with the blacks, sometimes using post merchandise for private gain.[59] Occasional feuds between commanders and vicars continued, but not always with the outcome in favor of the latter. For example, in 1605, when the vicar's vituperative letters and personal insults upon the governor because of the latter's use of church funds became intolerable, Cristóvão de Melo used the full powers of his office as commander and forcibly sent the vicar, Gaspar Soares, back to Lisbon. For nearly two years following this incident, the vicarship of São Jorge lay vacant until Soares's successor was chosen.[60]

One final element of São Jorge da Mina's personnel deserves mention. This was the large number of slaves kept at the post. Although these captives were not formally part of the garrison, they performed an essential part of the life of the post. Even before the erection of the station, Portuguese ships had sailed to the region of the Benin Bight and there acquired slaves. Some of these were sold as porters to Mina merchants who traveled to the coast and needed laborers to haul their goods back to interior markets. This thriving business in black slavery was continued after 1482 and grew to such a size that by the sixteenth century five to six hundred captives per year were being channeled through São Jorge.[61] Slaves offered for sale to visiting African merchants were kept in fetters in sheds in the riverside yard. As mentioned previously, a portion of these slaves were diverted from sale and singled out to serve in menial tasks as a labor force for the garrison. They worked in the kitchens, at the smith's hearth, and in the shops of the carpenter and cooper. Alongside these slaves was a group of female slaves, one to every three soldiers. These captives saw to the personal needs of their masters, assisting in the washing, cooking, and marketing required to keep the fortress operating. The height of the slave traffic between São Tomé and Mina was reached in the period from 1510 to about 1540 when four to six slaving vessels were kept continually occupied hauling captives.[62] The round trip from the island to the Portuguese Mina station averaged between twenty-five and thirty days barring accidents or storms. As late as

1535 the royal factor on São Tomé reported sending a slave shipment to São Jorge every fifty days.[63] The dispatch of each ship and
its cargo unloaded at São Jorge was governed by the same regulations as the Lisbon caravels. Extensive records exist for the period
1529–35 which show the method of shipping and receiving these
cargoes of captives.[64] As many as 100 to 120 slaves at a time were
brought to Mina by larger slave vessels. Smaller caravels could
haul between 30 and 80 slaves. In addition, shipments of blue
aggrey beads or *coris* were included with the slaves, and these
beads were sold as trade items by the factor of São Jorge.

Not all slave sailings were routine. On a voyage from São Tomé
to São Jorge in October 1535, the slaver *São Cristóvão* encountered serious misfortune. A week out of São Tomé, an epidemic
broke out on board. The ship was driven off course by a storm and
did not reach São Jorge until seven weeks later. When she arrived
22 of her cargo of 120 slaves were dead along with the ship's
clerk.[65] An even worse fate befell the slave ship *Misericordia* in
late 1532. Captain Estevão Carreiro sailed from São Tomé bound
for the Mina mainland with 109 slaves on board. At sea the blacks
rose up and seized the ship and murdered the crew except for two
seamen and the ship's pilot who escaped in a longboat. Eventually
these three survivors reached safety at São Jorge and reported the
loss. The *Misericordia* was never heard of again.[66]

The organization of São Jorge da Mina in the fifteenth and sixteenth centuries obeyed the tenets of strict regulation of the trade
contacts between the post and the mother agency in Lisbon, a complex system of checks and balances among the garrison members,
and a heavy emphasis upon the fortified nature of the station. John
II did not intend to lose his new outpost of empire to any but an
overwhelming enemy force. However, all the organization was
subordinate to the primary purpose of São Jorge da Mina—to conduct a profitable trade and acquire much-needed gold for the Portuguese crown.

3

Trade and African Relations, 1482-1540

Every regulation in the operation of the outpost of São Jorge da Mina and all functions of the personnel were directed toward the goal of a lucrative trade in gold. Even important religious activities were deemed secondary to this primary economic role of the post. The most important furnishing in the fortress was a massive chest kept by the governor under guard in his quarters (similar chests were issued to every outpost of the Portuguese empire). Containing the gold acquired in trade, the chest could only be opened with three separate keys, one each belonging to the governor, the factor, and the first clerk.

This chest with three keys *(arca com tres chaves)* at São Jorge symbolized the careful controls which were imposed on the gold trade. While the governor controlled the overall supervision of the station and its formal relations with neighboring tribes, he remained apart from the conduct of the trade itself. The sale of merchandise and administration of post accounts was under the authority of the royal factor, who had sweeping powers over the conduct of trade, and furthermore served as a check against the potential misuse of authority by a corrupt governor. Indeed, the factor stood within the ranking of the garrison as the second most important official in the post. In contrast to the governor's background, the crown preferred that men of proven economic abilities serve in this office of factor. Almost every appointee served in an important financial post within the royal bureaucracy prior to assignment at São Jorge. Considerable knowledge of accounts and trading techniques was required if transactions with African merchants were to be successful.

The factor drew an annual salary of 150,000 *réis*, or more than double that of any official at São Jorge except for the governor.[1]

Immediately beneath the factor's authority was a staff of seven persons: two clerks, one to manage post expenditures and the other for receipts; an overseer of provisions who kept account of the items needed for the operation of the fortress and who also sold surplus wine to the blacks; and four laborers. The São Jorge factor also supervised the activities of his counterpart, the factor of the small trading outpost of Axem to the west. Since ships from Lisbon were forbidden to pause at Axem, all trade between that post and Lisbon passed through the hands of the factor in São Jorge. Each month the factor at São Jorge prepared a statement or summary of the trade which had been conducted, as well as the general disposition of the fortress. At times in their correspondence, governor and factor were quite critical of one another's performances. This latent animosity was exactly what John II had planned by separating the functions of commander and factor and thereby establishing an internal set of checks and balances within the remote outpost.

Living quarters for the factor were located in the inner keep and convenient to the adjoining storehouses around the innermost courtyard where much of the cloth and other items of trade were kept. However, by 1500 inventories of the post warehouses had outgrown their cramped quarters within the inner keep, and at that time surplus cloth was even being stored in the living quarters of the factor. In 1500 governor Diogo Lopes de Sequeira requested in his dispatches to Lisbon that he be authorized to construct a new storehouse for trade cloth. He noted that for nearly twenty years the cloth in the keep was sometimes stacked in piles ten feet deep. The problem of storage was especially acute after the unloading of a provision caravel. The period immediately following unloading was the prime time for the coming of black merchants, who were apprised of the ship's arrival. Yet the cloth in the warehouses was in such a jumble that prospective merchants and the Portuguese factor had to walk on top of the merchandise. A larger storage area for the cloth would permit better displaying of goods and prevent soiling. In late 1502 construction was begun on a more spacious warehouse where cloth goods could be shaken and folded properly to prevent mildew. The new facilities consisted of a long, narrow shed, roofed with tiles, which ran along the inner wall of the outer courtyard on the side adjoining the double ditch. By late 1503 the new warehouse was operational and this shed soon became the primary *taracena* or storage shed for fabrics and the focal point of visits by black merchants who came to barter for tradegoods.[2] Metal goods, which needed no such large space requirements, were also stored in one or more small locked sheds in the outer courtyard.

To ensure the high quality of trade merchandise, the factor examined each new shipment from Portugal and should inferior or damaged items be discovered, such as torn or soiled cloth or broken basins, these were returned to Lisbon in the same ship. The number of rejected items was not insignificant. For instance, during a two year period, 1529–30, 929 woolen cloaks and 218 basins of various sizes were the major items among a miscellany of goods returned to Lisbon as unsaleable because of inferior quality.[3] The quality of the cloth then being shipped to Mina under a contract of Fernão Alvares was particularly poor. In fact, the number of damaged pieces returned to Portugal in 1529–30 actually exceeded the number sold at São Jorge by 66 pieces.[4] The same close inspection was made of slaves coming from São Tomé. If unfit captives were found for which there could be no sale, these were turned back to the captain who had brought them.

If by carelessness or because of water damage at São Jorge itself cloth became spoiled or torn while in the post warehouse, then these goods were turned over to an official known as the "factor of used clothing" (*feitor da roupa velha*). During the first several decades of São Jorge's operation as a trade center, the Portuguese found that blacks would purchase almost any sort of fabrics and clothing, and until the late 1520s, the Mina House shipped additional quantities of worn and used clothing from Portugal to São Jorge. At Mina such items were traded for handsome profits in gold, even though the prices secured were lower than the normal tariffs imposed on prime cloth.

For more than four decades, from 1482 to 1529, this official directed a lively trade. For example, Paio Rodrigues, the *feitor da roupa velha* for 1503–5, secured 293 marks, 2 ounces, 3 drams, and 37 grains of fine gold from the sale of the following damaged items: 924 cloth mantles (*lambens*); 1600 large and small north

African cloaks *(aljaravias)*; and a miscellany of bed clothing and table linen.[5] 293 marks of gold was sufficient to constitute in itself a caravel's treasure shipment to Lisbon. However, the construction of more commodious quarters for the cloth inventory at São Jorge apparently had the effect of reducing the volume of damaged cloth which would be consigned to the *feitor da roupa velha*. Important too was the increasingly discerning nature of black merchants who came to the Portuguese station to trade. Since the traffic in old or damaged cloth generally was consigned to the local coastal market, merchants from the interior demanded cloth of the highest quality and looked over the wares in the factory carefully before selecting their purchases. Black entrepreneurs in the Village of Two Parts purchased large lots of old and damaged cloth and peddled their wares along the Mina coast in various salt villages and small settlements.[6] By the 1520s the overall volume of the Mina trade had increased to new highs while revenues from the office of the *feitor da roupa velha* showed marked diminution. Over a twenty-seven month period from 13 December 1516 to 2 March 1519, the *feitor da roupa velha*, Gaspar de Villa Lobos, reported receipts of only 267 marks, 6 ounces, 2 drams, and 66 grains of gold from the disposal of old and damaged cloth.[7] In 1529, on the occasion of the issuance of a Mina *regimento* for governor Estevão da Gama, it was decided to abolish the office of *feitor da roupa velha*. Henceforth, all damaged goods were to be returned to Lisbon and to the Mina House. Rejected slaves would continue to be returned to the royal officials in São Tomé.

In his private quarters in the keep, the factor conducted the business of the post scriptorium. Two large chests, each of which could be opened only with the insertion of three keys, were in the scriptorium at all times. In one *arca* were kept the books of receipts and expenses, which recorded the daily and quarterly sales of the post. The other chest contained a precisely calibrated set of balances in which the gold was weighed following each gold transaction. These balances, with arms plated with silver and including over a hundred weights, were much more refined than those normally carried by ships' captains. To ensure further accuracy, the balance arms bore the stamp of the royal master of weights for the city of Lisbon. Periodically, the balance at São Jorge would be returned to Lisbon to be calibrated against a similar set of balances kept in the offices of the Lisbon Mina House.[8]

No transactions could be recorded at São Jorge by a single clerk. The two clerks and the factor all had to be present with their respective keys even to open the chests. The factor and at least one clerk were required to sign all records of the factory. In case the factor died or became incapacitated, the chief economic office of the post passed to the first clerk of the factory, the clerk of receipts. The second clerk, clerk of expenses, then advanced to the clerkship vacated, while the post commander, the new factor, and the first clerk selected a person from among the garrison to serve in the vacant second clerkship until Lisbon could be notified and a replacement sent.[9]

Trade between Negro merchants and the Portuguese officials normally was conducted within the confines of the castle's great courtyard. Occasionally, however, an atmosphere of caution or fear caused some merchants and visiting rulers to refuse to enter the fortress. This was especially the case for trade conducted during the first several decades of São Jorge's operation. It took many years to cement cordial relations with even the closest indigenous tribal states. As late as 21 years after São Jorge's foundation, in July 1503, the factor of São Jorge reported that the king of Commany still refused to be trapped within the walls of the fortress. The factor at this time, Diogo de Alvarenga, noted how that monarch, who did a lively trade by acting as an intermediary, had approached the post accompanying merchants who had come from the interior. About three bombard shots' distance from the post, the king's entourage paused on the trail and brought the merchants into the view of the post lookout. This was the customary signal that a trading session was desired. Alvarenga, accompanied by his clerks, eight armed crossbowmen, and several slaves who carried trade merchandise, went forth to meet with the king and his merchants and soldiers.[10] Bartering sessions might last for several hours or even continue through two or three days. Therefore, the site chosen was in the shade of one of those large trees which stood in isolated fashion throughout the landscape. When the Portuguese had secured the best possible price for their goods, which was usually the minimum price fixed by the Lisbon Mina House, the gold would be exchanged. Black merchants paid for the tradegoods by measuring out fine particles of gold in pinches between their thumb and index finger. Larger gold flakes and nuggets were weighed by the Portuguese with a set of balances. The gold thus obtained was recorded and poured into a small locked chest which was lined with leather and had a slit in the lid through which the dust passed. When a trading session had ended and the factor was back inside the quarters, the gold chest was unlocked in the presence of the factor, his two clerks, and the post commander. All the gold was weighed together in the accurate balances kept in the factor's quarters; the weight was then recorded in the ledger book of receipts.[11] Although in the formal weighing an increase would sometimes be noted from the price paid by the merchants for the goods, African merchants generally were skilled traders and knew the worth and amount of gold which they handed over.[12] The gold was placed in a large sealed chest, which was put in a larger wooden box in the post commander's quarters. The commander, factor, and clerk of receipts had respective keys to this *arca com tres chaves.* Once every three months the chest was opened to pay the salaries for the garrison and to dispense a small percentage of the quarterly profits which was allotted to the commander, the factor, and the two clerks. These officials were entitled to share one percent of the profit in gold which was obtained every three months.[13]

On special holidays or feast days, the factor customarily opened the post warehouses and distributed a small quantity of tradegoods to each member of the fortress according to his rank. The recipient could trade this cloth with local merchants in return for gold, or he could use it to obtain additional provisions, such as chickens, fresh vegetables, and the like, to supplement his rations. Superficially, this granting of private trade privileges by the garrison with the indigenous population would appear a serious infraction of the strict regulations imposed on the trade by the Mina House. However, the crown obviously realized that to attempt a total ban on private trade was an unrealistic policy. As in the other parts of the Portuguese empire there was a wide gap between the ideal standards prescribed in *regimentos* and the actual conditions that prevailed. This was especially true of Mina, where an abundance of gold could corrupt everybody. Such restrictions would have been impossible to enforce. Therefore, to keep private trade within acceptable limits, the ability of the garrison member to traffic with African merchants was circumscribed. In 1509 the factor of the Mina House noted that gold acquired through private trading occasionally exceeded an official's total salary, and new regulations were issued that year to curb this practice. An upper limit was imposed on the amount of privately-acquired gold which any individual could import into Portugal from Mina.[14] Henceforth no official was permitted to obtain a sum of private gold in excess of his own salary.

As a further check on private trade, the amount of personal possessions which any new official could carry with him to Mina was carefully circumscribed. Every new official was required to furnish all his personal clothing, blankets, towels, sheets and other linens. Since cloth items were such popular items for sale to the local merchants, limits on the number of each item were imposed. A Portuguese official who wished to dispose of any of his clothing allotment while at São Jorge could do so, but such sales could only be handled through the factor of the station, who acted as the intermediary between the private individual and the local purchaser.[15] Normally these items were sold at a regular trading session or *feira* which was held for local merchants. Gold received from such private sales was subject to a royal duty of twenty percent and was shipped to Portugal within the royal coffer. All gold belonging to individuals within the garrison, including the salary payments, was wrapped in individual paper packets and placed within the royal coffer. The importer of illegal gold into Portugal faced severe punishments if he were caught.

Figures for the amounts of private gold acquired during the *feiras* vary widely. A sampling of 26 yearly totals for private gold (*de particulares*) from Mina which reached the royal mint during the period between 1495 and 1560 shows an average annual receipt of 136.3 marks. However, individual yearly totals range from an extreme low of only 28.1 marks in 1525 to a high of 298.8 marks in 1532.[16] Private trading at São Jorge, expressed as a percentage of the royal portion of gold shipments, amounted to the following:

1495–99	10.0%
1511–20	14.4%
1521–30	8.8%
1531–40	7.6%
1541–50	19.6%
1551–60	23.2%

If the above figures are an accurate reflection of the extent of private trading, it would seem that the regulation first established in the Mina *regimento* of 1509 succeeded in gradually reducing the private commerce to acceptable bounds. Despite the king's allowance of private trading at São Jorge, a few officials continued to exceed the legal limits imposed and amassed fortunes at the station. One such case was in 1536 when officials in Mina reported that several former office holders at São Jorge had buried 18,000 to 20,000 *cruzados'* worth of illicitly-acquired gold before they returned to Portugal. Once back in Lisbon, these men sought to enlist the aid of other conspirators to recover their treasure. Unfortunately for them, their activities were reported to the crown in the monthly dispatches from Mina. The guilty parties were arrested and the gold recovered.[17]

Private trade did not begin to increase as a percentage of the royal revenues again until the 1540s. In absolute terms, private trade did not grow after that date—the overall volume of the gold trade was declining and being altered by foreign interloping. The private portion of the trade remained at a fairly constant level while total revenues dipped sharply. This accounts for the sharp rise in percentage rates after 1540.

Portuguese factors at São Jorge found that African merchants insisted that a wide range of trade goods be stocked before any trade in gold, ivory, malagueta pepper and assorted forest products was conducted. Often when a single commodity was sold out or not available for some reason, blacks refused to purchase any of the other goods. But this problem did not become acute until the second half of the sixteenth century when the Mina supply system began to break down. Basically, the tradegoods shipped to Mina from Portugal and from parts of the empire consisted of five categories. In their order of importance as to volume traded and the profit to be had for each item, they were: cloth, metal hardware, slaves, shells and beads, and wine.

Cloth. Despite a large population concentration on the Mina coast since a very early period, animal and vegetable fibers with which to weave cloth remained in short supply. The small quantities of fabric imported into the region from the Sudanese empires or from Nigeria before the Portuguese arrival brought high profits. However, this pre-European trade never fully satisfied local demands. When the Portuguese arrived at Mina in the late 1460s, they discovered that a ready market awaited them for any cloth which they wished to carry there. Among the most popular trade items during the late fifteenth and early sixteenth centuries were mantles, called *lambens,* which were purchased in north African marketplaces and in the Alentejo region of Portugal and shipped to Mina. Flowing full-length to the ground, these mantles consisted of a single piece of cloth sewn along the sides with armholes cut and a poncho-like opening in the center for the wearer's head. The modern *gandoura* or *hambel* worn today in north Africa is a modern version of the original design which the Portuguese purchased from Maghribine weavers. Similar shawls are also worn in the Alentejo region of Portugal.

Lambens came in a variety of styles and colors. Those destined for markets at Mina were shipped generally without being sewn into a garment. In Mina these *lambens,* about 2.7 by 6.5 meters in size, were cut and wrapped around the waist of the blacks in a series of windings which draped to the ground. The value of a *lamben* to a prospective African purchaser lay in the dye of the fabric, with the most popular designs having stripes of red, green, blue, and white about two or three inches wide. Portuguese merchants in north Africa purchased thousands of *lambens* of every hue in the cloth markets of Oran, Bone, Bougie, Tunis, Mazouna, Tenez, Stora (Argela), and the kingdom of Tlemcen.[18] In Mina the most popular designs commanded high prices, especially those from the north African market at Oran. A prime *lamben* from the village of Mazouna near Oran was valued in Mina at the same price as a male slave from Benin.

Equally popular, and also of north African derivation, were the thousands of *aljaravias* which the Portuguese transported to Mina for sale. They were similar to a *burnous* or cloak with half-sleeves and an attached hood. The modern version of the *aljaravia*, the *el-djalabiya* of north Africa, is still widely worn throughout the Maghrib today. Even in Mina, the Portuguese distinguished between several styles of *aljaravias* by their place of north African origin. Hence the derivation of the Portuguese terms in Mina documents mentioning *aljaravias tenezes* (Tunis), or *aljaravias da huara* (Oran).

Among other ready-made clothing stocked for trade were red capes, leggings, caps, neckerchiefs, and handkerchiefs. However, aside from *lambens* and *aljaravias* most blacks preferred to purchase unfinished cloth which could be dyed locally to conform with traditional styles of the region. At the Portuguese station black merchants could select from an almost endless array of fabrics, weights, and colors. The merchandise included, to mention only a few items: *panna*, which were lengths of cloth made from finely-woven cotton; *pano branco*, or white sailcloth; calicos; scarlet cotton cloth from Portúgal, Holland, and India; Bruges satins;[19] Muslim fustian, a type of cloth with coarse weave manufactured from cotton and flax; and a grouping of cloth known as *roupas pretas*. This latter derived its name from India fabrics. *Roupas pretas* were of two basic sorts: *caudeis*, a cotton Bengali muslin;[20] and *mantases*, a variety of cloth from the weavers of Cambay.[21] In addition to the above types, the Portuguese also imported cloth from other regions of sub-Saharan Africa. Account summaries for São Jorge during the 1520s and 1530s mention small amounts of Benin and Ijebu fabric being offered for sale.[22]

All cloth in the factory at São Jorge da Mina was sold according to two standardized lengths of measure. These were the *vara* and the *côvado*. The former was a linear measure of 1.1 meters and used for linen cloth. However, the *côvado* was generally employed when handling north African woolen and Indian fabrics. One *côvado* equalled three *palmos*, or two-thirds of a meter.[23]

Metal hardware. Next to fabrics and clothing, objects fashioned from copper and brass and, to a lesser extent, iron, lead, and steel, were the most sought-after items at São Jorge. Although restricted

by the scarcity of copper deposits, Mina blacks living in the forest
belt behind the coastal plain had knowledge of metal casting and
working. With the advent of new European sources of metal, a
plentiful supply became available and the local smithing industry
flourished. Items of copper and brass were offered in every con-
ceivable form and shape at São Jorge. There were basins ranging
in size from small shaving bowls and urinals to large cauldrons,
water jugs, thin sheets of copper, brass bells, small copper boxes,
small weights with which to weigh gold, lead crosses, iron ingots,
axes, knives, pruning hooks, and vast quantities of *manilhas*.
Most of the metal objects which the Portuguese sold were melted
and recast by local smiths into objects of African design. Therefore,
prices of *manilhas*, which were bracelets of heavy design, and
basins, were set by weight and not by shape or decoration. The
manilha, weighing about .6 kilogram each, became the standard
weight by which most other metal objects were valued. Black merchants purchasing these items became adept at determining the
quality of the particular item offered by testing its alloy content.
Basins or other metal items were tested by striking two pieces together and gauging the tone emitted.

From 1470 to about 1520, copper was the most popular metal
purchased from the Portuguese station at São Jorge. However,
brass began to replace copper as the most sought-after metal early
in the sixteenth century, and by about 1530 this changeover was
complete. In ensuing decades copper *manilhas* and basins were
only rarely offered for sale in quantity. Late in the sixteenth century, numerous iron ingots began to appear among Portuguese
trade inventories. Iron continued to be sold alongside brass items
until about 1620–30 when iron completely replaced brass as the
dominant metal trade item. During the seventeenth century the
Portuguese successors to the Mina trade sold thousands of iron
ingots to black Mina merchants.

Shells, Beads, and Coral. Alongside cloth and metal hardware,
there was a brisk demand among Mina blacks for a variety of deco-
rative beads and shells. Duarte Pacheco Pereira reports that certain varieties were treasured in the same manner Europeans
valued semi-precious stones. The beads consisted of small polished
stones or glass of varying hues and shadings. The stone varieties

originated in the forest region of interior Nigeria. A popular type which the Portuguese called *coris,* fashioned from a blue stone which had random streaks of red, came from a zone east of the Niger delta. When the Portuguese first arrived on the Mina coast, there was already an established trade in *coris* emanating from the kingdom of Benin. The Portuguese quickly became middlemen in this traffic and included *coris* in their inventory of trade offerings.[24] *Coris* were purchased in large quantities in Benin by the Portuguese factor assigned there and were shipped to São Jorge da Mina where blacks from the village polished, drilled, and strung them for sale.[25]

Other colors of *coris,* particularly yellow and dark-grey varieties, were even more highly esteemed than the blue stones. The Portuguese traded yellow *coris* very dearly in exchange for handsome gold profits at Mina. When the Portuguese discovered that *coris* sales could be supplemented by glass beads of European origin, quantities of Venetian glass beads (*margeritas* in Portuguese inventories) were sent to Mina. Some of these were already drilled and strung, but more often they were sold in small packets, or *maços.* These *maços* were assembled at São Jorge from larger sacks of glass or stone beads shipped there in supply or slave ships from Portugal or São Tomé.

To a lesser extent, there was a market for cowrie shells, coral, and conch shells brought to Mina. In the sub-Saharan regions of Ouadan, Timbuktu, and Djenne, at least two varieties of cowries possessed value for trading purposes—*Cypraea moneta* and *Cyprae annulus.* Both species came from the Indian Ocean and originally were carried overland from the east African coast. These shells were drilled, strung together on strands of grass, and carried to the northern regions of the forest belt where they served as a form of currency.[26] Given to an African bride in Mina, cowries offered good luck and guaranteed offspring. Shortly after the opening of trade between Portugal and India, quantities of the so-called "money cowries" began to appear in trade inventories at the Portuguese station in Mina. Pacheco Pereira mentions what may have been a brisk cowrie trade in Mina as early as 1504–8. In 1515 King Manuel I signed a contract with a Portuguese merchant which permitted the latter to import 500 *quintals* of cowries annually from

India to São Tomé.[27] These cowries *(buzios da India)* began to arrive on the Mina coast in appreciable quantities within a few years. In October 1519, several thousand *buzios da India* were included within an inventory of trade goods present in São Jorge's warehouses.[28]

Wine. Most of the time the Portuguese station scarcely had enough provisions to supply its own rations. By about 1500 the Portuguese had become accustomed to supplementing their meager diet of bread, honey, vinegar, olive oil, and wine with local vegetables and millet.[29] Portuguese gunners could secure a variety of wild game from the nearby river banks and especially to the west toward Axem. The only exception to a general practice of reserving food provisions for consumption by the garrison was in the sale of wine to the local populace. Mina blacks had their own variety of local alcoholic beverage made from the fermentation of palm fruit, but they preferred the sweet white wines of Portugal. A particular favorite was the muscatel produced at Caparica just south of Lisbon. White Caparica wines traveled well and could be kept in the damp climate of Mina much longer than most red varieties, which spoiled quickly.[30] This Caparica wine was the type normally sent to São Jorge da Mina for the garrison's consumption and also for sale. Portuguese officials at Mina reported that the local populace became quite addicted to the imported wine and prized it highly.[31] In the early years of trade any surplus wine at the fortress was sold in exchange for local produce or gold. By 1500 extra hogsheads of wine were purposely being shipped to Mina in supply caravels for sale. They were sold in *pipas* or pipes, which contained about twenty-five to twenty-seven *almudes* or approximately two hogsheads each. Often the pipes were broken and wine was sold in lesser amounts for local trade. Until about 1500 the wine usually came from royal cellars in Lisbon rather than private contractors.[32] However in 1500–1502 Manuel chose to contract the Mina wine shipments to private hands. Succeeding vintners supplied the wine and were required to ship it on royal vessels along with the regular provisions.[33]

Slaves. Finally, an adequate and continuous supply of slaves was indispensable for the success of Portuguese trade at São Jorge da Mina. Without such slaves, much of the remainder of the tradegoods would not have been sold. The bulk of the Portuguese Mina trade was conducted with black merchants who were not local, but came to the coastal stations from remote tribes in the interior. By the 1530s Portuguese goods sold at São Jorge were penetrating local African markets several hundred miles behind the coast. Since animal transport was unknown in the coastal regions of Mina, slaves were the only alternative and were widely used as porters.

From the very earliest years of Portuguese occupation of their Mina outpost, slaves were imported from other coastal parts of Africa to supply this labor need of the Mina blacks. The majority of black captives came to Mina on board slaving vessels from the kingdom of Benin and the Slave Rivers. From 1482 until midway through the reign of Manuel I, the captain-general of São Jorge dispatched a caravel at regular intervals to deal directly with the slave-supplying regions. Officials were sent from the Mina station both eastward along the coast as far as Benin and occasionally westward onto the Malagueta coast in search of slaves.[34] Beginning around 1515, the Portuguese Guinea islands of São Tomé and Príncipe began to function as entrepôts for the slave traffic. Slavers were outfitted and dispatched to Benin and the Slave Rivers from these islands on behalf of the Portuguese crown. Captives were carried back to the islands, where they were "seasoned" and sorted, and then taken to São Jorge da Mina. Regular supply boats plied between São Tomé and São Jorge da Mina bringing a steady influx of new slaves for sale to Mina merchants. When the royal revenues for the island of São Tomé were leased to private merchants, part of the agreement required that the contractor furnish at least 500 slaves per year to Mina for the conduct of the trade.[35]

The presence of a varied inventory of trade items at Mina represented a remarkable coordination of effort on the part of royal officials in both Lisbon and São Tomé. From the offices of the parent Mina House all merchandise shipped to Mina, save for *coris* and slaves, either passed directly through the hands of the factor and his clerks, or else authorization for its shipment to Mina from other parts of the empire originated in their scriptorium. Remittances of gold, pepper, ivory, musk cats, and hides from São Jorge da Mina further complicated economic supervision. This yeoman supply service performed by the Mina House is rendered all the more remarkable when one considers that only a small portion of the tradegoods sent to Mina originated within Portugal. For the most part, aside from the provisions sent, the Mina House tapped many foreign sources to secure the goods needed for the trade conducted at São Jorge da Mina. Subcontracts were leased to private business houses to supply specific goods. One of the early important Mina subcontractors was the wealthy New Christian entrepreneur, Fernão de Loronha. During 1502/3 this merchant's involvement with São Jorge da Mina included supplying all slaves and wine to the post. Simultaneously, Loronha held leases for Brazil and the Guinea pepper monopoly. Because of his varied contacts with the Mina trade and with the help of a close business relationship with Manuel I, Loronha was accorded a singular privilege of being permitted to assign a servant to live at São Jorge for the purpose of overseeing his interests. The contractor of slaves for Mina from 1516 to 1519, António Carneiro, was permitted a similar representative to reside at Mina during the term of his contract. [36]

The names of some other contractors who had dealings with the Mina House have also survived. For example, near the end of Manuel I's reign, in 1518 and 1519, the acquisition of Tunisian *aljaravias* for Mina was the monopoly belonging to Goncalo Vaz. [37] By 1520 this particular contract for *aljaravias* had passed to Fernão Alvarez, who supplied both *lambens* and *aljaravias* from 1520 to 1531. [38] From the account book of the São Jorge factor Goncalo de Campos (1529?–31), it is clear that Alvarez was remiss in the quality of goods which he sent to Mina, since numbers of his *lambens* and *aljaravias* were rejected at São Jorge as damaged and unsaleable and were returned to Lisbon. [39] In 1533 the contract for the supply of these two trade items passed to another Lisbon merchant, Francisco Lobo, for an indefinite period. [40] In 1541 Afonso Torres of Lisbon, a prominent Portuguese merchant, was listed among the contractors supplying tradegoods (unspecified) to the Mina station. [41] During the early 1550s and corresponding with the tour of Rui de Melo as captain-general at Mina, the contract for *roupas* belonged to Pedro Ruiz. [42]

The degree of Portuguese dependence upon foreign suppliers to meet the metalware needs of the Mina trade is striking. Because Portugal did not possess sufficient copper deposits of her own to supply the growing Mina and Indian trade, reliance upon foreign mining interests became commonplace. Contracts were assigned through the Portuguese factory in Antwerp to Genoese bankers and German mining consortiums to furnish large quantities of crudely-cast *manilhas*, basins, copper ingots, and other species of metalware. Northern European merchant houses, such as those of Erasmus Schetz and Anton Fugger, alternated with Italian merchants in furnishing the trade needs of the Portuguese. In 1515 Giovanni Francesco Affaitadi supplied 6,394 quintals of copper to the Portuguese crown destined for sale in Mina.[43] During the 1520s the amount of base metals utilized in trade with Mina was between 8000 and 9000 quintals per year (cf. Appendix A). The bulk of this metal was furnished through the Portuguese factory in Flanders.[44] The foreign monopoly on metals did not change appreciably until the final years of John III's reign when iron appeared on the Mina market as brass and copperware were phased out of the trade. The reason for this change was that competition in northern Europe combined with deflated profits from the Portuguese contracts prompted the foreign mining consortiums to drop their contracts.[45] The German firms desired specie in return for metal shipments, and they became increasingly reluctant to accept the spices which Portugal sought to barter in lieu of gold and silver. The firm of Erasmus Schetz permitted its contract to lapse in 1547 without seeking a renewal. Although a three-year lease to supply the Mina House with *manilhas* and basins was signed by João Rebelo, the Portuguese factor in Flanders, the availability of brass and copper metalware at Mina had dropped sharply by 1550.

During the height of the Portuguese trade monopoly in Mina, which spanned the decades between 1480 and 1540, the crown sought to impose a set of fixed prices on all commodities offered for sale at the trade stations. In 1509 King Manuel I decreed that "from this day forward, all merchandise in the post shall be sold at the prices which are commanded . . . without lowering them by any degree."[46] While a small quantity of damaged or spoiled goods was authorized to be sold cheaply by the *feitor da roupa velha*, after 1529 this official was eliminated and all damaged tradegoods were returned to Lisbon rather than disturb the price structure. Despite the absence of European competitors on the coast, the

Portuguese factor at São Jorge da Mina found that Africans were reluctant to purchase tradegoods without attempting to drive a bargain. Sometimes several days were spent in a trading session before one side or the other relented. Although the Portuguese could not legally lower their prices, this royal prohibition was surmounted by granting extra gifts of cloth and other merchandise to the traders to induce a sale. This practice was within the rights of the commander of the station and was widely practiced. When both trading parties were satisfied, the transaction was concluded. The only items which were not sold at standardized prices were *coris*, cowries, and slaves. Size and color were the primary determinant of the value of the first two items, while sex, age, and general health set the price for slave sales. Table 1 depicts a sampling of the major trade items at Mina and the average sale price per item to black traders during the years 1500 to 1540.

Table 1—Tradegoods prices at São Jorge, 1500–1540

Cloth	Sale price of each per *vara*, *côvado*, etc.
aljaravias	1,800 *réis*
lambens	10,800 "
capas (capes)	1,800 "
capuzes vermelho (red caps)	5,400–6,000 "
pano (fabric by the *vara* or *côvado*)	240 "
panna	5,400 "
mantas	2,400 "
pannellas cinzaladas	1,800 "
barretes	444 "
cintas (belts)	600 "
Metalware	
manilhas	120 *réis*
bacias (basins):	
de mijar (urinals)	600 "
de barbeiro (shaving mugs)	1,200 "
macho (large, shallow pans)	1,440 "
caldeiras (cooking pots)	1,200–2,600 "
Coris	8–60 "
Wine	570 *réis* per *almude*
Slaves	9,000–18,000 *réis*

Strong pressure was exerted constantly by the Mina black merchants to force these prices downward. However, the Africans seemed to have little success in altering the Portuguese price structure until the advent of French and English trading competitors on the coast during the 1540s. Even then the Portuguese crown strongly resisted competition with the cheaper products carried by merchants from other nations. After 1540 São Jorge factors had to rely on claims of Portuguese goods' excelling the interlopers' products, but the blacks soon discovered otherwise. Requests poured into the Lisbon Mina House after 1540 seeking permission to bring prices into line with those of goods offered by competitors. These suggestions generally went unheeded by the crown for more than a decade while Portuguese coastguard squadrons attempted to drive the invaders from the region. A price reevaluation during the last years of the 1550s came too late, since by that time Portugal's monopoly over the Mina trade had been irrevocably broken. Consequently prices of both Portuguese and foreign goods spiraled downward drastically as the coast was inundated by European tradegoods.

General estimates and samplings of scattered years in the period 1480 to 1540 show that cloth sales accounted for about 40% of Portuguese trade at Mina, while metal products made up another 37%. Revenues from the sale of slaves and from other miscellany comprised about 10% and 13%, respectively. Accurate records of the volume of individual trade items such as *aljaravias, lambens,* and *manilhas* are difficult to ascertain for the years prior to 1500. Those available records suggest an average annual purchase of between 1300 and 1800 *lambens* in north Africa during the 1480s for sale in Guinea.[47] Only with the beginning of Manuel I's reign in 1495 are any sort of accurate serial listings available for examination. For instance, a quittance issued the factor of the Guinea and Mina House for the three years of 1494 through 1497, indicates that the equivalent of about 71,000 *manilhas* was received annually for shipment to west Africa with perhaps as many as 80 percent of these items earmarked for Mina.[48] Quittances issued to factors of São Jorge da Mina are another major source of information on commodity sales at the post. They are usually most complete in listing the number and variety of metal trade commodities received and sold at the post. By utilizing these records, Appendix A indicates that purchases of *manilhas*, basins, and other metal items at Mina reached a peak during the final year of Manuel's reign, 1520/21, and during the initial years of his successor, John III.[49] Following this, a substantial decline ensued during the remainder of the 1520s. In the next ten years sales stabilized at about 70% of their peak in the previous decade.

Where the annual totals of gold acquired at São Jorge da Mina are known, the figures for receipts parallel the serial listings of individual trade merchandise. Receipts of gold at the Portuguese station for the years prior to 1495 may be viewed only indirectly through quittances issued to the factor of the whole Mina House in Lisbon. These figures show that gold receipts at Mina fluctuated within wide limits, which ranged from a high of 2,000 marks per year to a low of half that figure. Commencing in 1495 more reliable yearly statistics indicate a steadier trade between 1495 and 1510. During this fifteen-year period, an average of 1,800 marks per year were received. A slight dip in revenues followed during 1513 and 1514, down to 1,420 marks average for each of these years. Then, by the end of the second decade of the sixteenth century, the reorganization of the Mina traffic and a further tightening of regulations to check smuggling, coupled with an expansion of trade in Mina itself, served to boost the gold revenues at Mina to new highs. During the two-year term of Duarte Pacheco Pereira as governor of Mina from 1519 to 1521, gold shipments from Mina annually exceeded 2,100 marks. Governor Pacheco Pereira was quite active in opening new trade relations with gold-bearing areas in the interior behind the fringe of coastal states. By the end of his tour of duty, which was cut short by recall to Portugal to face charges of maladministration, the majority of Portugal's trade through São Jorge was being conducted with these distant merchants rather than local coastal rulers.[50]

A slump in the gold trade followed Pacheco Pereira's removal. Succeeding governors, Dom Afonso de Albuquerque (1521–24), João de Barros (1524–25), and João Vaz de Almada (1526–29) were unable to reverse this marked downward trend in revenues. Pacheco Pereira's immediate successor followed a totally different policy toward the Mina blacks. Albuquerque freely utilized forced labor drawn from the Village of Two Parts to supplement garrison slaves in maintaining the post. Infractions of the law by blacks were severely punished by fines and imprisonment. Consequently many villagers migrated to other settlements and trade declined even more sharply. As previously mentioned, the situation became sufficiently acute to warrant the Portuguese monarch's intervention in 1523, when John III dispatched instructions to his representatives at São Jorge, particularly the post commandant, admonishing them for their harsh actions and counselling moderation in future dealings with the black populace.[51]

Average gold receipts reaching the royal mint in Lisbon from Mina during the years 1522–29 never exceeded 1,300 marks in any year, with the annual average for the period fluctuating between 1,150 and 1,200 marks, or about half of the totals for the preceding highs for 1519–21. In 1529 a further effort to restructure the Mina trade was undertaken. At this time the new commandant, Estevão da Gama, was proceeding to Mina to replace Vaz da Almada whose term had expired. Da Gama adhered strictly to his new *regimento,* and trade recovered to about seventy percent of its 1519–21 totals by the end of his tour of service. Receipts remained at this level until the early years of the decade of the 40s. At that point the Mina trade and revenues became very erratic from year to year, due in large part to a combination of French and English interloping along the coast, privateering raids on returning gold shipments, and difficulties experienced by Portugal in supplying Mina with sufficient quantities of tradegoods and provisions. The Portuguese economic position at Mina deteriorated rapidly. In the five-year span between 1549 and 1554 the trade of São Jorge reached an all-time recorded low compared with previous individual years. In 1553 only 414 marks, 5 ounces, 7 drams, and 15 grains of gold were secured in trade.[52]

These statistics on the total Mina gold revenues are in considerable divergence with the reports of previously accepted authorities on the trade. For instance, Duarte Pacheco Pereira, in his *Esmeraldo de situ orbis,* claimed that each year a supply caravel sailed monthly to Mina and returned laden with 20,000 *cruzados* in fine gold.[53] This would mean that approximately 240,000 *cruzados* or nearly 4,000 marks of gold were taken in trade annually at São

Jorge. Even during the best years of trade, which coincided with
the tour of this same Pacheco Pereira (1519–21), Mina revenues
did not remotely approach the figures cited within the *Esmeraldo*.
Certainly receipts of gold prior to 1500 do not appear to have attained 4,000 marks annually. For example, all gold received by
Fernão Lourenço, factor of the Lisbon Mina House between August 1488 and March 1494, amounted to 15,290 marks, for an average annual receipt of only 2,698 marks.[54] Pacheco Pereira presumably had reliable knowledge of the Mina gold trade, since he had
accompanied Diogo de Azambuja there in 1481 when the original
fortress was erected. Later, during the 1480s and 1490s, Pacheco
Pereira had commanded a supply vessel which sailed between Lisbon and São Jorge da Mina and he had brought gold shipments
back with him.[55] Apparently the author of the *Esmeraldo* did not
include in his account the notation that not every ship which sailed
the *Carreira da Mina* returned laden with full treasure cargoes.

By no means was the gold traffic regular in terms of monthly
revenues. Trade at São Jorge fluctuated widely from month to
month and season to season. Black itinerant merchants often came
from remote regions several hundred miles behind the coast and
they followed no regular, predictable schedule. There was no advance warning given to the factor and his staff and no way of anticipating the next group of prospective buyers. Some small trade was
conducted with the local villagers and neighboring states on a more
frequent basis, but by 1500–20 the bulk of the business was conducted with merchants from distant interior states. Occasionally
tribal wars closed the roads leading to the Portuguese post and in
such situations the Portuguese exerted all their political influence
on the rulers responsible for the closure to reopen the trails. The
earliest firsthand report available on the state of the trade at São
Jorge was a dispatch from the commandant of the post to the Mina
House in 1500. Fernão Lopes Correa wrote his superiors that he
had finally succeeded in opening the road through the kingdom of
Commany to the interior.[56] This commercial route had been closed
for several years for an unknown reason. With the opening of this
trail in 1500, there was a substantial increase in the number of
merchants visiting São Jorge—so great was the demand for goods
in fact, the Portuguese factor simply could not fulfill requests. In

the following months after the initial rush of sales, 400 marks of gold were sent back aboard several returning caravels. Late that same year, a noticeable slump occurred in the trade at the post, and during the last third of the year, only 85 marks of gold were sent from São Jorge aboard one supply caravel.[57] A decade later, in 1510, warfare among neighboring tribal states again closed all trails leading to São Jorge. The post commandant, Manuel de Goios, reported that practically no merchants came to the station during the rainy season from January to September. During that time local sales to coastal villages had yielded the only gold in the fortress—between 90 and 120 marks per month.[58]

Only a single account ledger belonging to São Jorge da Mina has survived with which to examine the daily trade. It is the receipt and expense entries made by Goncalo de Campos, who served as factor of Mina under Governor João Vaz de Almada and Almada's successor, Estevão da Gama. The ledger is incomplete and covers only the period from 10 June 1529 until 31 August 1531. Although the document lacks the first twenty-three folios as well as folios 85–93, it reveals in intimate detail the day-to-day business transactions of the trading station at São Jorge da Mina.[59] Of 812 days included within the account ledger (including 150 Sundays and saint's days of note), there were only seventy-one days in which trading sessions were concluded. Each of the recorded sessions was preceded by one or more days of bartering and negotiation between the Portuguese factor and the black merchants over the proper prices and the quality of the merchandise for sale. The briefest period between sales sessions was but a single day, 10/11 September 1529, whereas the longest hiatus in trading was for thirty-seven days between 18 December 1529 and 24 January 1530. For the most part, trade seems to have been conducted on a weekly or bi-weekly basis with no absolute fixed schedule.[60]

In terms of gold received for the merchandise sold by the factor Campos, there were wide extremes between the high and low figures acquired at any one session. Vast quantities of goods sold to a large party of Akani merchants arriving at the post in early December 1529 brought in just over 200 marks in a single day. Varying quantities of almost every item in the post storehouses were sold at this particular trading encounter. The greatest number of any given item which the Akani purchased was 19,255 brass *manilhas*. Following this huge transaction, there was no further business conducted at the post until 24 January 1530, when approximately 51.5 gold marks were taken. Apparently the warehouses of São Jorge had been so depleted by the Akani purchases in December that further trade had to await the arrival of a supply caravel, since the session of 24 January 1530 followed by just three days the departure of two supply caravels on their return to Lisbon. At the nadir of trade, the smallest bartering session occurred on 15 July 1529 and netted the Portuguese only 3 marks, 4 ounces, 7 drams, 21 grains in return for the sale of 1 *lamben*, 19 basins, and 295 *manilhas*. [61]

The Portuguese had mistaken the golden wealth which came from certain trading villages along the coast (Axem, Takoradi, Shama, Aldea de duas partes, Cabo das Redes, and Accra) to denote the presence of nearby mining areas. Modern studies have demonstrated, however, that the gold finding its way to the Mina coast in the fifteenth, sixteenth, and seventeenth centuries came from small alluvial workings deep in the forest belt or from the region of the upper Senegal and the Niger plains. Only a portion of the gold produced in these latter two areas eventually reached the hands of the Portuguese in São Jorge. While some of the dust was carried by African traders down the Senegal and the Gambia to other coastal stations, the remainder of the gold made its way north along the ancient established caravan routes through the Sahara.

Throughout the history of Portuguese occupation of Mina, and particularly during the years prior to about 1550, the Portuguese commanders of São Jorge sought to widen their sphere of influence among surrounding African states in an attempt to secure more of this remote gold trade. One of the first tasks facing the Portuguese at Mina was to extend their political control over the Village of Two Parts. João de Barros reports that during the first captain-general's term, disputes over rights between the Portuguese and the villagers became so intense that armed conflict erupted. Because of increasing thefts from Portuguese stores in the sheds of the riverside yard and the *ramada*, Azambuja attacked the African settlement and burned a portion of it to the ground. [62] Following this aggression, the Portuguese commander sought to reaffirm relations with the local inhabitants by a combination of military intimidation and frequent largesses of gifts to local headmen and their warriors. Although the local village leaders at São Jorge eventually appeared reconciled to the Portuguese presence, they could not guarantee free access for more distant traders coming to the coastal station. The agreements made between Azambuja and Caramansa were not the sort of binding general trading rights to the area that the Portuguese had envisaged. To achieve these rights the cooperation of the paramount chiefs of Efutu and Commany was essential. Therefore the visit of a leader from either of those states to São Jorge was always an important occasion, and small gifts were always taken from the post stores to promote peace and trade.

Portuguese information regarding the inland African kingdoms was sketchy and vague until about 1500. The first direct evidence of inland traders at São Jorge occurred in 1502, when the son of an Akan ruler came along with several merchants from that country to visit the Portuguese. The Akans had come more than a hundred miles through the forest belt. Their closest town to the coast was five days' journey inland at Assingrud. At that time the Portuguese learned that the Akani confederacy of states was engaged in war with their neighbors, the Atis, over the murder of an Akan chieftain's son. In their early reports the Portuguese spoke of the Akani as if it were a single, powerful kingdom; however, supplementary Portuguese documentation applied the term *Akani* generally to a number of inland states which formed a loose association in the sixteenth and early seventeenth centuries.[63]

Trade with the interior states continued on an irregular basis for several years after the initial 1502 meeting. Gradually the Portuguese pieced together a general picture of the region immediately behind the coast. They knew that these inland states were powerful, well organized, and, most important, close to the source of the gold. The gold which was traded by the occasional Akani merchants at São Jorge assayed at nearly twenty-three carats and was among the purest which the Portuguese had seen.[64] Perhaps it was because of this high grade of gold, or else because Akan merchants had not been seen at São Jorge in over a year, that the Portuguese commandant was prompted in 1513 to send a Portuguese emissary to open the trail all the way to Akan territory. This ambassador was instructed to contact the Akan paramount king if possible and establish friendly relations. The Portuguese commandant at this time, Afonso Caldeira, selected Lopo Mexia from the garrison and sent him to the Akan country accompanied by an interpreter and gifts. There is no subsequent report on the outcome of Mexia's mission save for the notice of its dispatch.[65] In 1517 Governor Fernão Lopes Correa sent another emissary to seek out the land of the Akani. This second Portuguese messenger, Nicolão Garcia, traveled first by canoe to the kingdom of Akara (Accra) at the eastern edge of the Mina coast. There Garcia presented gifts to the local ruler: a *lamben*, an *aljaravia*, several measures of cloth, and a yellow cap. From Akara Garcia, accompanied by black interpreters and a small retinue of merchants, proceeded north five days' march to the land of the Akani. There the Portuguese ambassador made gifts and presentations to the Akani chieftains similar to those given at Akara.[66] Garcia's mission bore results, for within the year Akani merchants were making their way to São Jorge. The merchants were accompanied by an ambassador of the Akan king sent to deal with the Portuguese.[67] For over two decades following this 1517 exchange trade relations between the Portuguese and the Akani continued at a brisk pace. Only in times of serious civil conflicts were the roads closed for these merchants, and even then delays were of short duration.[68]

The administrations of Fernão Lopes Correa (1516–19) and Duarte Pacheco Pereira (1519–22) were among the most energetic in seeking new trade and inland contacts. At the same time that Garcia was venturing into Akan country northeast of São Jorge, attempts were underway to effect peaceful trading contacts with an African kingdom situated several days' march to the northwest behind Cape Threepoints. Wassaw had been a major contributor to the gold trade conducted with the tiny auxiliary post established by the Portuguese at Axem in 1502. Fernão Lopes Correa sought to encourage the Wassaw trade with Axem as well as with São Jorge itself by lavishing fine gifts upon merchants who came from this region. In late 1518 several goats were given to Wassaw merchants in exchange for their assistance in opening the roads to their kingdom. In addition, a female slave was selected and sent to the *Xarife*

The Mina Coast

Gulf of Guinea

AKAN

WASSAW

AKARA
Christiansborg
Accra

FANTE
Apam
Kormantin

EFUTU ASEBU
Moure
Cape Corso
São Jorge da Mina
Ampeni (Torto)

COMMANY
Shama

Axem

Cape
Threepoints

0   10   20   30   40
miles

of the Wassaws to encourage him to seek trade connections with the Portuguese.[69] Finally, Lopes Correa sent each Wassaw merchant home laden with a handsome *lamben* and *aljaravia* to give their king. When Wassaw traders returned to São Jorge in 1519, they were accompanied by one of the brothers of the Wassaw king. Although command of São Jorge had passed to Duarte Pacheco Pereira, gifts (basins, goats, and *lambens*) were tendered to this distinguished visitor.[70] Pacheco Pereira continued his predecessor's policy with regard to opening the Wassaw trade. Pereira valued these trade relations enough to send a Portuguese representative to the court of the Wassaw king in May 1520. João Vieira, accompanied by an African translator and a male slave, departed for the Wassaw kingdom bearing gifts of *aljaravias*.[71] A regular commerce ensued, and later the same year Pacheco Pereira was instrumental in settling a quarrel which led to warfare between the Wassaws and one of their neighbors, the Aduns.[72] The Portuguese had discovered that peace among the nations was essential if the gold trade were to prosper.

Along the coastal fringe, the Portuguese pursued a similar policy of trade expansion during the period 1482–1540. The Portuguese economic sphere of influence eventually encompassed all the coastal states and small villages from Cape Threepoints to the kingdom of Akara. Naturally, the closest and most frequent associations the Portuguese had with coastal people were with their immediate neighbors, the powerful states of Commany and Efutu. Permanent commercial contacts were opened between the Portuguese and these states prior to 1500. During the first governorship of Fernão Lopes Correa from 1499 to 1502, it was reported necessary to send an ambassador with gifts to the ruler of Commany to reopen the roads through that monarch's land.[73] Lopes Correa also reported that at the time (1500) Efutu merchants were at São Jorge awaiting fresh shipments of tradegoods. In 1502 the *xarife* of the king of Efutu and his family visited the Portuguese station.[74] Then in 1503 came the dramatic conversion of the Efutu paramount chief, described in great detail by Diogo de Alvarenga. The peace which ensued between Efutu and the Portuguese lasted for several decades and was interrupted only briefly in 1514 when a dispute arose between Efutu and the Portuguese. It was about this time that the

Village of Two Parts was asserting its final independence from the authority of both Efutu and Commany. The villagers looked to their Portuguese allies for support in this move, and Portuguese military assistance placed a strain on the Europeans' relations with their neighbors.[75] An Efutu attack against São Jorge, feared at the height of the 1514 crisis, did not materialize.

By 1500 Portuguese influence had expanded westward to the extent that the fortress of Santo António de Axem was founded to handle the growing commercial activity around Cape Threepoints. The small post was furnished with personnel, provisions, and tradegoods drawn from São Jorge, and all financial transactions conducted at Axem were included in the account records of the factor of São Jorge. In 1515 Axem was attacked by neighboring Ahanta warriors and almost overrun. The Portuguese governor at São Jorge, Nuno Vaz, ordered the western station dismantled and a new, stronger fortress erected nearby on a rock outcropping overlooking Axem bay. In the succeeding decades the fortifications of the new post were considerably amplified.

On the eastern flank of São Jorge contacts and trade developed more slowly. As late as 1514 the eastern limits of Portuguese coastal trade did not extend beyond Cabo das redes. Trade had been established with this small coastal settlement sometime prior to 1504. At that time Pacheco Pereira reported in his *Esmeraldo* that annually the local merchants of Cabo das redes carried 10,000 to 20,000 *dobras* of gold to trade at São Jorge da Mina.[76] The Portuguese also purchased occasional supplies of millet from the region around Cabo das redes to supplement grain shipments from Portugal.[77] It was not until 1517 that the first mission was dispatched to the kingdom of Akara farther east to arrange trade contacts. Three years later, in 1520, the Labade (Labida) who resided in the region just east of Akara sent an ambassador to São Jorge to initiate trade relations.[78]

The Portuguese never were able to extend their political influence far beyond the narrow limits of São Jorge da Mina, Axem, and the Village of Two Parts, or Edina as the latter was called. Continual attempts were made to interfere in the local affairs of Commany and Efutu whenever the peace was threatened, but these efforts met with only limited success. For instance, in 1519 one of the last duties which Fernão Lopes Correa performed as governor was to engineer a peace between the new rulers of both Commany and Efutu.[79] This helped pave the way for the successes enjoyed by Pacheco Pereira in the latter's dealings with the local merchants and rulers. On the other hand, no amount of Portuguese pressure could influence the selection of a new paramount chief for any of the local states. Nor did the Portuguese have any control over the internal politics of the states with which they traded. Customarily, on the occasion of a new king's ascendancy to the throne or on the arrival of a new European governor, gifts were sent to all the major states with which the Portuguese conducted trade. This was not a payment or a quitrent of any sort, rather it was a diplomatic gesture designed to encourage trade. On his arrival at São Jorge Pacheco Pereira went a step further and personally visited several of the coastal states, including Commany and Efutu, to cement Afro-Portuguese relations.

The most important figure in the gold trade was frequently not the king of an African state, but rather his chief advisor or *xarife*. The *xarifes* of Commany and Efutu were particularly essential to the Portuguese trade, for all of the inland merchants journeying to São Jorge had to pass through one of those two bordering states. Many merchants, particularly those from remote kingdoms, remained suspicious of the white man and his fortress and therefore they preferred to leave the conduct of trade with the Portuguese in the hands of local merchants. The latter usually had some command of the Portuguese language and knew the workings of the trade. Even inland merchants who ventured all the way to São Jorge itself were always accompanied by the *xarife* of the state through which they passed. The Portuguese quickly realized the essential nature of the *xarife* as the middleman or intermediary in the gold trade and they continually lavished this official with innumerable small gifts on each occasion of his visit to São Jorge. Without this African's goodwill and intercession with his king, the roads might be closed. Portuguese records abound with references to contacts with the respective *xarifes*, and every factor and commander of São Jorge was aware of this man's function and importance.

Ultimately, the question must be answered, How great were the annual profits from the Mina gold trade during the era of royal monopoly, i.e., 1482–1540? Except for a handful of years, complete statistics for the trade are lacking. Nevertheless, there are several approaches to the question which, when combined, permit a general summary of the volume of profit. For example, reports of contemporaries who were directly associated with the Mina trade are one valuable source. These men generally indicate that the sums of gold brought to Portugal from Mina were considered enormous for that day and age. Aside from these very general impressions of the gold trade, the gold receipts may be ascertained through the records of the Casa da Moeda in Lisbon, where all the gold from Mina, both royal and private portions, was sent to be refined. By making use of these records and their statistics, the expenses involved in administering the posts (e.g., salaries and miscellaneous outlays), and by deducting the latter, the amount of profit emerges. With further allowances for recorded losses of treasure at sea by shipwreck or through seizure of privateers, the resulting figures should reflect the crude royal profits from Mina. Of course, this would not include the cost of the tradegoods themselves or the salaries and expenses involved in maintaining the Casa da Mina in Lisbon. But in accounting procedures utilized at São Jorge by the factor and his clerks, these latter two expenses were never computed.

Gross receipts of the Portuguese crown drawn from Mina during the years 1482–1540 were quite handsome, but they did not reach the lofty sums cited by most contemporary writers. In the reigns of John II and Manuel I the royal portion of the trade remained nearly constant from year to year. During that time, it fluctuated between 1,500 and 1,800 marks per annum. Between 1522 and 1540, royal Mina revenues slipped to an annual average of only 1,266 marks, but accurate records are lacking for the years 1522 and 1527. Furthermore, the great disparity in revenues for the years 1530, 1531, and 1532 are not accurate indicators of the normal flow of gold from São Jorge da Mina. The Lisbon Mint received only 920, 650, and 925 marks respectively during these years while the factor's records at São Jorge noted sales nearly double these amounts.[80] The reason for this disparity is that the commandant of the post, Estevão da Gama, chose to hold back on gold ship-

ments until the final year of his tour in 1532. In those last twelve
months Da Gama shipped 2,960 marks of gold to Portugal in elev-
en caravels.[81] The governor judged that a grand entry into Lisbon
with enormous quantities of gold for his sovereign would make a
decidedly favorably impression on John III.[82]

From fragmentary records of the Mina trade, royal revenues
apparently stabilized at about 1100 marks annually for the rest of
the 1530s. The turning point in the trade came in the early 1540s.
During the final fifteen years of John's reign, 1542–57, gold receipts from Mina dipped to an annual average of only 687 marks.
Unfortunately, economic records pertaining to Mina following
John's reign are so scattered and fragmentary that any averages
then become totally unreliable.

In comparison with total royal revenues during the period 1480–
1540, Mina gold clearly enjoyed its greatest prominence prior to
the opening of the eastern spice trade in the sixteenth century.
Gold from São Jorge da Mina nearly doubled the total royal revenues during the last twenty years of the fifteenth century. By
1506 Mina gold shipments constituted about 25% of the crown's
income. At that time, however, Mina treasure was already exceeded slightly by the drugs and spices from Asia. A decade later,
in 1519, despite the fact that gold receipts at Mina had reached
their absolute peak, this gold had slipped to only about 15% of
crown income. By 1519 the value of commodities derived from the
Far East exceeded that of Mina gold by a ratio of 5 to 2.[83] During
the remaining decades, until about 1540, Mina gold continued to
contribute between 13% and 16% of the annual average income
enjoyed by the Portuguese monarch.

By examining the major expenses in the Mina trade, such as the
cost of tradegoods, freighting charges, and salaries and upkeep for
the post it would appear that between 500 and 600 marks of gold
per year were needed to meet the overhead of São Jorge until
about 1540. Of course this figure is approximate. For example, the
profit margins for only part of the tradegoods sold are well documented. In the case of metal hardware, *manilhas* cost 10 *réis* when
purchased in Flanders. At São Jorge these same *manilhas* sold for
120 *réis*. In like manner, all basins were valued according to their
weight and could reliably bring a similar profit/cost ratio of be-

tween 10 to 1 and 12 to 1 after deducting losses from breakage. Until about 1530, copper and brass *manilhas* were purchased by the Portuguese factor in Antwerp at an approximate cost of 2000 *réis* per quintal.[84] On the other hand, items made of cloth cost the Portuguese factor in Flanders more than metalware. Moreover, cloth came not only from Flanders but also from France, north Africa, and Portugal itself, provided by private contractors. In addition to costing more than metal, cloth goods suffered more from spoilage and damage, both en route to Mina and while at the station awaiting sale. A reasonable average profit/cost ratio of 4 to 1 would not be out of line for most fabrics traded at São Jorge. Profits from slaves varied from head to head. Captives taken in the Slave Rivers for a cost of 50 *manilhas* or about 500 *réis* brought between 9,000 and 18,000 *réis*' worth of gold at São Jorge da Mina.[85] However, other expenses had to be figured into the slave traffic: transporting and feeding the slaves cost another 500 *réis* each before they were sold; also, many captives died on board ship and the rate of rejection by the factor of São Jorge was high.

Supplies and provisions used by the garrison cost 50 to 75 marks in gold per year. Some grain and local produce were purchased from nearby villagers, but the bulk of the provisions originated in Lisbon. Likewise, all munitions came from Portugal. Another 75 to 100 marks were required to provide for the expenses, including crew salaries, of the caravels which plied the *Carreira da Mina*. Finally, salaries for those serving at the Portuguese station amounted to approximately 2.5 million *réis* per year, depending upon fluctuations in the size of the garrison. This amounted to slightly more than 100 marks annually for this major expense.

Even when the rough overall expense figure of 500 to 600 marks is compared with the amount of gold remitted from São Jorge, the royal portion of the profit was quite respectable. The Mina gold trade was a self-supporting enterprise throughout the entire period before the 1540s (cf. Appendix C). At no time during this period did gold receipts fall below this 600 mark level. The first annual losses from the trade were not experienced until the early 1550s. It should be noted, however, that a general downward trend in the amount of profit can be detected beginning about 1526. This

dwindling of the Mina treasure continued with only rare rises to
the high levels customarily taken in during Manuel's reign.

One of the earliest descriptions of the lucrative nature of the
Mina trade is the *Esmeraldo* of Duarte Pacheco Pereira. The *Es-*
meraldo, written about 1504, describes gold trade at São Jorge
during the late fifteenth century. Pacheco Pereira attests to a 5 to
1 profit margin overall on goods shipped there for sale.[86] Another
equally glowing account of the Mina trade is that of Vasco da
Gama, who in 1502 halted a Lisbon-bound treasure caravel from
Mina long enough to show its cargo of 250 gold marks to the Hindu
ambassadors on board the admiral's vessel. The statement was
made by da Gama that this type of treasure shipment was a monthly affair.[87] Later the same year, a Venetian resident in Lisbon reported the simultaneous arrival of two Mina treasure caravels. The
amount of bullion cited as having been on board these vessels was
so high that the Italian remarked that Mina treasure was one of the
great underpinnings of Manuel I's extensive empire.[88] Mina gold
was much in evidence around the court of Manuel I, for apparel
worn by that monarch was covered with decorations made from
this precious metal. Other items included gold daggers, filigree
belts, spurs, fragile baskets, crucifixes, and cups, all of gold. Most
of the gold was refined in Portugal and cast into objects of traditional Portuguese design. During the late fifteenth century, however, cast gold was occasionally brought from Mina for the king.
For instance, included among Manuel's many treasures in 1499
was a gold bracelet sent to him from Mina by Fernão Lopes
Correa, the governor of São Jorge.[89]

As already demonstrated, gold obtained from Mina was a significant addition to the Portuguese economy during the years 1480
to 1540. With it, the crown could purchase many of the necessities
required for the conduct of trade with the East as well as the luxuries of Manuel's court. Mina gold also paid for armies and fleets as
when in 1529 John III sent his brother-in-law, Charles of Spain,
forty muleloads of treasure, including a considerable portion of
Mina gold. The gold arrived in Barcelona while Charles was pre-
paring to depart for Italy and the war with France.[90] Mina gold also
purchased German silver which in turn helped to stabilize Portu-

gal's coinage in a major revision of the monetary system in 1489. A year later, gold from Mina was sent in large quantities to Italy to buy luxuries (silks, brocades, jewels, etc.) on behalf of the crown prince of Portugal.

Throughout most of John III's reign (from 1521 until 1557) Mina gold shipments to the king were deemed sufficient collateral to satisfy loans underwritten by John's foreign bankers. The earliest recorded instance of payment made against future Mina gold shipments dates from March 1535 when John III ordered that 10,000 *cruzados* be set aside from the Mina caravels to pay loans recently acquired as well as to meet salary payments for his officials serving in Safim and Azamor. In February 1537, John secured a loan of 35,000 *cruzados* from his bankers, again using the treasure from an anticipated Mina gold fleet as collateral. In May of the same year, the Portuguese monarch wrote to his overseer of the royal treasury that since there was no revenue more certain than that from the Mina caravels, a further debt of 5,000 *cruzados* could be assumed with security given in gold expected from a second fleet returning from São Jorge da Mina that year.[91]

While mint records are useful in determining profits, more gold was traded at São Jorge da Mina than reached Portugal. More than once Mina caravels became victims to shipwreck or piracy. The French were particularly active in waylaying Portuguese vessels suspected of carrying treasure cargoes. Each time the loss to the Portuguese crown ran in excess of 200 marks of gold. The first recorded attack and seizure of a Mina gold shipment by French privateers was in 1492.[92] Three years later another Mina caravel was overhauled and pillaged by French pirates led by a renegade Portuguese pilot, and they relieved the caravel of a gold cargo valued at 20,000 *dobras*.[93] By the 1530s French preying upon Portuguese shipping and Mina caravels in the *Carreira da Mina* had become so intolerable that steps were undertaken by John III to protect his treasure ships by providing them with escorts. In addition, armed galleons began to be used with increasing frequency to carry treasure shipments from São Jorge. The years of competition had begun. No longer could the Portuguese ply the *Carreira da Mina* unchallenged.

4
Years of Challenge, 1540-80

During the late 1530s João de Barros, historian and factor of the Lisbon India House, accurately summarized the gold trade with Mina up to that time in his *Décadas da Asia:* "I do not know in this kingdom any yoke of land, toll, tithe, excise or any other royal tax which is more certain in each yearly return than is the revenue of the commerce of Guinea. It is, besides, so peaceful a property, quiet and obedient, that—without our having to stand at the touch-hole of the bombard with lighted match in one hand, and lance in the other—it yields us gold, ivory, wax, hides, sugar, pepper, and it would produce other returns if we sought to explore it further."[1] Barros's statement offers a valid summary of Portuguese activities in African posts such as Mina. Within a decade, however, Mina would become a battleground of competitors, all vying to wrest control of the rich trade from Portuguese hands.

For more than half a century following the implantation of a permanent post on the Mina coast, the Portuguese crown enjoyed a relatively quiet possession of its holdings. Much of the period between 1482 and 1540 was spent in creating and perfecting the administrative machinery which would ensure a steady return in treasure for Portugal. An occasional Spanish, English, or French vessel might venture into west African waters, but none proceeded as far south as the Mina coast. For the most part, foreign privateers chose to lie in wait for Portuguese vessels farther north in the narrow waters around the Azores. Mina caravels were not exempt from the danger of capture, as has been noted, and the loss of even a single Mina vessel was a serious blow to crown revenues. Yet the Mina caravels had at least one advantage. They could rely upon their swiftness and ability to outmaneuver any enemy vessel which sought to give chase.

Despite the capture of a few Mina prizes, foreign interlopers were not yet so bold as to directly challenge Portugal's territorial claims. Between 1480 and 1540 Portugal's *mare clausum* in Mina remained intact, not because of its own defenses, but because the possible contenders—Spain, France, and England—were preoccupied elsewhere. Spain's interests were focused upon the New World and piecing together an empire in Europe under Charles I. England and France were both caught in internal difficulties over deepening religious and political problems. Furthermore, neither of these nations had as yet a maritime tradition sufficiently powerful to challenge the Iberian supremacy in naval matters. Nevertheless, powerful mercantile interests in both countries were beginning to apply pressure upon their sovereigns to sanction voyages to Guinea and Mina. Certainly Portugal's military posture in Mina, with only about sixty soldiers, was not a sufficient deterrent. Yet for French and English merchants, dispatching a trading ship to Mina in 1500 or even as late as the 1530s was at best a risky undertaking. Such an expedition had about a fifty percent chance of returning with a profit, for navigational skills which British and French seamen had developed gradually for sailing in European waters were of little assistance in the seas around Mina. The English had not yet found an accurate method of finding a position by utilizing the sun's declination, whereas Portuguese pilots had already recognized the value of compiling solar tables to aid them in sailing near the equator. In 1484 John II appointed a commission of scholars to work on this problem, and the commission's findings resulted in a simplification of the solar tables of the Jewish astronomer Abraham Zacuto of Salamanca. With São Jorge da Mina as base for the scientific enquiries, these tables were tested in Guinea waters in 1485 and found to be satisfactory.[2] The "Regiment of the Sun" (Regimento do sol) which resulted from these studies was jealously guarded by the Portuguese crown, as was other vital navigational information pertaining to African discoveries. World maps revealed to northern Europeans the continuing Portuguese explorations, but specific rutters and sailing charts for Mina and areas south of the equator were rigorously protected by royal ordinances. It is interesting to note that the first foreign vessels sailing to Mina were guided by rebel pilots who had fled from Portugal and had taken service with foreign masters.

The Portuguese crown went to some lengths to foster the rumor that though English and French vessels might successfully pene-

trate the latitudes of Mina, it was impossible for their ships to return because of persistent headwinds and contrary ocean currents.
Without exact information of offshore winds and currents, rumors
were purposefully circulated by the Portuguese that ships of the
type used by the English and French would be cast headlong upon
the leeward shores and founder.[3] As late as Henry VIII of England's death in 1547, the practice of oceanic navigation in that
country was still an obscure field to all but a handful of Englishmen. The study of geography in England still lagged seriously
behind that in the Iberian states. As an example, in 1547 the only
book in English describing the whole of the Portuguese conquests
and the areas which they covered was a thin pamphlet printed in
Antwerp in 1511![4]

Nonetheless, the encouragement to sail on a Guinea voyage was
present in both England and France. It was fostered and stimulated by each gold shipment unloaded from Mina caravels in Lisbon. Much of this same treasure eventually found its way into the
hands of northern banking concerns in Antwerp. As early as 1481
a voyage directly to Mina was contemplated by a consortium of
English merchants who were encouraged in their endeavor by the
Spanish Duke of Medina Sidonia. The duke agreed to supply
skilled pilots necessary for such a venture from among Spanish
pilots who already had sailed those waters. John II of Portugal was
able to forestall the combined Anglo-Spanish expedition's plans by
dispatching an embassy to Edward IV's court. After considerable
negotiation, the Portuguese ambassador obtained Edward's prom-
ise to publish a prohibition against such voyages in violation of the
agreements existing between England and Portugal. More specifically, the Portuguese pressed the English sovereign to bar the
sailing to Guinea of two English subjects, John Tintam and William
Fabian. These men were acting as the coordinators of the planned
trading venture to Mina. Thus John II succeeded for the moment
in protecting his Mina lands by resorting only to diplomatic pressure, but he realized that this action would not suffice forever.

The earliest recorded open challenge to Portugal's Mina lands
did not come for more than a half century following Spanish trading activities in the region in the early 1480s. Starting in late 1538
or early 1539, French and English privateers intensified their

attacks against Portuguese shipping. Corsairs and merchant adventurers tried to breach the Portuguese trade monopoly in the southern Atlantic, including Mina. The Mina House in Lisbon began receiving disturbing reports from São Jorge and from ship captains on the *Carreira da Mina*. These letters bear witness to the growing boldness of foreign interlopers. During the 1530s Portuguese vessels sailing along the Malagueta coast west of Mina reported sighting occasional French interlopers and these French pirates seized several Portuguese trading ships in these same waters.[5] Consequently John III began to send heavily-armed galleons, such as the *São João* and *Trinidade*, to accompany the Mina supply ships. Once in Mina, one of the warships usually returned with the treasure caravels to protect the gold shipment, while the other armed vessel remained on the coast for several months to pursue foreign traders.[6]

As foreign sailings into African waters increased, buccaneering ventures were supplemented by purely commercial voyages to Guinea in search of trade outlets. Voyages were further stimulated when, on 13 November 1540, the French monarch raised embargoes upon Mina voyages which had been in effect since mid-1536.[7] Associations of French merchants were formed to conduct trade with Guinea and Mina. One of the centers of the new French African trade was the city of Rouen, where a regular, highly organized consortium of merchants appeared in the early 1540s, led by a number of wealthy city burghers, including the brothers Dumochel (Jean and Pierre), Guillaume le Seigneur, Guillaume Deshayes, and Jean Ribault. As early as September 1541 they sponsored the Mina sailing of *L'Esperance* under the command of Guillaume le Mire. In 1546 these merchants again were sponsors of the Mina-bound *Catherine de Honfleur*. The *Catherine*, commanded by Gratian Perys, departed from France in January 1546 under explicit orders to proceed to Mina and conduct trade for gold with African merchants.[8] Frequent mention of other sailings suggests that voyages to Mina were made by the French every year during the 1540s.

Portuguese reports from officials of São Jorge da Mina confirm many of these French sailings. In February 1541 the governor of São Jorge, Antonio de Miranda, noted the presence of French vessels near his post. The French halted a Portuguese dispatch canoe manned by Mina blacks heading for Axem.[9] Anticipating an attack, Miranda hastened to repair and strengthen the defenses of Axem which had been neglected for almost a decade. In 1540 a fire had gutted most of the post's interior, destroying provisions, powder, and wooden gun mounts. By June 1541 repairs were underway, but the French attack never materialized.[10] The French vessel sighted by the blacks in late spring of 1541 had already returned to France with its golden cargo.

In February 1543 a Portuguese patrol from Axem encountered another French vessel about nine leagues west of their station. The factor and captain of Axem, Estevão de Limpo, immediately dispatched a canoe to São Jorge with news of this sighting, and in response, Captain Miranda sent a small squad of soldiers by canoe to ascertain exactly where the French were trading. Their instructions were to remain in contact with the French and to shoot any interlopers who might try to come ashore. Landing undetected near the trading site, the Portuguese found not one ship, but a squadron of six French merchant vessels. Unaware they were under surveillance, these ships weighed anchor and sailed eastward past Axem to a point between the post and São Jorge itself. The flotilla consisted of an armed galleon of considerable size, two vessels of about twenty to thirty tons and three very small picket boats, the latter of which could operate in shallow coastal waters, even sailing upriver a short distance. The French brought for sale the same commodities the Portuguese had been selling but their prices were considerably lower and thus they were eagerly purchased by blacks in villages remote from the Portuguese posts.[11] With no Portuguese warships in the area, no attempt could be made to intercept these interlopers. Captain Miranda noted that 1541 was the third consecutive year in which French vessels had visited Mina.[12] Each year the French arrived on the coast between the months of December and March and Miranda suggested to his superiors in Lisbon that the construction of two or three galleys to guard the coast during this season could prevent further incursions. This, he believed, would be more effective and cheaper than sending additional troops to Mina and using land-based forces to discourage landings along the coastline. But Miranda's suggestion fell on deaf ears. It took Lisbon ten years to adopt such measures. Galleys were first reported operating on the Mina coast during the 1550s, and they quickly became an essential part of the Portuguese Mina defenses.

The statistics of gold remittances from São Jorge during the 1540s clearly indicate how effective French interloping came to be. While during the period 1530–39 the Mina trade averaged 1400 to 1800 marks per year, beginning in 1540 these figures plummeted until they reached their lowest level in 1544.[13] The following year the traffic and trade rose briefly to its normal level. Nevertheless, the trend was apparent. By mid-century Portuguese trade at São Jorge da Mina was clearly in decline. Gold receipts from Mina from 1549 to 1553 show a 60% decline in the volume of trade there. The average annual income was reduced to only about 600 gold marks. Obviously French interloping was chiefly responsible for this. But also to blame were a series of disturbances and wars in the interior. Shortly before 1543 a civil war between several of the Akani confederation members seriously curtailed the flow of gold to the Portuguese posts. Only small numbers of Akani merchants ventured to the coast for several years. In 1548, for instance, it was reported that Akani traders were still fearful for their goods and safety on the interior roads. Moreover, heavy tributes were exacted by southern Akani states on all who passed through their lands.[14] In 1551 the commander of São Jorge reported the temporary opening of trade with merchants 150 miles away, but apparently that trade was curtailed again after a short time by new internal African struggles.[15] It was 1557 before direct, unhampered trade between the Portuguese posts and the Akani states was reestablished. That year gifts were sent to the *Grandes Akanes* and *Pequenos Akanes* to reopen the roads through their lands. Governor Afonso Gonçalves Botafogo reported that eight months after this tendering of gifts the first Akani merchants since the days of António de Miranda began to arrive at São Jorge to trade.[16]

The small fortress of Axem, where French squadrons first traded with nearby villages, showed a decline of gold receipts even more pronounced than at São Jorge. During 1538 the factor of Axem sent 144 marks of gold to São Jorge for shipment.[17] The following year 159 marks were logged by the Mina factor as originating from

Axem.[18] In 1540 this figure remained almost unchanged—157 marks.[19] Then, during 1541, following the appearance of the French, only 32 marks were reported traded with African merchants who came to Axem.[20] This reduced volume was not offset by any increase in the trade being conducted at São Jorge itself. The reduced level of trading at Axem continued for the remainder of the decade.

The diminution in the gold trade did not seriously hinder work underway to effect substantial improvements in the defense system at the posts. Major advances had been made in the design and accuracy of both naval cannon and gunnery during the sixteenth century. Italian engineers were at work devising means of greater resistance to bombardment techniques. Although Portuguese defenses at São Jorge da Mina had not yet been tested against naval bombardment, John III perceived the need to update the post's physical facilities and gun batteries. During the 1540s a major renovation of São Jorge was begun that continued for more than four decades before it was completed by Philip II of Spain. The curtain walls around the main courtyard were thickened by more than eighteen inches along their outer courses, and at the western and northern corners of the outer curtain wall the medieval vertical towers were dismantled and transformed into bastions resembling those being designed by Italian Renaissance engineers. The solid foundations of the original towers at these points were used as the core for these additions.

Modifications were also made on the land side of the fortress. The double ditch, which almost severed São Jorge from the rest of the peninsula on which it was constructed, was deepened. In this way, additional building material was obtained for the stonework of the walls. The inner ditch was blocked off at one end and used as a water reservoir. Ships using the harbor could take on fresh water from this ditch without depleting the water rations of the fortress, which were kept in two cisterns. Finally, defenses surrounding the riverside yard were strengthened, and a wall was also built across the peninsula to the west of the African town to protect the Portuguese's black allies.[21]

John III assigned the supervision of the alterations at São Jorge to a newly-created official on the post—the *vedor das obras*, or overseer of works. Often a stonemason by profession, the *vedor das obras* was required to ensure that all other workmen, masons, carpenters, and slaves used in the fortress modifications carried out their tasks properly. The office of *vedor das obras* continued to function at least into the 1590s; after 1572 the position was assigned for life.[22] It was one of the few offices at São Jorge which was not made for a specific, limited term. Every ship captain sent to São Jorge da Mina was given instructions to observe the progress being made on the fortress modifications and give a status report to the Lisbon Mina House.[23]

French and English interlopers were not alone in seeking to penetrate the royal Portuguese monopoly at Mina. During the 1530s and thereafter, Portuguese interlopers became an increasing source of annoyance to the crown and the Mina administration. Officials in the Mina House alleged that nearly one-half of all gold taken from Mina by illicit trading was in the form of Portuguese privateers operating without royal licenses.

The best documented case of private Portuguese ventures is the account of an illegal voyage made by António Roiz between 1545 and 1553. Roiz had secured detailed sailing information on the *Carreira da Mina* during several earlier voyages into Guinea waters. When he returned to Portugal, he and several of his relatives contracted with a merchant, Francisco de Andrade, to sail to Mina for trade. Arriving off the Mina coast in 1545, the Roiz-Andrade expedition carefully avoided the Portuguese posts, but despite the interlopers' caution, their presence was reported to the governor of São Jorge by African informants. The commandant sent a squad of soldiers and surprised the trading party about nine leagues from São Jorge, arrested those caught on shore and confiscated considerable merchandise. The prisoners were taken to São Jorge, tried for their crime, and imprisoned. António Roiz was not ashore during the attack and was able to escape with his ship to São Tomé. When royal warrants for his arrest arrived at that island, he fled to the Cape Verdes, where he was captured. Although he escaped again and was able to smuggle himself and 7,000 to 8,000 *cruzados* in gold back into Portugal, he was recaptured and sent to the galleys for life.[24]

In the 1550s the first English competitors appeared on the

scene. São Jorge's governor, Rui de Melo, first learned about them from African informants in 1553. On the basis of this information, Melo reported to the Lisbon Mina House that two large ships accompanied by a pinnace were sailing eastward along the coast. More importantly, Melo had learned from his informants, who had spoken with these foreigners, that a Portuguese renegade was assisting this squadron in trading with the coastal villages. The English ships did not tarry on the Mina coast. Special precautions had been taken to avoid detection by the Portuguese advance post of Axem; therefore, by the time Melo received the news of their presence the fleet had already departed from that portion of the coast and sailed eastward to Benin. Thus the Portuguese commander could take no punitive actions except to send out strict orders that any coastal village found trading with these or other foreign ships would invite serious punishment for their transgressions.

Captain Thomas Windham commanded this first recorded English squadron to penetrate the Portuguese monopoly at Mina. Financial support for the diminutive fleet of three ships had come from a syndicate of English merchants, the majority of whom were centered in London. Captain Windham was fortunate to have as his co-commander on the expedition a skilled Portuguese pilot named António Anes Pinteado, who had served extensively on Portuguese coastguard expeditions to Brazil and Mina during the reign of John III. Pinteado's navigational skills had earned him a customary admission to the household of the Portuguese monarch as an expert pilot. However, Pinteado had fallen from royal favor and had left Portugal for refuge in England.[25] His departure from Portugal without royal permission was a direct violation of the king's law prohibiting pilots from taking service with other nations. Nonetheless, John III's efforts to have him returned failed. Pinteado's services and the details of Guinea sailings which he brought with him could be added to the English rutters of the time. He was too valuable simply to hand back to the Portuguese. On this basis, he was selected to accompany the first Windham expedition when it sailed for Mina from Portsmouth harbor on 12 August 1553.[26]

After securing about 150 pounds of gold in trade along the Mina coast, Captain Windham insisted upon sailing eastward beyond Mina to load a cargo of Guinea pepper at Benin. Pinteado urged

Windham to trade the remainder of the goods for Mina gold and
return home. But Windham was obstinate in his decision and the
squadron sailed on to Benin, where Pinteado's worst fears were
realized. While waiting for the gathering of pepper, the crew became sick and several sailors died. Aboard the command ship
Windham himself fell ill and died. Of the 140 men who had left
Portsmouth in August 1553, only 40 were still alive when the single
surviving ship from the fleet reached its home port. The second
vessel had to be abandoned at sea because there were not enough
hands to man her. In spite of the tremendous human loss, the
cargo brought back by the surviving vessel caused a stir among
English merchants. 150 pounds of pure gold was an enormous
profit and certainly more than the trade in ivory could secure in
west Africa. The Windham expedition spurred merchants to begin
preparations for followup voyages to Mina. Windham's fleet had
proved indisputably that English vessels could make a voyage to
Portuguese Mina and return with a profit.

The London merchants who had sponsored Windham hastily
organized a second expedition for the fall of 1554 under the command of John Lok. His squadron, consisting of three merchant
ships and two small pinnaces for coastal work, cleared the Thames
on 11 October 1554, bound for Portuguese waters off São Jorge da
Mina. The outward passage was relatively uneventful, except for a
sudden gale in the Channel which swamped one of the pinnaces,
and by January 1555, the squadron entered the Gulf of Guinea and
turned its helm eastward. Lok sought to avoid Axem and keep the
Portuguese from receiving advance warning of their presence. If
the trading went as planned, the English captain expected to be off
the coast before news had reached the Portuguese at São Jorge or
the Portuguese had time to mount a counterattack.

But the expedition's departure from England had already been
reported by the Portuguese minister in London to his superiors.
Secret dispatches passed to Flanders and were then forwarded by
dispatch boat to Lisbon, where John III received them by the beginning of December 1554.[27] Actually, Lok was most fortunate.
Even before the English fleet had departed from London, an
armed Portuguese squadron of four or five vessels had sailed to
take up station in Mina. For reasons which remain unclear, the

fleet commander, Dom Luis de Melo, altered his course after taking on fresh provisions at Cape Verde and sailed to the northern coast of Brazil.[28] Had Admiral Melo continued for Mina, he would doubtlessly have overhauled Lok's ships.

On New Year's Day 1555 Captain Lok anchored his fleet off the village of Shama between São Jorge and Axem and opened trade with the Mina blacks. The previous year Governor Melo had sent a strong Portuguese patrol to Shama to punish the villagers for their willingness to trade with Windham's squadron. Formerly the Portuguese had maintained a small trading lodge at Shama, but this had been closed several years before the Windham expedition. On their return from Benin, the survivors of the Windham squadron reported that the entire village had been burned to the ground by the Portuguese force as a punitive measure. Thus Lok did not expect to find any Portuguese present in the small thatch lodge that had been used occasionally for trade during peaceful times. The English captain was surprised when he anchored and was met by a volley of cannonfire. Governor Melo had just recently placed two or three pieces of ordnance within the lodge and stationed a squad of men to guard them. Lok mistakenly attributed this act of hostility to fire coming from the blacks of Shama, who he thought were manning the battery. It seems clear, however, from subsequent Portuguese accounts of the encounter that Portuguese gunners were responsible for the direction of the fire.

Lok departed quickly from Shama and sailed east, putting far out from shore when his ships neared São Jorge da Mina to avoid detection by the Portuguese lookouts atop the fortress roof. If the English presence in Mina was already known, the best the English commander could do was to keep his exact location a secret. The squadron sailed beyond the lands of Commany and Efutu and reached the village of Cabo Corso. Here, the English were welcomed by the villagers, for at that time the Cabo Corso chief was at war with the Portuguese. A lively exchange in English cloth and Mina gold ensued. One of Lok's ships, the *Trinity*, was sent farther east to trade with other small coastal settlements. Together, the four English vessels canvassed the Mina coast to its eastern limits around Accra.

When Lok turned his fleet homeward on 13 February 1555, he

had been in Portuguese waters off Mina for almost a month, and there had been no reprisals forthcoming from Portuguese forces. The only opposition had been the brief cannonade at Shama, but when the fleet neared Shama once again the handful of Portuguese had departed, and the English traded with the local inhabitants peacefully. The return passage to England was painfully slow—almost twenty weeks. When the cargoes were finally unloaded, they included over 36 hogsheads of Guinea pepper, 250 elephant tusks (each weighing over 90 pounds), and, most important, 400 pounds of fine gold dust. The presence of so much gold from a single expedition was more than sufficient to whet the appetites of merchant adventurers.

John III of Portugal made vigorous diplomatic protests to the English crown regarding the incursions of Windham, Lok, and subsequent interlopers. In regards to the Lok expedition, John III instructed his envoy in London, João Roiz Correa, to demand of Mary and her Privy Council: (1) the surrender of all Portuguese nationals involved in the expedition; (2) a restitution of the goods seized at Mina; (3) and publication of a general prohibition against future expeditions under grave royal penalties.[29] Queen Mary assured Ambassador Roiz Correa that she would take these matters under advisement. However, at the moment she was quite occupied with her wedding plans, since that summer she and Prince Philip of Spain were to be wed at Winchester. Expectations that Philip could exert some influence upon his new bride to restrict English incursions into territories claimed by Spain and Portugal waned swiftly by early 1555 when Philip left England to assume the kingship of Spain abdicated by his father Charles. The Anglo-Spanish alliance lay shattered.

Lok's successful voyage to Mina was followed by a spate of English sailings to Mina during the next two decades. Among the more notable were three voyages by William Towrson, in 1555, in 1556/57, and in 1558.[30] Commencing with Towrson's sailings the Portuguese in Mina began to mount a stiffer defense. During his first voyage, which began in the autumn following Lok's return, Towrson managed to sail his two vessels, the *Hart* and the *Hind*, past Axem without detection. This forestalled any advance warning being sent to São Jorge by dispatch canoe. Cape Threepoints was rounded on 3 January 1556, and the vessels landed at the mouth of the River Pra near Shama, where the Portuguese were still engaged in the conflict with the local inhabitants. Consequently the Portuguese lodge at the village was empty. While Towrson traded with the blacks, he learned that the chief of Cabo Corso, Don John, was also involved in a dispute with the Portuguese. Leaving Shama, Towrson steered the expedition out to sea beyond range of the lookout of São Jorge and sailed for Don John's village, hoping to repeat the successful route followed by Lok the year before. When the fleet arrived at the handful of mud and thatch huts, there was no sign of Don John, but local fishermen told Towrson that news of the English arrival had been sent to their king who was then at his capital inland. They asked that the Europeans await the impending return of their ruler.

While waiting, Towrson divided his squadron in half. The *Hart* was ordered to stay at Cabo Corso and await the arrival of the African chief, while Towrson sailed eastward in the *Hind* accompanied by a pinnace. Towrson traded along the coast for two days. He cautiously refused the entreaties of the blacks on shore that he land a boat and unload its cargo. Towrson preferred to conduct trade from a ship's boat anchored just beyond the line of the surf. In case a Portuguese warship should arrive or the Africans should attack from shore, this method of trading would permit rapid recall of the boat.

The caution of the English captain was justified. News of his presence at Mina had reached São Jorge da Mina, and the Portuguese commandant there had learned of the *Hart* and the *Hind* departure from Shama. Again African informants told the Portuguese of the number, size, and other particulars of the new fleet. They also told the Portuguese commander that the next stop planned by Towrson was at Cabo Corso. At that time there were no galleys stationed at Mina, only a small supply caravel which was used to transport goods to Axem. Although an all-out naval encounter was not possible, Governor Melo decided to risk sending an expedition to Cabo Corso to intercept the English ships. An armed patrol of 30 to 40 soldiers, almost half of the Portuguese garrison at São Jorge, was issued muskets, crossbows, and a small cannon. Rather than send them overland and risk their approach being reported by unfriendly blacks, the men and cannon were loaded aboard the supply caravel. Their orders were to land a short distance from Cabo Corso, move along the shore path, and surprise the English while the latter were on land and therefore vulnerable.

On the second day of trading near Cabo Corso, the crew of the *Hind* sighted a Portuguese patrol on a low hill behind the coastal settlement. The Portuguese soldiers descended to the beach firing their weapons as they advanced. Don John and his subjects fled, leaving the English to take to their boats and pull from shore. A brief but bloodless exchange of fire followed. The Portuguese shot from behind shore rocks while English sailors returned the fire from rolling longboats. The Portuguese remained in control of the village of Cabo Corso and Towrson headed east. As the English boats passed along the shoreline, Towrson noted that the Portuguese patrol had preceded them, burning several African coastal communities.

Towrson directed his fleet east along the coast and at each stop he encountered Portuguese resistance. Upon reaching Cormantin, the English tried to land and open trade. After some hesitation, the Africans began to come to the beach where a small tent had been erected to shelter the English factor and his wares. Towrson felt that he was now far enough removed from the Portuguese forces at São Jorge to risk going ashore to barter. He was mistaken, for no sooner had the trading session begun than the English discovered they had stepped into a trap. Portuguese troops had been shadowing the English in a small caravel. A squad of soldiers and a small cannon had been put ashore near Cormantin. Hidden from view by villagers who gathered around the English factor, the Portuguese crept within range and fired their weapons. The English scrambled for their boats leaving their tradegoods behind on the beach. The Portuguese managed three more volleys before the interloping boats pulled out of range. However, no casualties were reported on either side.

Towrson had expected the inhabitants of Cormantin to be friendly to English trade overtures. There had been reports that these villagers were engaged in a war with the Portuguese at São Jorge. What the English skipper did not know was that the previous Lok expedition had caused a turnabout in the relations and allegiance of the Cormantins. When Lok had paused at this settlement in 1555 one of his commanders, Robert Gainsh, had seized the son of the local chief and three other blacks who had come aboard the ship to trade. The four captives were carried to England where it was hoped they would be of some assistance to later English voyages as interpreters. Unfortunately for Towrson, Lok's hostile act had driven the Cormantin chief into an alliance with the Portuguese against the English.

The Portuguese caravel which had brought troops to Cormantin continued to shadow the activities of the English after they departed from that village. When Towrson landed between Cormantin and São Jorge to trade, the Portuguese fired warning shots from their lone vessel during the night to warn blacks to stay away. But the warning was not heeded, for Towrson reported spending a week at this site trading. On 22 January 1556 the local ruler departed for his inland capital and Towrson sailed westward, occasionally pausing to trade while the squadron passed the settlements on the Mina coast. By the first week of February, when victuals and tradegoods were all but exhausted, the ships took on fresh water and ballast and set sail for England. Over four months were required for the return north, and the ships finally reached Bristol harbor on 14 May 1556.

The journey was a moderate success for its backers. Aside from 120 pounds of gold, the cargo included several elephant tusks and two hogsheads of Guinea pepper. No vessels were lost, and in his report Towrson cited only one death among the crew. One can measure the extent of the Portuguese loss in trade by the reports of the commander of São Jorge, Rui de Melo. Confirming the success of the English Mina venture, Melo noted how Towrson's factors had flooded the coastal settlements of Mina with cheap cloth of inferior quality. So great had the English trade been that for some months following their departure no black merchants came to São Jorge or Axem to buy Portuguese wares. By May 1556 Melo reported that only 55,000 *cruzados* in gold had been received through the trade.[31] Towrson himself felt the trip was successful enough to warrant a second expedition to Mina. In the same month as his return from his first expedition, the English captain secured the financial backing for a new venture. The *Hart* was refitted, and a large cargo ship, the *Tiger*, was added to the fleet. The open preparations of the new fleet for a Mina voyage were carefully reported in dispatches sent by the Portuguese minister in England to John III of Portugal.[32] Therefore, when Towrson set out in the fall of 1556, plans were well underway in Mina to meet this new threat. In 1556 a new governor, Afonso Rodrigues Botafogo, was sent to São Jorge to replace Rui de Melo, who had held the post for nearly five years. Botafogo was escorted to his new post by a naval squadron of five large armed warships and a caravel. They carried both provisions and strong reinforcements for the garrisons on the Mina coast. The new commandant's orders were very explicit: he was to engage any enemy ships before interlopers could land and open trade. The opportunity to carry out these instructions came almost immediately. While en route to São Jorge, in mid-December 1556, three ships in the Portuguese convoy encountered a French vessel at the western edge of the Mina coast. The ship was the *Roebarge*, on a voyage for Mina and accompanied by a small trading pinnace. Portuguese warships engaged the two Frenchmen in a running sea fight off Cape Threepoints. The action was finally curtailed and the supply ships recalled to press on to São Jorge.

While the cargoes were being unloaded at the fortress an expected enemy was approaching. William Towrson had departed Harwich on 14 September 1556, determined to repeat his success of the previous season. On December 30, after an uneventful voyage, the English squadron reached the western approaches to Mina. At this point they encountered a French fleet of five ships which were also bound for Mina to trade. The Frenchmen included the *Espoier* out of Hableneff, captained by Admiral Denis Blundell; the *Leuriere* of Rouen, with its master Jerome Baudet; and a third unnamed French vessel from Honfleur accompanied by two pinnaces. Towrson met with the French commanders and a compact was signed. The eight ships then sailed on to the Mina coast. On 8 January 1557 the now familiar red cliffs which lay twenty to thirty miles west of Cape Threepoints were sighted. These cliffs were the landmark signalling the beginning of the area patrolled by Portuguese warships. A week later, secure in the size of their fleet, the squadron sailed within open view of São Jorge da Mina.[33] Before committing his forces, Captain Botafogo dispatched African allies to ascertain the destination of the enemy. Informants reported that the squadron had divided into two parts. One element continued to the east; the second half was trading with coastal settlements between São Jorge and Axem. A small contingent of Portuguese troops were already in the latter area conducting reprisal raids against villagers who had traded with earlier interlopers and a brief skirmish occurred between Portuguese soldiers and English sailors near the mouth of the Pra on January 19. Just before sunset Portuguese gunners opened fire on the English coming ashore to trade with the villagers of Shama. The Portuguese could not press their attack too vigorously since they were heavily outnumbered by the black forces of Shama who were still hostile toward them.

In the interim, Botafogo completed the unloading of the convoy and he swiftly dispatched his ships in pursuit of the intruders. Late in the afternoon of January 25, the squadron of five armed Portuguese vessels encountered the English and French ships near Cape Threepoints. Decks were cleared for a sea fight. The entire following day was spent in maneuvering by both parties to gain sea room and wind advantage. The fight did not begin until the 27th. Richard Hakluyt transcribed Captain Towrson's account of the fight in the pages of the *Principal Navigations:*

". . . about eleven of the clocke wee had the wind of them, and then wee went roome with them, which when they perceived, they kept about to the shore againe, and wee after them, and when they were so neere the shore that they could not well runne any further on that boord, they kept about againe, and lay to the Seaward, and then wee kept about them, and were ahead of them, and tooke in our topsailes and taried for them: and the first that came up was a small barke which sailed so well that she cared not for any of us, and caried good ordinance: and assone as she came up, she shot at us, and overshot us, and then she shot at the Admirall of the Frenchmen, and shot him through in two or three places, and went foorth a head of us, because wee were in our fighting sailes: then came up another caravell under our Lee in like case which shot at us and at the Frenchman, and hurt two of his men and shot him through the maine maste. And after them came up the [Portuguese] Admirall under our Lee also . . . both our Viceadmirall and the two Frenchmen, & our owne pinnasse left us in the laps, and ran to seaward, and wee ran still along, and kept the wind of them to succour the French Admirall, who was under all of their Lees, and when they met with him, every one went roome with him, and gave him the broad side, and after they cast about againe, and durst not boord him, because they sawe us in the weather of them . . . three of the [Portuguese] caravels which were the smallest, went so fast that it was not possible for a ship to boord them, and earied such ordinance that if they had had the weather of us, they would have troubled three of the best ships that we had, and as for their Admirall and Viceadmirall they were both notablie appointed."[34]

Half the crew of the *Espoier* were killed, along with sixteen on the smaller French pinnace. On January 29 it was decided that the pinnace, her rudder shattered and shipping water badly, was not salvageable. The cannon were removed, and the ship was set afire and driven onto the shore. In spite of the defeat which had been suffered, Towrson and his remaining French allies chose to tarry for another month on the Mina coast. They kept on the move, trading for only a day or two at each coastal settlement and avoiding further contacts with the Portuguese coastguard squadron operating out of São Jorge. The only portion of the coast where the English felt secure enough to venture inland in search of trade was in the kingdom of Efutu. Towrson sent some men a few miles back from the coast to the large African settlement at Eguafu, where King Abaan was holding court. Relations between Efutu and its Portuguese neighbors at São Jorge da Mina had been strained for months. When the English approached him looking for trade Abaan asked them to build a fort in his land and even offered them a site for such a fortress.[35]

On 3 March 1557 Towrson set a course for home. Passing São Jorge, he sighted the five Portuguese warships still riding at anchor in the harbor. That same afternoon the English encountered a new Portuguese fleet coming from the west and heading for São Jorge. This new squadron had been sent from Lisbon to relieve the vessels then on coastguard duty. Even more powerful than the first, the new squadron included two very large warships estimated at 200 and 500 tons respectively. The Portuguese gave chase to Towrson, but he managed to slip away under cover of darkness and proceed for England.

As a result of the second Towrson expedition, about 70 pounds of gold was acquired. This was less than 20% of the amount secured by his first expedition. Still it did represent a respectable sum and was sufficient to further encourage Englishmen in a series of Mina sailings over the remaining years of the 1550s and well into the 1560s. The exact number of English and French voyages to Mina during these years will probably never be known. It appears that interlopers sailed from these countries every year bound for Mina. However, none of these squadrons were to enjoy the successes of the early expeditions, for succeeding ventures met with increasingly stiff Portuguese resistance. John III died in 1557, but his regents, first his widow Catherine (1557–62), and then Cardinal Henry (1562–67), did not neglect Mina. The Portuguese could not eliminate interlopers entirely from the vast stretch of the Mina coast, but they could and did make interloping voyages a very hazardous occupation.

In 1557, as in the last several years, corsairs' forays into the Mina monopoly had made deep inroads in the trade at São Jorge da Mina. In April of that year, the factor of the Portuguese post wrote complaining that nothing had been traded so far that year because of the cheap goods carried by Towrson and his French allies. The factor, Simão Rodrigues, noted the activities of the coastguard squadrons against the interlopers, and he suggested to the regent Catherine that an annual fleet be maintained at Mina during the peak sailing season. This would increase the Portuguese share of the trade more than enough to justify the additional expenses incurred.[36] The commandant of São Jorge, Botafogo, also wrote that only 5,371 *cruzados* had been obtained since the beginning of the year. This small amount had all been secured in early January before the arrival of the Anglo-French squadron. While São Jorge could draw upon black auxiliary forces from the adjoining settlement to protect any direct assault on the fortress, the Portuguese could not secure the allegiance and cooperation of more distant settlements. For example, Botafogo noted that the inhabitants of Accra to the east had refused to trade with Portuguese envoys sent there, claiming that there was no gold that year, but when foreign ships paused there in the spring of 1557 a lively trade had ensued. Obviously the local merchants of Accra preferred the favorable prices offered by English and French factors to the fixed prices of

Portuguese goods. An ounce of gold bought eighty *manilhas* from the English and French, while the same amount of gold at São Jorge bought only half as many *manilhas*.[37]

In mid-March of 1557 Captain Botafogo dispatched an armed force of soldiers to Accra to punish the villagers for their disobedience. The coastal settlement was burned and looted, and the blacks fled into the interior until the Portuguese departed.[38] In 1558 Botafogo dispatched a major Portuguese force from São Jorge against the settlement of Shama and subjugated that town. There had been intermittent disputes with these Africans over trade since the Lok expedition of 1555. To ensure that no further undesirable trade would be funneled through Shama, Botafogo established a permanent European garrison there. On the site of the thatch lodge used in 1555, the Portuguese threw up a bank of earth enclosing an area about seventy feet on each side and crowned by a wooden palisade. In the center stood a tall stone tower to shelter the squad assigned to the new outpost. A tiny battery of four *berços* was mounted so that the Portuguese could dominate the African town. To support the soldiers, the Portuguese demanded and collected a levy of one-tenth of the fish brought in by Shama fishermen. In the years immediately following 1558 the Portuguese also raided other recalcitrant coastal settlements who trafficked with foreign merchants. A major raid upon the inland capital of Efutu in 1562 was also designed to reopen roads to inland merchants who attempted to reach São Jorge and barter.[39]

Portuguese tactics ashore were paralleled by a renewed aggressiveness against foreign shipping. During the 1540s and 1550s, coastguard patrols of armed galleons were sent from Portugal whenever advance intelligence indicated the presence of an enemy fleet. On the other hand, galleons were limited in their activities off the Mina coast because of a strong eastern current offshore. This Guinea current, which normally set easterly up to about two knots, increased to three knots from May to July and made westward sailings extremely difficult. Even when advance warning of an approaching enemy fleet was sent from Axem to São Jorge, several days were required for Portuguese ships to reach Cape Threepoints. To correct this problem, small galleys, powered by both sails and oars, were used extensively in defense of Mina. A small galley of ten to fifteen benches and about sixty feet long could overhaul any sailing vessel hard against the wind. Also, galleys could remain on the coast year round and, moreover, they could be built in the workshops at São Jorge. The only drawback to the galley system was the large number of men required. Twenty or thirty persons per galley could not be spared from the garrison at São Jorge without depleting the fortress's defenses. A remedy was found by making use of slaves and English and French prisoners as a labor force. The advantages of the galley system far outweighed its drawbacks, for galleys also provided rapid communication between São Jorge and outlying Portuguese lodges at Axem, Shama, and later, Accra.

Galleys were used only intermittently in the period 1540–60. After 1560, two armed galleys became a permanent element in the Portuguese defenses. Some of these vessels were quite large, carrying up to seventy-two rowers and thirty armed soldiers.[40] Each vessel, equipped with one or more smallbore cannon, was a formidable foe for all but the largest warship. They were highly effective against lightly armed merchant vessels, such as the English ship *Minion*, who in 1562 was badly mauled in a fight with one of these Portuguese galleys.[41] Only with a supreme effort did the English vessel manage to escape. The two Portuguese galleys then attacked another vessel in the *Minion*'s squadron. Shortly after this second combat the entire English fleet left the coast for safer trading areas. They had been on the Mina coast for only a week and no trade was made. Denying this lack of profit, the English merchants who returned home claimed that over 300 pounds of gold was secured from Mina.[42] However, in view of their brief sojourn at Mina, it seems scarcely possible to give much credence to the English reports. So long as the galleys remained patrolling the coast, they served as a major, if not absolute, deterrent to interloping.

In 1564 when the *Minion* revisited Mina waters, she was again attacked by the same galleys and driven off the coast after only a brief sojourn. At the same time a French vessel, the *Green Dragon* out of Newhaven, was forced to leave Mina and sail to the West Indies. While this combined Anglo-French squadron was attempting to initiate trade, the fleet's commander, Captain David Carlet, ventured ashore to observe the trading sessions firsthand. He was betrayed by the Africans and captured by a Portuguese land patrol. Carlet and a dozen of his men were taken to São Jorge and imprisoned. Carlet himself was a prize catch for the Portuguese commander. Because of the Englishmen's activities he had already been officially declared a pirate by the Portuguese crown.[43]

It must be noted that a large portion of the credit for Portuguese successes against the 1564 squadron was due to advance intelligence coming from Portuguese agents in England and France. A carefully prepared description of the fleet's exact composition, preparations, and projected sailing orders was secured by these secret agents and passed to Portugal in early August 1564. This information was then forwarded to Martim Afonso, commander of Portuguese forces at São Jorge. In a dispatch dated 5 July 1564 Francisco da Costa Pontes, ambassador in England, had relayed to his superiors in Paris the size of the fleet, the name and disposition of each ship, and the names of the financial backers of the fleet. Costa Pontes noted that it was imperative that Martim Afonso be informed of these activities.[44]

Another documented instance of galleys successfully repelling foreign ships at Mina came much later. In 1581 the French vessel *Cherubin* out of Dieppe was captured. She was a large merchant vessel, somewhere between 80 and 100 tons. After beating off one assault by two galleys on Easter Sunday 1581, she was attacked again on April 25. In the melee, the French commander was blown overboard by a cannon shot and 16 of his crew killed. The *Cherubin* suffered more than a hundred hits from the galleys' cannon. When the Portuguese soldiers in the galleys finally boarded the crippled Frenchman, the survivors among the defeated crew had managed to escape in one of the longboats which was hurriedly loaded with provisions and put over the side. The prize vessel was towed to São Jorge with her rich cargo of cloth and metalware valued at 32,000 *écus*.[45] Next year, the same Portuguese galleys sunk another French ship, the *Esperance*. Again, in 1588 two Portuguese galleys captured a fifty-ton French merchant vessel after a dramatic fight in which most of the French crew was killed.[46]

In 1572 Mina officials suggested that to improve the galleys' effectiveness, no further shipments of white *degredados* should be made from Portugal. White convicts sent to Mina as rowers sickened and died at such an alarming rate that they were of little help. Condemned black slaves from São Tomé were much more desirable. To prevent smuggling among galley crews, the captain of Mina ordered that henceforth, rowers *(remeiros)* who were not kept shackled in the fortress must remain in their galleys. This was especially important while loading and unloading of cargo from the supply ships was being conducted. Another suggestion from São Jorge in 1572, to use the galleys as trading vessels or escorts to trading caravels along the entire Mina coast, was never put into effect.[47]

Prisoners captured by the Portuguese suffered one of two possible fates. More frequently, ordinary seamen were condemned to galley service as *remeiros,* and most died in their chains.[48] In the attack on the *Minion* in 1562, the English crew reported hearing a fellow countryman shouting encouragement to his free comrades from the attacking galley. If the captive were a wealthy merchant or ship's officer, however, the Portuguese commander usually detained him as a prisoner at São Jorge. In due course prominent captives were shipped back to Portugal to stand trial. One of the notable English prisoners taken by the Portuguese at Mina was Martin Frobisher, who was captured in 1555 and spent almost nine months at São Jorge before being sent to Lisbon where he was eventually released. Frobisher left a detailed, if somewhat prejudicial, view of Portuguese garrison life at the main Mina post. He reports that captive Englishmen were kept in irons in the slave lockups at São Jorge.[49] At times as many as two dozen captives were detained in this fashion.[50]

Successful patrolling by the galleys and severe reprisals against recalcitrant black traders helped only slightly to reduce the English and French threat to Mina. For each vessel captured or driven off the coast, perhaps two more eluded Portuguese vigilance and were able to secure cargoes of gold at more remote coastal settlements. English interest in Mina as a source of profitable trading continued throughout the remainder of the sixteenth century, with the high water mark of English incursions into Mina being reached about 1567. By then expeditions were departing from English ports for Mina every sailing season. In addition, serious consideration was being given in some quarters to erecting an English trading station

on the Mina coast as a permanent base of operations for English
ships to compete with those of the Portuguese.

In early 1567 English merchants were approached by two Portuguese, fugitives from their native land because of their own privateering activities. These men, Antão Luís and André Homem,
sought an audience with Elizabeth I of England to offer their services in leading an expedition to Mina. Luís and Homem claimed
that they could guide ships to a good port in Mina where a fortress
could be built. They also stated that such a voyage would net a
profit of at least 300,000 pounds sterling.[51] In return for their services, the two Portuguese asked for the command of the expedition
and the privilege to make land grants in the area around the new
fortress.[52]

The proposal of the Portuguese had been reinforced by reports
brought from Mina. There were certain African rulers chafing under Portuguese rule who sought an alternative to the monopolistic
trade policies of the Portuguese. Whenever the opportunity arose,
these rulers offered English merchants the chance for land on
which to erect their own post. The English could then join in an
alliance with the blacks against the Portuguese. But unwilling to
challenge the Portuguese while she faced Spain and believing that
such an exposed station would be too vulnerable, Elizabeth I declined the offer of Luís and Homem. Nearly sixty years more
would pass before England created her first outpost on the Mina
coast.

A major turning point in the lingering conflict between England
and Portugal over the Mina trade came during the five-year regency of Cardinal Henry, 1562–67. Henry redoubled efforts to
bolster Mina's defenses. He also secured from Elizabeth the prom-
ise that she would continue an earlier prohibition issued by Queen
Mary against English sailings to Mina. The cardinal soon discovered, however, that officials of Elizabeth closed their eyes to a
series of commercial ventures to Portugal's African possession of
Mina. For example, after the interloping expeditions of both 1562
and 1564, embassies were sent from Portugal to the English court.
They lodged strong protests in both instances against such piratical
activities. Elizabeth's reply was that since Portugal claimed the
Mina blacks were subjects of the crown, the king should command

them not to trade with English merchants. If the Africans continued to defy the Portuguese orders, then it was clear that Portugal's claims to sovereignty did not extend over the entire Mina
coast.[53]

When Henry received the queen's reply, he did not completely
abandon the hope for a diplomatic solution to the problem. But to
protect Mina in the interim, Henry dispatched occasional coastguard expeditions throughout his regency. In 1567, his final year
as Sebastian's regent, Henry increased his efforts to bring his dispute with England to a satisfactory conclusion and to protect Portuguese trade in Mina. The cardinal raised the issue of the English
prisoners who had been captured by the Portuguese in Mina.
Henry suggested the possibility to Elizabeth that these prisoners
might be brought to trial in Lisbon and acquitted rather than simply being condemned to the Mina galleys. An entire English crew
had been captured in February 1564, and many of these men were
still languishing at São Jorge da Mina. In September 1565 a coastguard squadron sent by Henry had seized an English vessel and its
crew near São Miguel in the Azores. In addition, all English merchants then residing on the island of São Miguel had been arrested. Even English merchants in Lisbon had been taken into
custody and charged with interloping and smuggling. Henry thus
was applying pressure on Elizabeth to force a settlement. In 1566
the cardinal went so far as to threaten to close all Portuguese ports
to English shipping.

Henry had another cause for complaint. In 1565 Portugal had
been inundated with great quantities of counterfeit copper money
emanating from somewhere in England. The counterfeiting activities, which had first begun in the Netherlands, were directed by
two Portuguese. One man operated a secret mint in Antwerp while
the other was in Middleburg. Margaret of Austria published strong
decrees to end this illicit commerce, but it was merely transferred
to Germany. In August 1565, similar injunctions against the counterfeiting were enacted by Maximilian II. The minting operations
moved again and found relative safety in England.[54]

Cardinal Henry left the way open for Elizabeth to reply to Portugal's demands that England desist from the African trade and stop
the counterfeiting ventures. But in April 1567 William and George

Winter petitioned the queen to assist in recovering goods taken by a Portuguese squadron off the Sestos River in west Africa in September 1565. On 26 April 1567 the proposals of Antão Luís and André Homem were presented. Elizabeth solicited Sebastian's and Henry's aid in freeing English subjects then in Portuguese prisons and in Mina and dispatched Dr. Thomas Wilson to Lisbon to negotiate the matter of the Mina trade. The English position was that the captured Englishmen were not corsairs, but merchants. Wilson claimed that the areas where they had been seized could not be considered as being within the jurisdiction of the Portuguese crown since the black inhabitants there did not recognize Portuguese sovereignty.[55]

Henry and the Portuguese Council of State refused to accept this argument: yet to continue negotiations, Henry proposed to send Dr. Manuel Alvares to London in turn. Henry insisted that Portugal could not permit the free commerce of Mina because of the economic harm such an action would cause. Besides, Elizabeth had recognized in the past the Portuguese monopoly in west Africa. To demonstrate Portugal's good will Cardinal Henry ordered that those prisoners taken at São Miguel, though their crimes deserved punishment, were to be released and their goods were to be restored. Henry further ordered that English prisoners at São Jorge da Mina would be sent to Lisbon where each would receive a fair trial.[56] Manuel Alvares did not depart for England until 18 January 1568, only two days before the end of the cardinal's regency.[57]

The Portuguese ambassador arrived in London and conducted a series of inconclusive exchanges with Elizabeth over the next year, until in early 1569 negotiations broke completely when it was learned that Elizabeth had granted a letter of marque for George Winter to recover his losses by taking Portuguese prizes.[58] When this was discussed by the Portuguese Council of State, the ministers recommended to Sebastian that all Englishmen and their goods then in Portuguese ports should be seized and all commerce with England terminated.[59] Portugal based the legality of such drastic action on the following points: the ship belonging to Winter had been captured legally; Elizabeth's concession of a letter of marque justified the reprisals recommended by the Council of

State; and finally, the letter of marque would have to be withdrawn, Portuguese goods restored, and commerce with Mina prohibited. England could ill afford to lose the considerable trade she
enjoyed with Portugal. If the grain trade with Portugal were
halted, more than 120 large English wholesale merchants would
face ruin.[60] Although Elizabeth and her ministers accepted the first
two demands, they were unwilling to forgo the profits of the Mina
trade. The English trusted that in time Portugal would concede
this third point. Reports were beginning to filter into England that
a major reorganization of the Portuguese commerce with Mina was
underway.

The rumors circulating in England during the summer of 1567
were well founded. The advent of French and English interlopers
in the Mina economy had precipitated a financial crisis in Portugal's trade with that area that reached its peak by the mid-1560s.
For nearly half of the years between 1544 and 1567, royal revenue
from Mina had failed to meet the expenses of maintaining the garrisons. Several factors contributed to this dilemma, most notable
of which was the competition from foreign trading, which poured
enormous quantities of goods into Mina with a resulting drop in
prices which African merchants were willing to pay. Also, occasional seizures of treasure caravels by French and English corsairs
compounded the problem. For defense the Portuguese crown had
armed annual coastguard patrols and had begun a rebuilding campaign at São Jorge and Axem to strengthen the fortress defenses.
Two fully-manned galleys had been stationed in Mina waters along
with an added unit of soldiers. When the cost of coastguard patrols, supply caravels from Lisbon, and the cost of trade merchandise were added together, the total cost of maintaining the Mina
posts averaged roughly between 600 and 1000 marks per year.

Caught between rising expenses at Mina and diminishing revenues, the Portuguese crown began to consider alternative systems
of administration aside from direct royal monopoly. Cardinal
Henry struggled with this dilemma throughout his regency while
negotiations were underway with England. A few months prior to
his regency's termination, Henry formulated a new plan for the
administration of Mina. In November 1567 M. de Fourquevaux,
the French minister in Madrid, reported that the Portuguese

Council of State had agreed to lease Mina to a private consortium of twelve to fifteen merchants. King Sebastian of Portugal would relinquish his royal monopoly over the area and its trading stations in return for the defense of the Mina coast and payment of all officials' salaries by the contractors. The crown would supply the ships and crews, while the contractors were to furnish all goods for the Mina trade. An impost of ten percent on all commodities would be assessed and paid before the ships left Lisbon. On their return the royal fifth on all gold and other items secured in the trade would be levied by the king's officials at São Jorge before the vessels could depart from the post.[61]

A contractual system had already been in force in other parts of Portuguese Africa and in the Atlantic islands since the latter part of the fifteenth century. Even the supply of tradegoods which the Mina House sent to São Jorge under the royal monopoly had been leased on a contractual basis to private entrepreneurs. However, the crown had been reluctant to consider extending this policy to the gold trade. The dramatic turnabout in 1567 which brought Mina under the same administrative operation as the rest of Portuguese west Africa was prompted largely by the rapid decline in revenues which had reached crisis proportions. Apparently, Cardinal Henry decided to take this drastic step rather than leave the Mina problem and its solution in the inexperienced hands of the fourteen-year-old Sebastian. The initiation of a Mina lease offered several positive advantages. It relieved the royal exchequer from the mounting expenses of defense which were required on land and sea at Mina to repel interlopers. Second, such a private leasing system offered the crown a higher and more regular return on the traffic. The ten percent levy on merchandise before leaving Portugal meant that even if foreign competitors flooded Mina with cheaper trade merchandise, the crown would have derived a moderate income. Depending upon the success of trading in Mina itself, the crown stood to gain another twenty percent of the total revenue at little or no expense on its own part.

The first Mina contract, which was signed in 1567, remained in force for only three years. Gold receipts did not increase during this period, and the original contractors declined to renew their lease in 1570.[62] At that time Mina once more became the financial responsibility of the crown. In 1571 Sebastian relented to English demands in order to forestall further armed interventions in Mina. The Portuguese king agreed to permit English ships to sail to Mina and trade, provided they went unarmed and paid the same duties as had been required in the lease of 1567–70. English vessels attempting to circumvent these regulations would be severely punished when captured. Before cruising along the coast to trade, all English captains were required to stop at São Jorge.

At the same time that Sebastian was attempting to blunt English armed intervention, the king and his cardinal-uncle were seeking a more permanent answer to Mina's administration. Advice came from many quarters, including crown ministers, ship captains, and officials stationed at São Jorge and Axem. There were widely divergent views as to the most feasible long-range solution needed in Mina. However, everyone agreed that reversion to a policy of a restrictive crown monopoly in the area had slim chances for success. Not only were reforms required in the economic life of the Mina post, but the garrison required a major restructuring.

The galley system to patrol the Mina shoreline had added the element of convict labor to the garrison of São Jorge after 1550. *Degredados* were sent from Portugal in large numbers during the 1550s and 1560s to supply the galleys with rowers. They received no pay and were given only a small clothing allotment and basic garrison rations. Men who came to São Jorge in chains were constantly falling ill, and they required considerable expense when treated in the post infirmary. Their presence at São Jorge only accelerated the already deteriorating condition of morale within the garrison. Most garrison soldiers spent their off-duty hours in the African village and occasionally maintained black mistresses or wives. Many of the officials who retained residences in the fortress spent their idle hours gambling and living in a dissolute fashion. Frequent complaints were made by the clergy that São Jorge was filled with black prostitutes and Portuguese rabble.[63] Illicit trading by some garrison members was so commonplace by 1570 that few local African merchants bothered to purchase commodities from the factor through legitimate channels.[64]

In the fall of 1572 and throughout the following year, the Portuguese crown actively debated the Mina problem. Pressure from

English interlopers in Mina began to slacken. In general, privateers had shifted their focus northward along the west African
coast and into Spanish lands in the New World. There were three
courses of action for Sebastian and Cardinal Henry. The alterna-
tives were: (1) reform of the present system, (2) rental of Mina to
other interested merchant groups, or (3) settlement of the area as
a colony similar to Brazil.

The first alternative, reform, involved a major overhaul of the
monopoly, the reduction of the garrison staff by half, and utilization of galleys as mobile trading vessels as well as patrols. If the
galleys assisted in commerce the Portuguese could tap the gold
traffic on the entire coast. The second possibility, rental, called for
a lease to be signed similar to the contract of 1567–70. Though
this proposal was perhaps the most feasible economically of the
three plans under discussion, at that moment there were no merchants in Portugal willing to underwrite the Mina lease. A third
solution was to import colonists. The major proponent of this position was Jorge da Silva, a member of the Council of State. When
the Mina question had first been brought to the attention of the
Council in 1567, da Silva immediately had opposed the regent's
decision to contract the region to private hands. In 1572/73, during
the new round of debate on Mina, da Silva again voiced his oppos-
ing views in letters to Sebastian.[65]

Because of the impressive economic gains made in Brazil by the
1570s, da Silva and his supporters cited a number of advantages to
colonizing Mina. The land in the coastal plain of Mina was fertile
and could support a number of valuable crops: citrus fruits, pepper, sugarcane, and cotton. Experimental plantings at São Jorge
and Axem had already been made during Manuel's and John III's
reign. By 1572 there was a small orchard of oranges and lemons
near São Jorge maintained by the garrison. Bananas had also been
introduced to Mina and were cultivated along the wetter portions
of the coast, as well as some sugarcane. Some Portuguese who
advocated the creation of a colony at Mina claimed that virtually
any seeds or graftings planted into the Mina soil could not fail to
grow and render a profit.[66] While it was true that the climate often
had a debilitating effect upon whites coming to the region from

Europe, this could be overcome easily by bringing acclimated Portuguese immigrants from the island of São Tomé.[67]

The one decisive drawback to da Silva's proposal was the political power of the African states situated along the Mina coastal fringe. Kingdoms like Commany and Efutu were much more advanced politically than had been the Brazilian Indians when the latter's lands were appropriated by the Portuguese. It was unlikely that the Portuguese could implant a colony of agriculturalists on the Mina coast without incurring war with at least one of these states. Moreover, King Sebastian seemed unwilling or unable to commit money and manpower to implement such a colonial enterprise in Mina. During the 1570s the king was actively engaged in preparations to recover his grandfather's lost north African patrimony.

The choice which the Portuguese crown finally made was based upon expediency. Mina would continue to be held by the crown as a royal possession until a contractor could be found. In the interim, the galley system would continue. Little is known regarding Portuguese operations at Mina from about 1574 to 1579. It would appear, however, that in 1574 or 1575 the crown either licensed private trade with São Jorge da Mina or someone came forth willing to undertake a private lease of the area. This is the conclusion to be drawn from the dispatches of the apostolic nuncio in Lisbon during this period. Monsieur Caligari mentioned the Mina traffic in a letter dated 15 September 1575 and again on the 26th of the same month. In both, he reported the capture by French corsairs of a Mina caravel laden with 400,000 *escudos* in gold.[68] The caravel was the *Vitoria*, which had sailed to São Jorge the previous December, unloaded her cargo, and on 6 February 1575 had begun the return journey to Portugal. Becalmed off Cape Palmas, the *Vitoria* was seized by a French vessel. The Portuguese captain threw the official Mina dispatches overboard to prevent their falling into enemy hands. The caravel was put to the torch and her crew was put ashore on the mainland. Survivors of the mishap did not reach Portugal until September 1575, and Caligari apparently drew his report from the testimony of these survivors.[69]

Of the total gold taken from the *Vitoria* by the French, Caligari noted that the royal portion consisted of only 180,000 *escudos*, while another 220,000 *escudos* was classified as *de particolari*, or belonging to private parties.[70] This much "private treasure" was too substantial to be merely post salaries. The only possible explanation is that private trade, either from individual ships or by means of a new lease, had been conducted at Portuguese posts in Mina at least over the previous year. Any contract made for all of Mina would have been of brief duration, for in 1576 the contract for the region was definitely taken for a ten year period by Giacomo de la Bardi, a Genoese merchant in Lisbon at the time.

The new contractor was beset by misfortune from the outset. Beginning in 1576 the Portuguese became embroiled in a succession of armed confrontations and open clashes with two major African powers on the Mina coast, Efutu and the eastern kingdom of Accra. The difficulties with Efutu had not risen suddenly. As competition increased during the 1540s and 1550s, there had been an active trade between that African state and the new foreigners. On the other hand, the Portuguese claimed in European diplomatic circles that their sovereignty extended over the entire stretch of Mina coastline. It was clear, however, that powerful states such as Efutu did not recognize Portuguese claims. The Portuguese commandant in Mina had repeatedly insisted that the king of Efutu cease trading with interlopers. Considerable gifts and outright bribes were given this ruler and his nobles to induce such a move. When this policy had failed, the Portuguese launched punitive raids on the Efutu capital of Eguafu in the 1560s. After a series of skirmishes, the Efutu king retreated with his warriors temporarily into the bush country north of Eguafu. Portuguese troops entered the enemy capital and burned it to the ground.

More than a decade passed after this assault in the 1560s with the question of Efutu interloper trade remaining unresolved. There were occasional skirmishes between the Efutu and the Portuguese; but during the early 1570s trade began to move once more through this kingdom to São Jorge. Then in 1577/78, the issue flared again. Nuno Vaz, a *caboceer* (military captain) of the African village of Edina (the Village of Two Parts), killed two sons of the Efutu king in a dispute. Despite protests from the Efutu the Portuguese governor made no moves to punish Vaz.[71] The Efutu king then made an alliance with tribes of the Akani confederacy to fight the Portuguese and their black allies, the Elminans. Efutu-Akani forces gathered at Eguafu and began a march on the Portuguese fortress. When the danger became fully apparent, the Portuguese governor mustered all the Portuguese soldiers he could spare along with 500 to 600 Elminan warriors. Armed with guns, pikes, crossbows, and two cannon, they met the enemy about five leagues from São Jorge on the trail to Eguafu. Although the Efutu and Akani greatly outnumbered the Portuguese-Elminan force, the latter's superiority in weapons decided the contest. However, the victory was costly, for thirty European soldiers were killed and an unknown number of casualties were suffered by their Elminan supporters. The Portuguese governor, who had left São Jorge to command the defense, was mortally wounded and died eight days later.[72]

On another portion of the coast, the Portuguese fared worse. Since the time of Manuel I they had sought to establish permanent contacts with the coastal kingdoms far to the east near Accra. The quality of gold from this area was reported the best in all of Mina and occasional visits had been made by Akara merchants to São Jorge since about 1520. With the advent of foreign interloping, however, Akara became a favorite trading site for English and French ships. Gold was plentiful, and the African merchants were eager to trade with the newcomers. When Portuguese emissaries went to Accra in March 1557 to reopen trade routes, the merchants demurred, saying that there was no gold that year. However, the Portuguese commander at São Jorge, Afonso Gonçalves Botafogo, soon learned that the Akaran blacks were actively soliciting trade with passing interlopers, and sent a detachment of soldiers and Elminan warriors by ship to Accra. The expedition burned out the coastal settlements in that region and drove the Akarans into the foothills to the north.[73] To ensure that further trade between interlopers and the Akarans would be terminated, the Portuguese erected a small fortified lodge on one of the coastal bays near Accra, permanently manned by a squad of Portuguese troops.

When the new contracts for Mina were signed with de la Bardi in 1576, it was decided to expand the Accra lodge into a fortified trading post similar to Axem. Work was begun shortly thereafter on the erection of strong stone walls and outlying bastions. The climax to the Portuguese-Akaran struggle came sometime during 1577/78, when an assault was launched by the Akarans upon the half-constructed, ill-defended station. Akan traders arrived from the north and Akarans went to the fort to act as intermediaries and linguists in the trade. However, once inside, the Akaran warriors attacked the tiny garrison, murdered all the Portuguese, and razed the fortifications.[74] The cannon taken from the fortress was the most prized possession for the victorious Akarans, since the station did not contain any substantial quantity of tradegoods at the time of the assault. When news of this disaster reached São Jorge, the governor sent two galleys to Accra to investigate. However, the Akarans remained near the beaches and would not permit the Portuguese vessels to land.

By 1575/76, the attention of the Portuguese crown was shifting from the problems of west Africa and Mina to focus on preparations for King Sebastian's north African campaign. The final act in this tragedy came at Alcaçar Quivir in August 1578 when Portugal lost her young monarch and the flower of the nation's nobility. While the problems of Mina and the rest of the empire had to be set aside temporarily by Sebastian's successor, his aged great-uncle, Cardinal Henry, the years between 1578 and 1583 would prove to be crucial for the tiny African outpost of São Jorge da Mina. In 1579 King Henry sent a small relief squadron to the remote Mina station with stores of provisions, tradegoods, and replacements for the garrison. At the head of this modest squadron was a new governor for Mina, Vasco Fernandes Pimentel.

5

Spanish Takeover and Reorganization at Mina, 1580-95

Political events in Portugal between 1578 and 1582 were to have resounding repercussions for the life of the Portuguese garrisons in Mina. Upon Henry's death in January 1580, two major claimants to the vacant throne came forth. Don Antonio, the illegitimate grandson of Manuel I and the Prior of Crato, enjoyed popular support from among the citizenry of Lisbon. He had taken up his residence in Lisbon and was determined to defend his rights to the throne. The second claimant was Philip II of Spain, whose mother, Isabella de Avis, had been Manuel I's daughter. Philip settled the matter definitively when he dispatched the Duke of Alba to Portugal with an army and routed Antonio's forces at the battle of Alcântara in August 1580. Lisbon surrendered to Spanish forces, and on 16 April 1581 Philip I was sworn in by a Portuguese *cortês* and formally assumed the throne of Portugal. Letters were dispatched to Portuguese colonies and fortresses throughout the world, including Mina, demanding the allegiance of the officials stationed at the remote posts. The garrisons were instructed to swear fealty to Philip as their rightful sovereign. Response to these dispatches was less than enthusiastic. In the Azores and on the island of Príncipe, officials refused and instead swore fealty to the fugitive Prior of Crato. Other colonies and outposts, including São Jorge da Mina and Axem, simply did not respond to the decrees, but instead adopted a wait-and-see attitude.

Meanwhile, Don Antonio had escaped from the disastrous defeat at Alcântara and succeeded in fleeing from Portugal to France in early 1581. At the French court and in neighboring England, Antonio found considerable sympathy for his claims to the Portuguese throne. He received news that he still held the loyalty of most of the Azores, and that only two islands in this group, São Miguel and Santa Maria, had welcomed the Spanish representatives. During 1581 Catherine de Medici began to assist the Portuguese pretender with a French fleet of fifty ships and 5,000 soldiers to reduce São Miguel and Santa Maria.

While preparations were underway in France for the Azores expedition, Antonio turned his attention to the question of Mina's allegiance. There had been no news from this post for more than a year. If Antonio could secure the gold treasure awaiting shipment to Portugal from this *presidio*, this revenue would make a significant contribution to the pretender's depleted treasury.

News had already reached Antonio that the representatives sent to São Jorge by Philip had not been well received. No firm commitment had been given by Pimentel to the Spanish. Governor Pimentel's brother, Antonio de Brito Pimentel, had already cast his lot with Antonio and was traveling with the pretender in France.[1] Thus Antonio could expect that the Mina governor might be sympathetic. Pimentel should be reached immediately and reinforced to prevent the fortress's falling into Spanish hands. In December 1581 Antonio made a contractual agreement with the same merchant consortium which had lost the *Cherubin* to Mina galleys that same year. This French merchant group, including Eustache Trevache, owner of the ill-fated *Cherubin*, Pierre Lubin, and Guillaume le Blanc, had already been granted a letter of marque by Henry III to recover 600,000 *écus* at the expense of Portuguese shipping. In addition, the upcoming voyage of the French to Mina was sanctioned by Antonio. The contracting parties agreed to outfit four ships at Havre de Grace. These included the main vessel of the squadron, *l'Esperance*, which carried a crew of fifty-five seamen and was a large vessel of around 120 tons' burden. Command was vested in Jean Croix. Accompanying the admiral's flagship was *l'Aventureuse* (100 tons), commanded by Jean Scot; and two smaller barks, *la Petite Esperance* (35 tons) and *la Petite Aventureuse* (25 tons), were commanded by Guillaume Malerbe and Guillaume Grandcamp of Saint-Adresse, respectively. Altogether the fleet would transport merchandise valued at 180,000 *écus* to Mina along with a delegation of six or seven Portuguese. Led by Sebastião de Abreu, one of Don Antonio's squires, these men carried dispatches from the exiled king and instructions to Pimentel to permit some of the Portuguese coming in the fleet to remain at the fortress. One or two Portuguese would return to France with the governor's replies.[2]

The Franco-Portuguese squadron sailed from Le Havre on 22 March 1582. The outward passage to Mina was exceptionally long, about eleven weeks' duration, and further misfortune struck when the smallest bark was lost at sea in a storm. The remaining three vessels reached Mina on June 16 and cautiously approached the Portuguese post at São Jorge. Rather than sail openly into the shelter of the harbor and pass under the lee of the main batteries, Admiral Croix anchored offshore beyond the range of the post's artillery. The French factors on the journey, Richard Senecal and Romain Lezart, accompanied by Abreu and the other Portuguese, cautiously rowed toward the harbor mouth under a flag of truce. They had no idea of what the reaction of the garrison might be to this French vessel. However, their fears were eased as they passed under the silent ramparts of the fort and saw the governor and his factor coming to meet them on the beach.

The French squadron arrived at a critical time for São Jorge da Mina. The fortress had not been without its problems during Pimentel's governorship. Pimentel had fared well during the first eighteen months of his tour: roads leading to the station had been opened to trade with the interior, and two galleys at São Jorge were overhauled and put into operation, with Negroes replacing white *degredados* as rowers. The galleys went on continual patrol off the villages of Kormantin and Takoradi, the two most popular trading sites for foreign vessels. Villagers in these two settlements had been repeatedly burned out of their homes by the Portuguese, but despite this intimidation they refused to recognize exclusive rights to trade claimed by the Portuguese. Occasionally, the governor himself accompanied galley patrols. On one such reconnaissance, the governor encountered a small French squadron of merchant vessels near Kormantin and had ordered his galley to give chase to the French cargo ship *Cherubin*. In the light midday breezes the galley quickly caught up with the Frenchman and the ensuing fight lasted most of the afternoon of 25 April 1581. When firing from the French ship ceased and the Portuguese boarded her, twenty-two of the French crew were dead or wounded and the remainder had fled in a ship's boat. Pimentel towed his prize back to São Jorge and unloaded the cargo. Because the ship was so badly damaged, it was broken apart and its timber and iron hardware were used for salvage. The captain of the captured vessel, Louis de Mire, had been blown overboard during the fight, was fished out of the water by the Portuguese, and died several days later at São Jorge. Other prizes captured over the following six months yielded an additional 60,000 *escudos* in tradegoods and gold to the Portuguese.[3] The trade with African merchants at São Jorge increased when it became evident to blacks that the Portuguese were succeeding in restricting the illicit trade. During Pimentel's administration, from 1579 to 1582, the factor at São Jorge received between 300,000 and 400,000 *cruzados* in gold which filled several large chests in the governor's quarters. Such a sum would be a valuable addition to the treasury of either Don Antonio or Philip I.

After late 1581 the Portuguese position at Mina began to worsen considerably. There had been no relief squadrons sent from Portugal after the governor's arrival, and supplies brought by Pimentel in 1579 were nearly exhausted by early 1581. Consequently, after that date trade with local merchants began to wane once more. Pimentel clearly realized the position of his post. It was becoming seriously undermanned through normal attrition of the garrison, and there were no immediate prospects of relief from Portugal. The post's physical defenses and those of Axem were stronger than they had ever been. Even with a current shortage of powder, shot, and manpower, São Jorge could probably repel an assault. But because of conditions after 1581 it was clear that the galley patrols would have to be curtailed, which meant that much of the Mina coast would again lie open to interloping. Therefore, when the opportunity to regain the initiative came in July 1582, and the French vessel arrived with representatives from Don Antonio and a fresh supply of powder and shot, the governor of Mina took the advantage to improve his position.

The recent French arrivals in 1582 were unaware of the shortages of gunpowder, slaves, food, and personnel in São Jorge. They did not realize that the two galleys hauled up on the beach inside the harbor were no longer fit for sea duty. But the governor carefully concealed these shortages from his visitors by conducting all discussions on the beach and refusing admittance to the fortress

itself. In this way, Pimentel could argue his position from an outward appearance of strength.[4]

On 27 July 1582, after more than five weeks of this awkward
negotiating in the shadow of the fortress, an accord was reached
between the Mina governor and the French and Portuguese visitors. The goods from the ships could be unloaded at the beach
ramada and would be stored in the fortress warehouses. The two
French factors, Senecal and Lezart, could remain and conduct the
sale of tradegoods. Sebastião de Abreu would be allowed to remain
at the fort as the personal representative of Don Antonio. Pimentel
agreed to recognize the pretender's claims. On the other hand, the
governor insisted that the remaining bark, *la Petite Esperance*,
should be ceded to the fortress. It would be needed to conduct
trade along the coast and also to supply Axem with provisions.

The French ships remained at São Jorge da Mina for a month
before departing for France on 21 August 1582. During that time,
trade with the local villagers was brisk. About 20,000 *cruzados* in
gold were obtained and carried back to France aboard the *Esperance*. When the fleet sailed, letters from the Mina governor to both
Pierre Lubin and Don Antonio were on board. Pimentel wrote
Lubin noting that he had taken *la Petite Esperance* over the protest
of Admiral Croix. However, the vessel was deemed necessary to
conduct trade profitably, and Pimentel suggested that Lubin might
recover the cost of his ship from Don Antonio. The governor also
sought the Frenchman's forgiveness for the damages inflicted upon
the *Cherubin* in 1581. Pimentel stated that the victuals which had
come in the recent squadron were quite welcome.[5]

In his letter to Antonio, the governor agreed to deliver the gold
and the fortress to the next fleet sent by that monarch. However,
since he could not hold out against any Spanish fleet sent by Philip
to deliver up the post, Pimentel informed Antonio that he would
have to surrender his post to whichever of the claimants' ships
arrived first with assistance.[6] From supporting documents it would
appear that Pimentel's letters to Antonio were a ruse to encourage
the Spanish in dispatch of supplies. The governor had no intention
of surrendering the fortress to Antonio's lieutenants; Pimentel's
wife and children were still in Portugal and to declare for Antonio
would place them in jeopardy. Also, the governor judged correctly

that the military and naval strength of Philip would determine the outcome of the struggle. News carried to Pimentel by way of a slave ship from São Tomé in July 1582 told of an impending naval battle between Antonio's forces and the Spanish admiral sent to the Azores to reduce them to submission. Though the Mina governor did not know it, the Marquis of Santa Cruz, Alvaro de Bazan, had already led his Spanish and Portuguese squadron to an overwhelming victory over the French fleet supporting Antonio.

Even before Pimentel became aware of the outcome of the battle of the Azores, he demonstrated his loyalty to Philip I by sending a full account of the French arrival with Antonio's men in July. He sent his dispatch to Philip via a slave ship to Antonio Monteiro Maciel, royal factor for São Tomé. Pimentel reported that he had received a packet of letters from Antonio via the Portuguese in the French squadron. The Portuguese on board the vessels had sent them on ahead of the fleet's arrival by entrusting them to Elminan fishermen whom they had met several leagues west of São Jorge. Pimentel stated that he would forward these letters to Philip as soon as possible. For the moment, however, there were not enough men at the post to spare a caravel's crew to sail to Lisbon.[7] Other than the most recent slave shipment from São Tomé, the most pressing necessity of the fortress was soldiers. At least fifty armed soldiers should be sent at once, along with flour, cannon gunpowder, and two new galleys. The latter were vital to protect the coast from interlopers. In his dispatch to Philip, Pimentel professed his loyalty and asked the king to send an armed ship to collect the gold which was then at São Jorge. About 400,000 *cruzados* in fine gold had been taken in the trade at São Jorge over the previous three years and no shipments to Lisbon had been made for that time.

The officials at São Tomé forwarded copies of the Mina dispatches from Pimentel to Lisbon by two vessels. Only one of these ships reached Portugal safely. The other was captured by supporters of Antonio off the Azores. The letter from Pimentel fell into the enemy's hands before the caravel captain had a chance to throw it overboard and was forwarded to France and Antonio.[8] Both Philip I and Antonio now began to make active preparations to send squadrons to Mina to claim their gold. In October or November 1582 Antonio received the dispatches from Pimentel given to Admiral Croix. The captured letter addressed to Philip I arrived in Antonio's hands a month later. The pretender had great difficulty in securing a boat and enough Portuguese to provide reinforcements for Mina. It was not until mid-March of 1583 that Antonio's ships left Rouen bound for Mina and São Jorge. On 7 March 1583 Edward Prim wrote Elizabeth I of England's secretary, Sir Francis Walsingham, that "There departed for the castle of the meyne a small bark, which goes for the king's [Antonio's] coffer, and in her go 40 Portugals, men of good *vydo*, whose names are, of some part of them, these: Nuno Alvares, the Farya captain, Manoel Alvares da Costa, Belchior Payes, Manoel Castanyo, Antonio Botelho, Antonio Beyram, John de Brito. The same captain has the king's order to receive his coffer into the ship from the castellan of the castle, whose name is Vasco Fernandes Pimentell. The value of the treasure is counted at 300,000 ducats and the money of the fatherless children is counted at 115,000 ducats, all which money the king sends for by his bark."[9]

The ship never reached São Jorge da Mina. It was forced to disembark the troops in the Azores to bolster Antonio's defenses on Terceira.[10] Antonio then arranged with French merchants at Dieppe to send a second vessel to São Jorge. Antonio contracted with Bellenger Parmentier, captain of the hundred-ton merchantman *La Levriere* to transport the king's representatives and a new French factor to Mina. All was in readiness by late April 1583, and on the twenty-fifth of that month the ship weighed anchor bound for the Azores and then for Mina.[11] After an outward passage of sixty-four days, Captain Parmentier finally sighted the Mina post of Axem and anchored a half league offshore in front of that station. A signal shot was fired and, after a brief pause, six Negroes in a canoe rowed out to the French vessel. They carried disappointing news. The delays experienced by Antonio in securing a ship had cost him the race. São Jorge da Mina was already in Spanish hands. The Negroes told Parmentier that a powerful Spanish fleet of four ships, including two large galleons, had arrived a week or so before, in mid-June. One of the Spanish vessels had already departed just two days before Parmentier's arrival. The remaining three ships still were at anchor in the harbor of São Jorge.[12]

Philip I's recovery of Mina had long been delayed by more pressing military matters. Although the new king had appointed a new Mina governor in February 1581, it was almost eighteen months before ships and money could be found to send João Rodriguez Paçanha to his post in Africa.[13] During this time the Spanish crown was beset by the problem of the Netherlands, which had formally declared its independence in 1581. The prince of Parma's requests for men and ships to suppress this rebellion took precedence over all other matters. Also, before Philip could supply remote stations like Mina, the king had to send a squadron to drive Antonio's forces out of the Azores. It was only following the victory of Santa Cruz over the Franco-Antonio fleet in July 1582 that preparations could once more be directed to dispatching relief squadrons to Mina and other parts of Philip's empire. When Santa Cruz's fleet returned from the Azores victory late in 1582, eight of the Portuguese vessels in it were immediately refitted for new overseas sailings. Four ships were to go to India to resupply Portuguese posts in the Orient. The remaining four warships were given orders to carry Governor Paçanha and reinforcements to São Jorge da Mina. Accompanying the Mina fleet was a force of several hundred soldiers to recover the post by force of arms. To guard against attack from roving French corsairs, Philip included two galleons among the four vessels. These were the *San Mateus* and the *San Miguel*, both among the largest and most powerful warships in the Spanish-Portuguese navy. Their combined displacement was well ovr 1500 tons.[14] When the king received news of Governor Pimentel's correspondence with Don Antonio, Philip had changed his orders to Governor Paçanha. The new governor was not merely to replace Pimentel, but he was to arrest the commander of São Jorge and send him to Lisbon where he would stand charges of treason.

The Luso-Spanish fleet departed from Lisbon about the same time that Captain Parmentier left France.[15] However, the outward passage time of this squadron was much shorter than that of the French vessel. Parmentier apparently paused in the Azores to deliver supplies and dispatches to Antonio's supporters. When Parmentier did at last arrive at Axem and learned the bad news from the blacks there, he decided to sail to São Jorge and confirm these reports for himself. On June 29, as the French vessel came within

a mile and a half of the main Portuguese post, a canoe manned by
Negroes came from the adjoining village. Aboard was a Portuguese
soldier sent by the fortress. The Portuguese, Enrique Ribeiro,
carried letters from the captain of the fortress. The letters assured
Parmentier that it was safe to land and unload the supplies for the
post. A letter, supposedly signed by Pimentel, went on to assure
the French captain that the fortress remained securely in the hands
of Don Antonio and his supporters. The French captain ordered
Ribeiro seized, bound, and tortured to extract the truth. Under
threat of torture, the soldier confessed that the post truly was in
Spanish hands. He declared that only two days before, the *San
Mateus* had departed for Lisbon with the former governor in chains
and a cargo of seven chests filled with gold.

Ribeiro reported that when the Spanish galleons had first arrived, Governor Pimentel had surrendered the post without of-
fering resistance. The ex-governor claimed that he had always
supported Philip and that he was only using Don Antonio as a stalk-
ing horse to gain needed provisions for the post. Apparently, once
the post was securely in Paçanha's hands, the *San Miguel* sailed
south, leaving the *San Mateus* behind along with two new galleys
brought from Portugal. Thus, when Parmentier arrived, there was
no indication that the Spanish fleet had yet arrived save the testimony of Ribeiro, who warned the French captain to weigh anchor
and sail as swiftly as possible, since the new governor was prepar-
ing the galleys to move against the French ship. Parmentier en-
quired as to the fate of his two countrymen left at São Jorge as
factors the year before, and was told that both had died along with
Sebastião de Abreu during an epidemic which ravaged the garrison
shortly after the earlier French squadron had departed. The sickness apparently was still virulent when the Spanish arrived ten
months later; many of the ship's crews and soldiers had to be left at
São Jorge to replenish the depleted garrison. When the *San
Mateus* departed, she sailed short-handed.[16]

Parmentier left the Mina coast on June 29. It would have been
foolhardy to remain and attempt to trade independently with two
new galleys and a reinforced garrison present at São Jorge. Therefore, the French captain directed his ship to São Tomé and from
there to Príncipe. The latter island still remained in Antonio's

hands. Antonio himself did not learn of his loss of São Jorge and Axem until the end of 1583 when the French vessel returned home.

Governor Paçanha's arrival at São Jorge with provisions, galleys, and a strong armed force infused new life into the faltering station. It marked a significant alteration of the formerly haphazard supply link between Mina and Lisbon. Previous governors had had to make their own arrangements to maintain the posts when supply ships failed to arrive. At times the officials could call upon assistance from the Portuguese on the island of São Tomé. Slave ships still came from the island with small numbers of captives. Nevertheless, it became increasingly clear that without a reinstitution of a regular supply of foodstuffs, powder, shot, and tradegoods, the day would arrive when the Portuguese in Mina would be pushed out of their fortress by aggressive powers like England, France, or possibly Holland. The arrival of Paçanha and reinforcements was a welcome reprieve. More important, the new governor made it clear that arrangements were being made in Lisbon to correct the resupply deficiencies of the previous decades. This is certainly the conclusion to be drawn from Paçanha's returning of many of the tradegoods then at São Jorge in the hold of the *San Mateus* when that ship departed for Lisbon. Only about 25,000 *cruzados* of the best merchandise was retained in the factory warehouses. The governor of Mina expected to be resupplied before these few goods were exhausted. Because of a shortage of ships to police and furnish the far-flung empire of Portugal, there was no way to reinstate the monthly sailings of supply caravels which had been customary during Manuel I's era. However, the stations at Mina could at least expect annual visits by vessels bringing goods from Lisbon. Over the next decade and a half until the death of Philip I, Mina did enjoy at least an annual renewal of its stores and a replenishment of its garrison. These were the same fifteen years, from 1583 to 1598, in which a second reorganization was effected in the financial structure of the Mina trade. The man primarily responsible for restructuring the Mina trade was not Philip himself. Rather it was Cardinal-Archduke Albert of Austria, governor of Portugal and nephew to the king. Two specific aspects of the Mina trade received the archduke's attention. These were the defense of Mina and the attempt to renew trade and boost revenues.

When Governor Paçanha departed for Mina in 1583, he carried royal orders not only to secure the Portuguese post to the allegiance of Philip I, but also to restore the Mina defenses against any potential assaults from interlopers. One of the major areas of concern to Archduke Albert and Philip was the improvement of the fortifications in the area. In 1583 when the new governor arrived, the fortress of São Jorge da Mina was already commencing its second century of operation. While improvements had been continuing on the post to upgrade the living conditions and accommodations for the garrison as well as to bolster its defenses, São Jorge was becoming dangerously antiquated as a military station. It was increasingly vulnerable to the new weapons of war. The curtain walls of the fortress along the outer courtyard were no longer sufficiently thick to withstand hits from the heavier cannon which many naval vessels now mounted. The two towers guarding the seaward approaches of the fortress (the east and south towers) mounted the heaviest cannon in the fortress. But there had been little renovation or repair effected on the masonry supporting these towers for several decades. The vertical outer walls of both gunplatforms were vulnerable to cannonfire. The riverside yard with its workshops provided an area for the transfer of supplies into the fort, but it had only the protection of a low earth and masonry wall which dated from the period 1500–10. Its original purpose had been to prevent blacks from pilfering goods which were temporarily kept on the beach until they could be stored in the fortress.

Paçanha brought new masons and craftsmen with him. He also brought new plans for updating the fortifications. Three years earlier, in 1580, Philip had engaged an Italian military architect, Filippo Terzi, to modernize royal fortifications in the Iberian peninsula as well as *presidios* in north Africa. When Philip became the king of Portugal, similar assignments of remodeling Portugal's overseas posts were given to Terzi and other Italian engineers. In 1583, when Paçanha's fleet had secured Mina, half of the squadron continued to India with supplies and reinforcements. On board one of the India-bound ships was a new chief architect for India, sent there to carry out the remodeling of fortresses in the Orient. He was Giovanni Battista Cairati, who served in India until his death in 1596.[17] It is not certain whether the new master plans used in rebuilding São Jorge originated from designs executed by Terzi or from some unknown Portuguese engineer. Cairati himself may have made some suggestions. But during the following two decades São Jorge da Mina underwent extensive modifications in its design.

There were certain elements in the basic layout of the fortress which were retained out of necessity. One of these was the quadrilateral plan of the keep and the outer courtyard. During the years of construction on the original fortress during the fifteenth century, the original rock outcropping on which the fortress was situated was cut down until there was a sheer drop of six to ten feet all along the outer course of the courtyard walls down to the level of the beach. The rock removed from this area provided stone for building and the absence of outcroppings served to accentuate the height of the outer walls, which made attempts at scaling more difficult.

One of the first improvements was the thickening of the outer walls of the fortress to secure them against heavy cannon. New courses of stone at least a foot thick were added to the outer casing of the rectangular keep where the walls formed the riverside defenses.[18] The rooms in the keep were small and cramped in their original 1482 design, and no attempt was made to put additional stone courses on the inside of the wall. When Paçanha's masons began to repair the walls surrounding the outer courtyard, however, it was decided to strengthen their course on both sides with new masonry. The additional stone reinforcing put up in these walls doubled their original thickness. The small gun mounts and towers at the corners of the fortress were completely transformed into modern outflanking bastions. Each tower was thoroughly covered with layers of stone and mortar until their outer walls were angled outward at the bottom rather than perpendicular. Two of these improved flanking towers faced the riverside yard and harbor; the other two looked out to sea. All four towers mounted heavier cannon with greater bore and range. These bastions offered a flanking fire to defend the vertical curtain walls against the threat of sappers or scaling attempts by an enemy force.

While repairs at São Jorge were proceeding, Paçanha and the succeeding governor, João Roiz Coutinho (1586–94), resumed an active campaign to drive foreign interlopers off the entire Mina coast. In this regard, the governors were aided by an annual coast-guard patrol which operated on the coast during the months of heaviest interloping, i.e., December through April, and a pair of galleys which maintained a continuous surveillance on the coast for the remaining months of the year. In the early months of 1584 the first relief squadron arrived. It had sailed from Lisbon in late December of the previous year, bound for Cape Verde, Mina, São Tomé, and Angola with supplies for each of these colonies. This fleet was not intended to act as a coastguard patrol for Mina, since Philip I was already busy making arrangements for a sizeable coastguard unit to sail for Mina.[19] In late November 1584 a fleet of six ships, including the galleons *São Felipe* and *São Luis* accompanied two supply transports and two new galleys from Lisbon to take stations on the Mina coast.[20] This fleet and subsequent coast-guard patrols proved highly effective in curbing interloping over the next several years. Privateers whose vessels were seized are recorded for the years 1586, 1588, and 1590.[21] Few of the captives taken from these prizes lived to tell their stories. For instance, in 1590 the São Jorge galleys *São Vicente* and *Santo António* attacked and burned a French merchant vessel trading at Cape Coast. The captured crew was locked in the slave prison at São Jorge. An attempt was made to escape; it failed, and Governor Coutinho ordered a dramatic punishment meted out. Members of the garrison and Elminan blacks watched as a prisoner was chained to one of the post's cannons and blown apart.[22] By utilizing such harsh tactics the Portuguese were able to curb the interloping considerably. However, it was practically impossible to keep the entire stretch of coast free, because the bays and inlets along the coast were too numerous. There were simply too many coastal villages willing to risk trade for the cheap goods offered by foreign merchants.

The renewed interest of the Portuguese crown after 1583 in protecting its holdings in Mina was tied in to a new examination of the economic possibilities of reestablishing a profitable Mina trade. The Mina commerce was about to undergo a second major scrutiny to raise its level of income. When Governor Paçanha arrived in 1583, he was accompanied not only by troops and a new staff for the post, but also by the new factor for Giacomo de la Bardi, Mina's new contractor. When the *São Mateus* arrived in Lisbon from its 1583 expedition to Mina in August, the vessel unloaded 300,000 *cruzados* in gold. This was the amount traded at Mina over the previous three-year period.[23] The arrival of the *São Mateus* caused a stir among the Lisbon business community. As late as December 1583 the Mina galleon and its rich cargo was a topic for discussion in private correspondence. From the Mina gold brought by the galleon, the royal mint had been able to coin small quantities of large gold *cruzados* (75 to the mark, 306 grains each), some double *cruzados*, and even a few impressive 4 *cruzados* coins.[24] Such mintings were the first strikings made in gold in many years.

Despite the notoriety that the treasure shipment of 1583 received, Bardi and his associates did not secure a great profit from their contract during these years. On Christmas Eve 1583 the apostolic collector in Lisbon wrote to Rome that such a treasure shipment (300,000 *cruzados*) should be considered in the light of the fact that no other ship or gold had come from Mina for such a long period.[25] When the royal fifth and twentieth, salaries, and operating expenses were deducted from this amount, Bardi's share of the shipment amounted to approximately 200,000 *cruzados*. The average annual amount taken, therefore, was only slightly in excess of the 50,000 ducats which the contractors had to pay for the lease. Bardi had done little more than recover his expenses. Revenues brought from Mina in returning ships in 1584 and 1585 helped somewhat in enabling the contractors to recover their investment. But it was no surprise that the merchants made no attempt to renew their contract in 1586. So, for the third time in less than twenty years, the issue of the disposition of Mina fell upon the shoulders of the Portuguese crown. In this particular instance the man who was responsible for finding a solution to the problem was Archduke Albert, Governor of Portugal.

In January 1586, on the suggestion of the Portuguese governor in Lisbon, Philip began to make several new appointments to the staff of the Mina garrisons. The terms of office for many ranking members at São Jorge who had gone there in the company of Governor Paçanha would expire soon.[26] Included among the new appointments in 1586 was a governor to replace Paçanha and a new chief captain of the Mina galleys. For the former post, Philip selected João Rodriguez Coutinho. Coutinho was the son of Lopo de Sousa Coutinho, who had served as *capitão-mor* of Mina during the reign of John III between 1548 and 1550. However, João Rodriguez had distinguished himself in his own service to the new Portuguese monarch. Philip's choice of governor and the other appointments were forwarded to Lisbon and to the attention of Archduke Albert. At that time there were several issues already before Albert pertaining to Mina. The region had been brought up for discussion many times in recent meetings of the Council of Portugal. There was the question of how the Guinea, Mina, and India Houses in Lisbon might be reorganized and made more efficient in supplying the overseas needs of the Portuguese empire.[27] Also, there was underway a major overhaul of the *alfandegas* of Lisbon and their administration.[28] Finally, there was Mina itself. Should a new contractor be sought to assume the lease? Or should the region be opened to all the king's vassals if they agreed to pay the proper duties for participation in the trade? Or would it be feasible for the crown to reassume direct royal control over the supply and trade with Mina and permit all the gold to revert to royal coffers? Archduke Albert ordered a list to be drawn up of all revenues and expenses to the crown in Mina over the previous six years, since the accession of Philip I. This list was sent to the finance council where it was tabulated against the revenues derived from the Bardi contract. The archduke believed that if there was no profit from the expiring contract, then continuation of the same scheme in the future was worthless. On the other hand, Albert did not feel it would be advantageous for the crown to reassume the entire financial burden of supporting the Mina commerce. If there was no profit found in the current lease, then Albert proposed to the king that the Mina trade be opened to all the crown's subjects.

The financial accounting ordered by the archduke is no longer extant. However, from subsequent events in 1587 and 1588, it would seem certain that the crown felt itself sufficiently compensated by the contract system to warrant the issuance of a new Mina lease. This was the opinion voiced by the archduke in a letter to

Philip dated 25 September 1586 which dealt at length with Mina.[29] Final action on the governor's suggestions was taken by the Council of Portugal on 6 December 1586. By that date the Bardi contract had officially lapsed. Dispatches sent to officials of the Lisbon Mina House and to the staff at São Jorge had been received and replies had been sent back to the Council. Statements from the Council of Finance were examined. Both Albert and the rest of the Council of Portugal agreed upon the necessary solution. Mina should continue to be rented to the merchant who offered the best price for the contract. Bardi's contract of 1576–86 for 50,000 *cruzados* per year would likely have to be revised downward to attract interested contractors. Among the recommendations made by the Council of Portugal was the stipulation that the expenses of the galleys would be borne by the new contractor. The king would reserve the right to select the chief captain of these vessels.[30]

Following the archduke and Council's decision and Philip's subsequent approval of the suggestions, the Mina contract was placed open for bids in the Mina House in Lisbon. In the early months of 1587 it was assumed for a five year period by Pero Borges de Sousa. Borges de Sousa already had had considerable financial dealings with the crown. Among his various business enterprises the native of Madeira had contracted to collect royal revenues for the Atlantic islands for the five years before, in 1585. Borges de Sousa now agreed to supply the tradegoods, pay the garrison salaries, maintain the galleys, and pay a flat fee of 40,000 *cruzados* annually for the Mina contract. The new contractor petitioned the crown to modify its requirements regarding the naming of the chief captain of the galleys. This was a lucrative post, since the captain of a vessel capturing interlopers was entitled to half of the value of the prize. Borges de Sousa wanted his own choice assigned to this office. Philip relented to the request to expedite the signing of the contract. The right to assign some minor officials to São Jorge and Axem was also relinquished to the new contractor. However, the crown maintained its insistence on the right to make assignments of the remainder of the garrison, including the important positions of governor and factor.[31] All the new terms of the contract were drawn up and compiled in a new *regimento* given to Governor João Roiz Coutinho to carry with him to Mina.

Roiz Coutinho departed for São Jorge in the summer of 1587 with the first squadron sent out under the new contract.[32] But things went badly for the Mina contractor. The reasons for the sudden failure of Borges de Sousa's contract are unclear. The last fleet sent to Mina by this merchant departed in April 1588, less than a year later. It went in the company of the fleet then sailing for India, Brazil, Cape Verde, and São Tomé.[33] In the early months of 1589 Borges de Sousa surrendered his contract and a new lease for Mina was drawn up. This time another Lisbon-based merchant, Giovanni Baptista de Rovelasco, assumed control over the fate of Mina for the next nine years.

6

Ordeal with the Dutch:
The Opening Phase, 1595-1615

Commencing with Philip's accession to the Portuguese throne, the future of Portuguese Mina became inextricably bound up with the economic fortunes of Spain. Even before the Spanish takeover in the 1580s, Mina had ceased to be a profitable portion of the Portuguese overseas empire and had instead become a liability. The vigorous attempt by Philip I to reestablish Portuguese hegemony in the Mina trade was possible only because of Spain's income from American silver fleets. Mina gold and the contracts contributed little to the continuance of the Portuguese garrisons at São Jorge and Axem, and Spanish silver made up the growing deficit.[1]

By the early 1590s it was also increasingly apparent that Philip's bid to dominate the Atlantic was doomed to ultimate defeat. Protestant victories in Europe, the drying-up of revenue sources, excessive governmental spending, and the decline of Spanish and Portuguese shipping all seemed to bode ill for Mina and the Portuguese continuance in the area. Losses inflicted by the English upon Portuguese shipping during the late 1580s as a result of the Spanish conflict began to be felt during the next decade. Sooner or later, priorities would have to be established in defending the Portuguese overseas empire. In such an event, Portugal probably would choose to defend the more productive portions of her Atlantic empire, i.e., Brazil and Angola. Philip's bankruptcy in 1596 marked the beginning of a gradual reduction of Spain's and Portugal's huge commitments that was to continue unabated through the reign of Philip III (of Portugal). In the case of Mina, this meant first the end of coastguard patrols, then the gradual elimination of a regular schedule of provisioning. Vessels were ordered to sail for Mina only when the direst needs of the fortress for resupply became evident, and even then only if the necessary ships could be spared. It was not that the Portuguese lost their desire to preserve their stations in Mina. They simply lost the capability of maintaining regular contacts with this remote portion of their empire. It was not possible to combine Mina's resupply with that of either Brazil or the east, because a stop at Mina would carry the India fleets far from the optimal sailing route, and the same was true for Brazil-bound vessels.

At this time a new and powerful enemy appeared on the scene. The Dutch began to make occasional forays to the Guinea Gulf in the 1590s, and by 1600 Dutch ships had largely supplanted the English and the French as the major competitors to the Portuguese in the coastal gold trade. As Dutch power and trade in Mina increased, the sphere of Portuguese influence and trade on the coast contracted.

Philip I's embargoes on Dutch shipping in Iberian ports had impelled the Netherlanders to look overseas in search of needed commodities previously obtainable in Spain and Portugal. In the aftermath of the embargo, instead of securing salt from Setúbal, south of Lisbon, the Dutch established their own salt factories in the Caribbean. Instead of obtaining much-needed Spanish silver through legitimate trade with Spain, Dutch merchants sought bullion, both silver and gold, at its sources in the Iberian overseas empires. Direct trade between Holland and Brazil was started in 1585. Ten years later, the first Dutch ships sailed for the Orient to break the Portuguese monopoly in the east. The first recorded voyage of a Dutch vessel to Mina dates from 1594. Three years earlier a Dutch skipper sailing for Brazil had been captured by the Portuguese and carried to São Tomé. While a prisoner on the island, the Dutch skipper secured valuable information on the conduct of the island's trade and also on the mainland trade at Mina. Upon his release, this Dutchman outfitted a ship in Holland and conducted a successful trading foray into Mina despite the threat of Portuguese reprisals. Encouraged by this voyage and also by the grants of freedom from duty for all imports of Guinea gold brought into Holland, successive Dutch squadrons were fitted out and dispatched to trade in Mina.[2] By 1600 scores of Dutch ships were sailing annually on their own newly-fashioned *Carreira da Mina*. These expeditions were financed by such men as Jonas Witsen, Hans Simons, Jacques de Velaer, Pieter de Hasselaer, Gerard

Lubbertsz, and Jan Jacobszon Melcknap, some of whom were founders of the East India Company in 1602. Among the earliest to venture to Mina were four businessmen from the province of Zealand: Balthazar de Moucheron and his business associate, Pierre Lemoyne; Cornelis Meunicx; and Andre de la Faille. The ships sailing in these men's names became familiar sights to Portuguese lookouts at Axem and São Jorge by 1600.[3] Rumors circulated in Holland and Portugal during 1600 that these Dutchmen were massing a great squadron of warships to assault the Portuguese posts in Mina. Though the Portuguese confirmed nine sailings of Dutch merchant vessels to Mina within the first seven months of that year, the expected military assault never materialized.[4]

By 1600 the Dutch were far better equipped to conduct a successful trade in Mina than were the Portuguese. First and most obvious, they possessed the necessary ships with which to trade while the Portuguese were straining to maintain even minimum contact with far-flung outposts like Mina. Equally important, the Dutch controlled the source of much of the metalware and cloth trade commodities which the Portuguese had customarily bought to trade in Mina. Throughout the sixteenth century the Portuguese had arranged for the purchase of Mina commodities through its factory in Antwerp. Even after the formal closing of this factory in 1549, considerable trade had continued between Flanders and Portugal. However, with the outbreak of the Dutch rebellion against Spain and the annoying embargoes imposed by Philip, the Portuguese gradually lost their financial position in northern markets. Antwerp, the main center of Portuguese trade, began to lose its own trade preeminence to Amsterdam and other Dutch towns whose commerce with Portugal had been less highly developed.[5] To compensate for this major loss of trading commodities, the Mina House in Lisbon tried to import quantities of Asian fabrics. Soon Indian muslin began to replace Flemish textiles in Portuguese Mina trade. There apparently was a wide market for this item among the blacks and it helped to alleviate the losses of Flemish cloth. On the whole, however, after 1550 the Portuguese could not meet the demand of African merchants. Thus the Dutch traders found a ready market for their own goods in Mina.

By 1600 the Portuguese maintained very small inventories at São

Jorge and Axem compared with the multitude of goods stocked a century before. Whereas *manilhas* had been the chief item of trade in 1500, a century later they had been replaced by iron ingots. North African woolens had given way to eastern fabrics like *matanzes, chaudeis,* and *guandares.*[6] Regular shipments of all-important slave cargoes from São Tomé had ceased. By 1600 the Brazilian demand for African labor was so strong that the Portuguese crown permitted slaving operations to be conducted within Mina itself. To maintain friendly relations with neighboring tribes, proposals were made after about 1590 that the king set aside a strip of coast ten leagues on either side of São Jorge and exempt this area from slaving activities. In 1616 this proposal was formally enacted, but the pressure was great to permit open slaving operations all along the Mina coast. In Pernambuco or Bahia, a prime Mina slave brought a premium price of about 20,000 *réis.*[7]

Portuguese measures to revive trade in Mina at the beginning of the seventeenth century generally ignored the problem of the growing Dutch power in the area. Dutch traders found blacks eager to engage in commerce everywhere save under the guns of São Jorge and Axem. A particularly favorite site for Dutch-African trade was the settlement of Moure, about fifteen miles east of São Jorge. Despite its proximity to the Portuguese post, the village did not recognize the authority of the Portuguese governor. Between 1595 and 1600 Dutch merchants founded a small, unfortified lodge at Moure to tap the local gold trade, and in 1601 it was suggested in the States-General that a company should be formed and an armed Dutch fortress built at Moure to secure the rich gold trade. A Mina company might even attempt to capture the Portuguese post of São Jorge itself. The profits of the Mina gold trade were already widely known in Holland by this time,[8] but no immediate decision was made since the Dutch were busy with the chartering of the East India Company.[9] Proposals to found a company for Guinea were made to the States-General again in 1605 and 1606, but in both instances the motions were not brought to a formal vote.[10] The chief proponent of the scheme for a West Indian company to compete with Spain in the Atlantic was William Usselincx, who introduced his plan to the States of Holland and the States-General. He was opposed by John Oldenbarnevelt, the leader of the assembly, who arranged the 1609 truce with Spain.[11] The establishment of a similar company to administer west African trade had to wait until 1621.

Despite the sterile political debate over a formal company's creation, Dutch interest in Mina mounted. Each year between 1600 and 1605, the Dutch extracted about 500,000 *cruzados* in gold from the area. More than a dozen ships annually were working the coastal trade.[12] In 1606 the Dutch were presented with an opportunity to initiate aggressive action against the entrenched Portuguese positions. That year a renegade Portuguese deserted his post at São Jorge and sought refuge with Efutu tribesmen who carried him to Dutch traders at Accra. The renegade, whose name is not known, was transported back to Holland and questioned on the disposition of Portuguese forces in the major fortress of São Jorge. He told the Dutch of the low morale, the shortages of supplies which the Portuguese experienced, and further suggested that with seven or eight ships and a few hundred soldiers, the Portuguese could be driven from São Jorge. The deserter proposed to accomplish this by placing siege cannon atop Santiago Hill, overlooking the Portuguese station.[13] At the time, the Dutch States-General had not yet reached a decision regarding the proposal to create a company to direct west African trade. Nevertheless, Usselincx and his supporters arranged a private squadron and the private recruitment of troops for the venture. It was agreed that the time was propitious for an attempt to capture São Jorge with the assistance of this Portuguese renegade. The Dutch vessels sailed for Mina in the late summer of 1607 and on the evening of September 6 they anchored at Moure and began unloading soldiers. São Jorge was a four-hour march overland from Moure.[14] The garrison at Mina was on the eve of its first major land battle with another European power for control of the Mina region.

The Portuguese had not been idle in the previous ten years. In Mina, the Portuguese governor who faced the initial thrusts of Dutch trade into the area up to 1607 was Dom Cristóvão de Melo. Melo had come to São Jorge in 1596 and served at that post for one of the longest terms of any governor—eleven years, until 1607. He was an experienced soldier who had campaigned with King Sebastian at Alcaçar Quivir, was captured, ransomed, and had then

taken service with Philip I. Just prior to his appointment to the
governorship of Mina, Melo had commanded a regiment of Portuguese troops defending the Portuguese city of Cascais at the mouth
of the Tejo River against a threatened English assault which never
materialized.[15]

By the time Cristóvão de Melo arrived at Mina, much of the
major repair work on the fortress and also at Axem had been finished. Stonemasons continued with minor repairs and installed
wall facings on the new stone bastions. One of the last major alterations completed by the Portuguese at São Jorge was the disman-
tling of the small chapel atop Santiago Hill overlooking the post
from the other side of the Benya. The king of Efutu had by now
become openly hostile to Portuguese attempts to control the roads
through his state. Thus, relations between these two powers after
1600 were on no friendlier a basis than armed neutrality. Governor
Coutinho realized the military significance of the Santiago church
and its site: it dominated the Portuguese fortress from high ground
across the river. There had been a small chapel in the main courtyard of the fortress since the late fifteenth century, and in 1595 the
governor ordered this chapel enlarged and furnished with the ornaments and vestments taken from the Santiago church. The clearing
near the summit of Santiago Hill where the church had stood was
garrisoned by a squad of Portuguese soldiers operating behind
earthworks facing the line of march of a potential enemy coming
up the far side of the hill.

During the years of growing Dutch involvement leading to this
encounter of September 1607, Governor Melo also had been
struggling with the basic issue of supply. When he first assumed
office, the contract for the resupply of Mina belonged to Giovanni
Baptista Rovelasco, an Italian merchant residing in Lisbon who
simultaneously held a large contract for the transport of pepper
cargoes to Portugal from India.[16] Rovelasco obtained the Mina
contract in June 1589, for a period of nine years, because the previous contractor, Pero Borges de Sousa, had defaulted on the contract and it had reverted to the crown. According to the terms of
the new Rovelasco contract, the lessor agreed to pay 60,000 *cruzados* annually, plus the salaries of the Mina garrisons and all other
expenses involved in operating the posts. Moreover, two galleys

would be kept on the coast at all times; these also would be maintained at the contractor's expense.[17] A further clause in the agreement stipulated the lump-sum payment of 6,000 *cruzados* toward
a pious work of the crown's choosing along with the supplying of
three *arrobas* of wax per year or its cash equivalent.[18]

It is apparent that Rovelasco placed the Mina contract subordinate to his more lucrative lease of the Indian pepper trade. Most
of the merchant's available ships were dispatched to the Orient
over the period of the contracts, with only an occasional caravel
maintaining the Mina posts.[19] Because of the consequent dearth
of reinforcements to replace sick and dead artisans, Governor
Coutinho had to curtail some of the construction work. Also, galley
patrols were limited to the portions of the Mina coast close by the
Portuguese posts.

Governor Melo had arrived on the scene in 1596 accompanied
by the last provision ships to be sent out under Rovelasco's contract. When the lease expired eighteen months later, in 1598,
Rovelasco chose not to renew it and the contract was picked up by
a new merchant consortium. One of the major participants in this
new lease was the Portuguese merchant and banker João Gomez
da Silva.[20] Da Silva's group soon discovered that they too were
financially unable to maintain the terms of the agreement with the
crown regarding Mina, and when the initial term of the lease
lapsed in 1603, it once again was not renewed. At that point there
was considerable debate within the Council of Portugal as to the
desirability of freeing the Mina trade to all the crown's subjects.
Several members of the council made this recommendation, but
the chief advocate of this plan was Estevão de Faro. His basic proposal was designed to improve trade. If free commerce were
adopted, all Mina-bound ships should be required to register in the
Lisbon Mina House and also at São Jorge. A flat duty of 40% would
be imposed on all goods sent to Mina. This duty would be collected
at São Jorge in kind. Once the merchants and ships' captains had
paid the proper excises, they would then be free to trade anywhere
along the Mina coast and with whatever villages they desired. Any
gold acquired in the coastal trade would be subject to no further duties, either in Mina or upon importing the bullion into
Portugal.[21]

Archduke Albert, viceroy for Philip II, found Faro's proposals unacceptable. Albert raised serious objections to them in letters to the king. Instead of following the Faro plan, the viceroy chose to lease the Mina trade on 26 April 1603 for a period of ten years to Pero Borges de Sousa, the same merchant who had defaulted on his contract during the previous reign. The new contract carried essentially the same provisions as the previous leases. One notable exception was that the lump-sum annual payment to the crown was lowered to only 40,000 *cruzados*.[22] Borges de Sousa's performance under the new contract proved no better than that under his contract of 1587–89. After only three years, and just prior to the Dutch attack upon São Jorge in September 1606, the contractor surrendered his lease to the crown because of financial insolvency. For the second time in less than two decades the only merchant willing to assume a lease over Mina was the aging Giovanni Baptista Rovelasco.

An assessment of the impact of the contract system upon Mina during the years after 1567 is difficult. There is very little in the way of firm economic records for the Mina trade during this period. From those records extant, it appears that in terms of boosting royal revenues, the Mina contracts were a moderate success. Receipts rose gradually from 1567 until near the midpoint in Philip I's reign. By that time the Mina lease was providing about 1,000 marks (circa 300 kilograms) of gold annually for its contractors and a small income for the crown. The suppression of interloping through the energies of King Henry and Philip I was largely responsible for this modest trade revival. However, by the end of Philip's reign, the picture had become gloomy as the trade of the Netherlanders in Mina grew at a fantastic rate. At the same time, the value of the Portuguese Mina contract dwindled. By the end of the contract era, in 1607/8, the value of Mina as a provider of gold for Portugal had fallen to a point fluctuating at about 650 marks per year. This figure included all the privately traded gold taken in at São Jorge and Axem by the Mina contractors. A drastic slump in revenues occurred the following year (1609) after the lapse of Rovelasco's contract. Two caravels reached Lisbon from Mina during the early months of that year with combined gold cargoes of only 38 marks, 2 ounces, 3 drams, and 8 grains.[23] This was the only treasure forthcoming from Mina for the year. The registry books of the Casa da Moeda outline in striking detail the precipitous drop in Mina gold receipts during the early seventeenth century. Mint records for the years 1570 to 1603 are missing; however, the surviving registers for 1604–37 (save volumes for 1605, 1634, and 1637, which are lost) show a total average receival of only 374.1 marks of gold annually. By no means was even a majority of this gold derived from the Portuguese stations in Mina. For instance, receipts for Mina treasure in 1609 cited above constituted only five per cent of the gold accepted by the mint that year. After 1600 the vast majority of Portugal's gold came from other African stations such as Arguim and Cantor, and most especially from purchases of Spanish American gold in Seville.

Very little is known of the extent of the Mina gold trade between 1567 and 1607, that is, during the years when the contract system was functioning. Scattered receipts for this thirty-year period do not accurately reflect the total gold secured at Mina, only the gold which safely reached the royal mint in Lisbon. Much of the gold never reached Portugal. For instance, in 1577 a Mina caravel laden with seven quintals of gold was captured and plundered by French corsairs, and similar unrecorded losses cut deeply into treasure shipments. It would appear that the trade with African merchants at São Jorge was still active whenever trade merchandise was available in quantity. In 1578, for example, supply ships from Mina returned to Portugal with 200,000 *cruzados* in gold. Five years later, as mentioned previously, the next gold shipments to reach Philip I from Mina totalled about 300,000 *cruzados*. Gold receipts began to diminish during the late 1580s and continued to decline as the supply system broke down and the contractors failed to furnish Mina with the necessary trade merchandise because of a lack of shipping from Portugal. The frequency of the galleys' patrols was cut back. Consequently, the amount of gold taken by the Portuguese in proportion to the total traded along the Mina coast was reduced. In 1597 three ships accompanied Governor Melo on his journey to São Jorge. No more relief ships were sent out by Rovelasco during his first contract and only one relief ship arrived at Mina during the lease of João Gomes da Silva, during 1598 or the early months of 1599. It is possible that other vessels were dispatched but either captured or lost at sea. The *Carreira da Mina* was becoming increasingly hazardous for merchant vessels, and few captains were willing to risk the loss of their ships. The next known relief for São Jorge—two caravels—was sent to Governor Melo in 1604 by Pero Borges de Sousa, the new contractor. Both ships eluded capture and reached Mina safely with precious cargoes of provisions, cloth tradegoods, 15,000 brass *manilhas*, and 50 quintals of *búzios* from India and the Maldives.[24] These were the first *manilhas* to come to Mina in several decades. Also included in this relief squadron were replacements for the Mina garrison. Some officials had been at São Jorge for nearly a decade awaiting the replacements to assume their offices.[25] Between 1604 and the time of the Dutch attack in September 1606, no further supply caravels were sent out from Portugal. What small outside assistance Governor Melo received came from the island of São Tomé, but the officials on the island could spare only a limited number of slaves and few provisions. No spare troops were available to bolster Mina's sagging defenses.

The fault for the lack of provisions at the Portuguese stations in Mina lay not entirely with the Mina contractors. There was also a serious shortage of available vessels in Portugal with which to supply the colonies, and the few seaworthy royal ships were used primarily in the Brazilian and Indian trade. Philip II had not done much to alleviate the problem. In April 1605, the king reissued an injunction prohibiting the use of foreign ships or foreign crews in any of the overseas possessions of Portugal save for the Azores and Madeira.[26] Simultaneously, Philip also ordered new ships built in the royal yards at Lisbon. But such construction required money and material, both of which were in short supply at this time. By 1605/6 there were simply not enough vessels to meet all the shipping demands of the Portuguese empire. Consequently, Mina's reinforcement had to be delayed. At that time also, the Mina lease had been returned to the crown by Pero Borges de Sousa and a new contractor had not yet signed a lease.

One final problem confronting the Portuguese commanders at São Jorge was that of low morale. For the most part, by 1606 the fortress garrison subsisted entirely off a meager fare of local produce and fishing. Occasional shipments of flour and oil which came from São Tomé and a rare supply caravel from Portugal helped somewhat, but there were serious deficiencies in the provisions at the post. More crucial was the arrears in salary payments which persisted among the garrison personnel. Revenues derived through the gold trade were not sufficient to meet even the salary requirements of the staff during recent years and most of the soldiers, officials, and clergy went unpaid. When not on duty, soldiers from the garrison lived outside the fortress with native wives or mistresses in the adjoining village. This situation had created serious friction among elements within the garrison. Of particular note was the controversy which grew up between 1598 and 1604 between Governor Melo and Gaspar Soares, the vicar of São Jorge. The latter official leveled open complaints against the governor for permitting the lax habits and corrupting morals of the soldiers to go unchecked. Vicar Soares's complaints commenced almost as soon as he arrived at his post in 1598 as dispatches sent to Portugal carried the cleric's repeated invectives against the governor.[27] In 1604 Melo took a firm stand against the vicar's attacks. When a relief caravel arrived that year, the governor removed Soares from his post and sent him forcibly to Lisbon. Melo dispatched letters justifying his action by complaining about the vicar's own laxity in performing his duties.[28] Soares's adventure on the return voyage to Portugal is illustrative of the communication difficulties between the remote Mina outposts and their base of supply in Lisbon. The vicar embarked on the caravel *Nossa Senhora da Piedade*, which was subsequently seized by the Dutch. He was robbed and taken to Holland as a prisoner, where he remained for fifteen months before being released.

According to testimony which the vicar gave on his return to Portugal, Governor Melo's major crime at Mina had been to dip into the funds of the church to assist in purchasing provisions for the post. There were several hundred thousand *réis* in separate accounts held by the treasurer of the church as salaries earned by deceased members of the garrison before their deaths. Rather than send these monies back to Portugal to the heirs of these persons, the Mina governor kept the gold for the welfare of the fortress.

When the last relief ship for 1604 departed, São Jorge da Mina

was staffed by about fifty whites, including officials, common soldiers, and craftsmen. In return dispatches the governor thanked
the king for the supplies. However, Melo noted that severe shortages still existed in certain areas. The post was dangerously short
of powder, muskets, iron for making crossbow bolts, lead for shot,
and medicines for the infirmary. There was sufficient food to sustain them thanks to the governor's purchase of millet in local African markets using the gold from the church's account. The critical
needs were in the area of defense. In addition to the provisions
mentioned above, the fortress was short of iron fittings for gun
mounts of several cannon; the old fittings had rusted away. Also,
to complete the fortress's continuing renovation, Melo asked that
lime, 100,000 tiles and bricks, two masons, and two smiths be sent
in the next supply ship to make necessary repairs.[29]

This, then, was the situation of São Jorge on the eve of the first
land encounter between the Portuguese and Dutch in 1606. During the first week of September, Governor Melo received advance
warnings from Elminan fishermen that six ships had neared the
coast about fifty miles to the windward of São Jorge. As was customary, the governor dispatched a Portuguese soldier in a canoe
manned by African rowers to reconnoiter the new squadron and
ascertain their destination. After several days, African merchants
visiting São Jorge told the governor that his man had been captured and that the six ships were not trading vessels, but contained
armed Dutch troops. They were now anchored at Moure unloading
a great number of men and guns. Melo decided that the fortress
of São Jorge could probably repel any single assault by this force,
but in its present condition the post could not survive a prolonged
siege. Therefore it would be best to meet the enemy in combat
before they surrounded the fort and constructed siege lines. The
Portuguese could muster about forty whites from within the fortress, in addition to 130 Negro warriors from Elmina who were
allies of the Portuguese.

On September 6 Dutch troops began disembarking at Moure and
by early the following morning, six hundred Dutch soldiers commenced the march toward the Portuguese post. At nine o'clock,
the Dutch column reached a position a half-mile from the Portuguese station where their commanders called a halt to rest the

men. Simultaneously, a smaller force of Dutch troops had been sent westward by ship to capture the Portuguese station at Axem.

Governor Melo was awaiting the Dutch. About eighty Negro warriors and ten Portuguese gunners were lying in ambush to strike the Dutch from cover along both sides of the path from Moure. The governor's battle strategy was to halt the enemy before he gained the commanding heights of Santiago Hill. With his remaining forces, Melo collected the women and children of the village and put them inside the fortress along with their cattle and livestock. The ambush was sprung on the resting Dutch troops. Apparently the Dutch were overconfident in their numbers and had not covered their flanks by skirmishers and lookouts. There had been little Portuguese activity during the past few years and this had lulled the Dutch into believing that São Jorge was on the verge of collapse. When the fighting began, the Dutch closed ranks into a fighting formation, but they were no match for the Elminan warriors who carried the advantage of surprise and cover. Close quarters made the guns a disadvantage when pitted against lances, axes, and crossbows. Musket fire from concealed Portuguese and African gunners poured into their ranks. Within two hours, the battle was over. The Dutch retreated in disorder trying to reach their boats, leaving behind them almost a hundred dead in the forest clearing. Governor Melo, who had risen from his sickbed to direct the attack, ordered the remaining garrison to pursue the fleeing enemy. In scattered clashes that followed during the afternoon, the Portuguese sank two launches and a ship's longboat, captured or destroyed large stores of munitions, and killed an additional sixty-five Dutch. By their own count, the Portuguese suffered thirteen dead and twenty-seven seriously wounded, including both Portuguese from the garrison and Elminan troops from the village.[30]

The Dutch had fared equally poorly at Axem. The factor at this post, Luis Soares, was forewarned of the enemy's arrival, and he proceeded to defend his redoubt bravely with the assistance of Negro allies from the neighboring village. African warriors were paid with tradegoods taken from the storehouse of the post. At the time Axem had only eight whites in the entire garrison; however, the enemy could not close on the fortress. Dutch ships experienced great difficulty in negotiating the shallow bar at the mouth of the small harbor. When troops finally went ashore, they found themselves trapped on the narrow beach and overshadowed by the cannon of the fortress. After several hours of exchanging fire, the enemy withdrew to their ships and departed.[31]

But the Dutch did not leave Mina following their stinging defeats of September 7. Warships established a blockade of São Jorge by sea until late January 1607, to prevent any supplies from reaching the post. In December, Dutch soldiers put ashore near São Jorge made repeated assaults on the fortress walls, and burned the nearby village. In each attack they were beaten back by the strong defenses of the fortress and by the Portuguese and Elminans manning the walls.[32]

When the siege was finally lifted in January 1607, an English vessel appeared at the entrance to São Jorge harbor with a cargo of slaves which it had contracted to haul from São Tomé to Mina. From the ship, the Portuguese governor was able to purchase a small quantity of powder, a few muskets, and several crossbows and for the first time since September 1606, he was able to send news of the Portuguese victory to the outside world. When it sailed on 8 February 1607, dispatches accompanied the English vessel first to São Tomé and from there were forwarded to Lisbon. The viceroy of Portugal and his council received the news from Mina in late August. The Mina governor's message from his besieged post was brief and succinct: if São Jorge did not receive outside help and soon, the crown would not find anyone alive at either São Jorge or Axem when relief eventually came.

The elaborate preparations to succor Cristóvão de Melo after 1607 are indicative of the difficulties that were being encountered in Portugal in maintaining her west African *presidios*. A century earlier, an average of a dozen caravels per year sailed for Mina laden with provisions and reinforcements. However, by 1607 delays of one to two years between squadrons had become commonplace. Much time was consumed with the mountain of paperwork required by the bureaucracy before outfitting the ships. There were hundreds of letters to be processed which dealt with various parts of the planned expedition. There were also letters of appointments to be issued. Matters of funding the ships expended additional time. Interim status reports and many other dispatches all had to pass through numbers of councils and agencies both in Portugal and in Spain before approval was made by the king himself.

The initial steps toward organizing a relief expedition for Mina began late in 1605 with the nomination of candidates as governor to succeed Cristóvão de Melo. On 18 October 1605 the viceroy of Portugal forwarded his recommendations for this post to Philip II in Spain. From the list, the king selected the name of Duarte de Lima as the new governor. No further action was taken until August 1606, when news reached the king of the impending Dutch attack. This information produced another flurry of activity.[33] Philip II ordered the viceroy to make ready six caravels and 150 soldiers with provisions for a full year to be sent immediately to bolster Mina's defenses.[34] To oversee the preparations of this flotilla, Philip charged Estevão de Faro, a member of the viceroy's council and a strong proponent of Mina's defense, with the chore of coordinating activities in Lisbon.

Faro's first discouraging report on the situation in Lisbon, dated 7 September 1606, reached the Council of Portugal in Madrid by special courier a week later, on the 14th. There were no funds available to purchase provisions or to equip vessels for the trip. Moreover, Faro complained to the king that the present contractor of the Mina trade, Pero Borges de Sousa, was unwilling to assist the relief enterprise by providing victuals and other supplies for the posts. Furthermore, the master of a Pernambucan caravel had sighted eighteen Dutch ships off the African coast and said the vessels appeared to be heading southward for Africa and possibly Mina.[35] Despite the urgency of the situation, the matter of the projected expedition dragged on for another two months. By November it had been decided to send one caravel immediately with the most needed supplies.[36] Philip II also ordered that construction be started on two galleys which the crown had agreed to furnish under the new Mina contract recently made with Rovelasco.[37] Because of the previous contractor's reluctance to assist in the dispatch of relief, his grant had been revoked.

The year 1607 passed with no ships being sent to Mina. The necessary caravel had not yet been outfitted because of a complete lack of royal funds.[38] In addition, the new governor of Mina,

Duarte de Lima, was still in Spain and too ill to travel. In July 1607 the first news since 1604 arrived directly from São Jorge when the second clerk of São Jorge da Mina, Ambrosio Ferreira, carried personally from Governor Melo the dispatches reporting the victory over the Dutch the previous September. After reading the letters of the governor imploring further assistance, on 15 August 1607 Philip II reiterated his insistence that caravels should be made ready with provisions to accompany Duarte de Lima when he departed for his post.[39] Governor Lima was ordered to leave as soon as possible for Lisbon and to continue to Mina with all dispatch.[40] Three days after the king's orders had been received, the Council of Portugal replied that no funds were available for outfitting any vessels. Instead, council members suggested that six or seven ships be detached from the Spanish squadron of Admiral Fajardo, who was in the midst of collecting vessels for a coastguard expedition to the Indies due to sail in October 1608.[41] The detached ships could sail to Mina and return in time to rejoin their original squadron before it departed. This recommendation was sent on to the Council of the Indies for its approval.[42] The council accepted the plan, but recommended that only one ship be sent from the Fajardo squadron for the voyage to Mina.[43] The relief of Mina had dragged on for so long that the Council of Portugal took a prudent action by suggesting to Philip II that when Duarte de Lima eventually left for Mina, he should be issued special instructions in the event that he should find São Jorge in enemy hands.[44]

When the Mina relief expedition finally sailed, it consisted of three ships: one transport—the *Nossa Senhora da Ajuda*—and two caravels. The galleys which were supposed to accompany this fleet were not yet finished and did not reach Mina until 1609.[45] Governor Lima left Lisbon in late May or early June 1608, and arrived at São Jorge in July. Altogether, thirty-four months had been required to dispatch this small relief flotilla. In contrast, during the same period more than three score Dutch ships had sailed to Mina and returned with gold and ivory cargoes![46]

The new governor's arrival at São Jorge brought eighty new soldiers to bolster the garrison. Lima found the fortress in such dire straits that severe emergency measures were necessary. The most

pressing problem was finding money to pay the troops already at
the station. Receipts of the factory over the previous five year
period were insufficient to meet even the annual salary requirements. In fact, the account books of Afonso Martins Albernás, the
factor during this time, showed a shortage of 350,000 *réis* when
they were totaled by the new governor.[47] Governor Lima ordered
the arrest of the factor and both of his clerks and he threatened the
three men with immediate execution if the embezzled funds were
not returned. Albernás confessed that he had taken the gold and he
showed the governor where the money was hidden. While Lima's
action drew a sharp rebuke from the Council of Portugal when
that body learned of the governor's threats, the king supported his
new governor. Philip II noted that Lima was deserving of thanks
for his zeal in prosecuting the matter to a successful conclusion. In
his letter to the Council of Portugal on this matter, Philip remarked that at the moment it was quite inconvenient to restrict
the powers and authority of the Mina governor.[48] Governor Lima
also sanctioned the actions of Cristóvão de Melo by following his
predecessor's example and dipping into the accounts of the church
to make up salary deficits within the garrison.

While Duarte de Lima was occupied in putting Portuguese affairs at Mina in order, negotiations were underway in Europe to
reach an accord with the Netherlands over overseas disputes with
Spain and Portugal. On 9 April 1609 a twelve year armistice was
finally signed between Philip and the Dutch republic. Articles four
and five specified that the Dutch would not traffic in the Spanish
empire, but they were free to trade in all lands not subject directly
to Spanish suzerainty. It was clear from the outset that Dutch
jurists interpreted these articles to their own favor with regard to
the Mina trade. The Dutch claimed that Spanish authority in Mina
was restricted to those areas under personal control by the Portuguese fortresses there. This was interpreted to mean the small
territory of the commonwealth of the Elminans and the village immediately adjoining Axem. Neighboring kingdoms such as Efutu,
Commany, Asebu, Accra, and others, were considered independent of Portuguese authority and thus not prohibited under the
truce from trade with the Dutch. As a matter of fact, the Dutch
could argue with regard to the coastal state of Asebu that this area

was a dependency of theirs. For several years the Netherlanders had maintained a small trading lodge there. The Asebu village of Moure was the focal point of Dutch power on the Mina coast.

Duarte de Lima received news of the twelve-year truce through a supply ship and two new galleys which ported at São Jorge on 22 December 1609.[49] The Portuguese governor disregarded the treaty in the same fashion as the Dutch. In fact, Lima had already begun to wage the most active military campaign against the Dutch since the attacks made on French and English corsairs in the early 1580s. In late September 1609, despite the absence of Portuguese galleys on the coast at the time, Lima successfully attacked a Dutch vessel belonging to Elias Trip sailing out of Amsterdam for Moure. The Portuguese commander sent his soldiers out in war canoes manned by Elminan blacks and overwhelmed the small crew of Trip's sloop. Dutch prisoners from this fight were carried to São Jorge along with the merchandise seized from the ship.[50] The arrival of two new galleys in December 1609, added measurably to Portugal's military position at Mina.[51] Lima wasted no time and he sent the galleys out on patrol immediately. On their maiden patrol, the galleys encountered a Dutch sloop belonging to Maerten Papenbroeck. It too was attacked and plundered of its cargo and the crew imprisoned.[52]

In 1610 Lima felt emboldened enough to challenge Dutch power on land. During the night of January 6/7 Portuguese troops from São Jorge's garrison were loaded aboard the two galleys.[53] Accompanied by about eighty war canoes full of Elminan warriors, the Portuguese-African force rowed silently toward the Dutch station at Moure. Just before dawn the Portuguese landed a short distance away from the Dutch post, surprised the enemy sentries, and before the Dutch could gather their weapons, the Portuguese had fallen upon them. Elminans attacked the African town adjoining the station and burned much of it while the Portuguese fought their way to the shore, intent on setting fire to the ships anchored there. These consisted of ten merchant vessels in the midst of unloading goods. Portuguese troops boarded a small sloop which they found pulled up near the beach and made off with it and its cargo. However, they were not as successful in their attempt to burn the other Dutch ships lying offshore and they had to content themselves with this prize. The Portuguese returned to São Jorge with their spoils without having suffered any casualties. The attacks on every passing Dutch ship continued. On 11 January 1610 the galleys fought off São Jorge with a Netherlander squadron which reported receiving 146 shots from the enemy guns.[54] Nine days later, January 20, Portuguese galleys captured the Dutch trading sloop *Sonne* laden with trade goods. A week after this, on the 28th, a 200 ton supply ship, the *Eendracht* of Amsterdam, was sighted by the São Jorge lookout. The largest galley gave chase to the interloper until the Dutch ship finally reached the safety of Moure's guns.[55]

Naval encounters between Portuguese galleys and Dutch vessels continued unabated throughout February and March 1610. On February 13 a sloop returning to Holland loaded with a cargo of ivory was captured and towed to the Portuguese fortress. On March 1 Governor Lima learned that a Dutch ship had sailed alone to Takoradi to trade. Again the *Capitanea,* or lead galley, sallied forth. Its commander Francisco Soares had orders to hunt the Dutchman down. The Dutch skipper had taken the precaution to arm his ship with ten small cannon in case of attack. However, his defenses were of little avail against the single larger gun of the galley with its greater range. The Dutch ship was outmaneuvered in the shallow coastal waters and captured. The prize was boarded by her Portuguese captors, fires were extinguished, and the vessel was then towed back to São Jorge. It joined a growing assortment of damaged Dutch craft lying beached in the shallow lagoon behind São Jorge. On 6 March 1610 three more Dutch vessels appeared off São Jorge and the Portuguese galleys fought with them all the way to Moure before breaking off.[56]

In a move intended to counter Dutch influence in the kingdom of Asebu, Governor Lima opened negotiations with the rulers of Efutu and Fante. The Portuguese actively sought to forge an alliance between themselves and these two African states because Efutu and Fante encircled Asebu and the Dutch center of trade at Moure. If an alliance could be concluded, the trails from the interior gold fields to Moure would be closed. However, despite months of negotiations and lavish gifts sent from São Jorge to the chiefs and princes of the two states, the Portuguese commander was unable to obtain a positive commitment from either state.

At the same time as Efutu and Fante were being approached, the Portuguese governor began discussions with the ruler of Accra. The king of that portion of the coast appeared fearful of the growing Dutch power and perhaps he sought to balance the position of the European states. While relations between the Portuguese and Accra had been marred several times by open warfare, and earlier the Africans had even burned the Portuguese out of their small fortress there, nevertheless in 1610 the Accra ruler appeared friendly toward Lima's overtures for an alliance. The king even agreed to permit the Portuguese to refound the fortress. The Portuguese commander reported all of these negotiations to the Council of Portugal in Lisbon with the recommendation of proceeding immediately with the erection of such a post. On 19 July 1610 the council recommended that an armed squadron of eight vessels be prepared and sent to sweep the Mina coast free of Dutch shipping. Moreover, materials necessary for constructing a new post at Accra were to be included in this fleet.[57] When this coastguard fleet was finally sent in 1614, the plan for extending Portuguese defenses to include a station at Cara had been abandoned for want of sufficient funds. Instead, efforts were now concentrated upon reinforcing and modernizing the bastions at São Jorge.

Governor Lima's aggressive policy had serious repercussions both in Mina and in Portugal. In Portugal, news of continued Dutch encroachments into Portuguese African territories raised the issue of whether the Twelve Year Truce was indeed valid for this area. In late November 1610 a caravel returning from a provisioning expedition to Mina reached Lisbon with the spoils taken during the spring offensive of the galleys. The caravel carried six high-ranking Dutch prisoners in addition to tradegoods, ivory, and gold. These captives were commanders and officers of the merchant vessels taken during the fighting. Presumably the remainder of the crews had been consigned to galley service in Mina.[58] Declarations taken from the six captives by the judge of Guinea were forwarded to the king in Spain. In Spain the Councils of the Indies and Portugal deliberated the fate of the prisoners being held in

Lisbon. The penalty for violating Spanish trade restrictions was specific: death. However, considering the claims of the Dutchmen, namely, that they were merchants and were trading in areas not under the authority of the king of Spain when captured, the matter became more involved. Also there was concern for the recent treaty signed with Holland. Consequently, the Council of Portugal waffled in its recommendations to Philip II, by suggesting the crown show clemency for these particular captives. In the future, however, the monarch should decree that all Dutchmen captured in Mina be consigned immediately to the galleys.[59] Orders to this end were sent to Governor Lima.

The Portuguese's renewed energies at Mina and preparations to send out new galleys from Lisbon also caused reverberations in the Netherlands.[60] Heretofore the Dutch had been divided on whether to initiate an openly hostile policy toward Spain's overseas possessions. Oldenbarnevelt counselled caution and opposed any overt acts. Against him stood the representatives of the East India Company. The States-General remained undecided. However, as Portuguese attacks at Mina mounted, shippers and merchants suffering losses made their complaints and relief requests to the States-General. Pressure for positive action increased, and finally, in 1611, the States-General gave way to these demands. On 25 August of that year the Hooge Moogende decided to build a fortress on the Mina coast at Moure in the land of Asebu to protect their merchants.[61] Two representatives of the king of Asebu had made a trip from Mina to Holland to request Dutch help against Portuguese reprisals.[62] Following the attack upon Moure in January of the previous year, merchants trafficking there had attempted to construct a new palisade of their own. Cannon were taken off ships in the harbor and mounted in temporary batteries around the post. But work on the early fortress progressed very slowly, and by the time of the Hooge Moogende's decision of August 1611, fortifications were only partially completed.[63] On 8 November 1611 Jacob Adriaansz Clanscius was appointed as the first Dutch governor general of the ships and post in Guinea. A month later, on 10 December, the new governor was given command of a 500 ton warship and a company of soldiers to form a regular garrison for the new outpost.[64] The Dutch did not experience the sort of delays which had plagued the Portuguese in building up their forces in Mina. By 1 March 1612 Governor General Clanscius had already reached Moure with his command galleon and three supply frigates carrying 140 soldiers.[65] Work was begun immediately on the new fortress. First, a rampart of timber packed with tamped clay was erected. Later, in 1614, stone walls began to replace these crude defenses.[66]

Open hostilities between the Dutch and Portuguese forces on land commenced shortly after Clanscius's arrival. The commander of Portuguese forces at São Jorge was no longer Duarte de Lima, but João de Castro. Castro had been the commander of a provision ship sent to São Jorge in 1610. When he arrived at the fortress, he found that Lima had died of fever earlier that year. Therefore, Castro exercised his prerogatives in the instructions given him and assumed command of the post. He remained there until 1613, when he was finally replaced by a regular, royally-appointed governor, Pero da Silva. Silva in turn served until 1616 when he was replaced by Manuel da Cunha e Teive. Manuel da Cunha had been one of the candidates for the Mina governorship in 1605, but at that time he had been passed over in favor of Duarte de Lima. After he assumed the São Jorge headship in 1616, he proved to be one of the ablest governors of the Philippine era. He served at the headship of Mina for seven years, until 1623. On the enemy's side, Governor General Clanscius remained at Moure until 1615. Thereafter a regular succession of Dutch military governors were sent to the outpost of Moure which was named Fort Nassau two decades later.

Alarmed by the new turn of events in Mina and the Dutch construction underway at Moure, the Portuguese managed for once to muster their energies in Lisbon. The curbing of Holland's Guinea trade was of more than immediate interest to Mina along with the recovery of Portuguese commerce, for the belief was widely held in both Spain and Portugal that the Dutch were able to effect their incursions into the two Indies of Spain and elsewhere chiefly through the gold revenues derived from the Mina trade. Philip II of Portugal enunciated this popular notion in 1613 when he ordered a renewed attention to the supply of Portugal's stations on the Gold coast.[67]

At least one relief ship was sent to reprovision Mina annually between 1612 and 1620. In 1614 a coastguard squadron of five warships of Portuguese vessels sailed to Mina waters and scoured the coast, picking off lone Dutch merchant vessels.[68] No attempt was made to attack Fort Nassau directly. In addition to the warships, the 1614 fleet carried two new galleys to São Jorge. Together, this naval force hampered Dutch coastal trading, but it did not stop Dutch commerce altogether. Dutch ships continued to arrive in Mina at Moure at a rate of approximately sixty vessels per year, and with each vessel came provisions, troop replacements, and bricks for the construction work. However, the numerical advantage of the Dutch in shipping and personnel was offset by an extremely high death rate among new arrivals. Because of the location of Fort Nassau and the period of acclimatization required, Samuel Brun, who attended the sick at the Dutch post, stated that only one person in five survived beyond six months at Mina. Brun further declared that for every hundred soldiers and officials who came to Mina, scarcely ten lived to return home. Malaria and fever were the chief causes of death at the Dutch station.[69]

Portuguese fortunes in the life and death struggle with the Dutch between 1612 and 1616 swung back and forth. 1615 was a particularly bad year for the forces at São Jorge da Mina. One of the valuable provision ships sent from Lisbon to succour the Portuguese post never reached its destination, having been dismasted in a storm and driven to seek shelter at Vigo in Spain.[70] The loss of even a single supply ship was a major setback for the Mina station and created severe shortages of provisions and medicines at the Portuguese post. To correct this situation, Governor Silva sent a small picket-boat with a skeleton crew to São Tomé in search of homemade medicines and herbs for the infirmary chest. This left only twenty-five whites in the entire garrison at São Jorge at the time, many of whom were too ill with fever to stand guard duty. Also in 1615 the fortress was racked by a violent earthquake which shook the coast. For several months there were occasional aftershocks, and one such tremor was so intense that one of the large bastions collapsed, destroying the gun battery located there. Permanent repairs on this part of the fortress were impossible for several years, since the only stonemason at the post had died in 1614. In the interim, makeshift ramparts were erected.

When Governor General Clanscius learned of the damage caused at São Jorge by the earthquake, he decided to attempt a land attack on the Portuguese position, and three separate assaults were made in as many days. Luckily for the Portuguese, the enemy was not aware of the true size of São Jorge's garrison and failed to press the attack. There was sufficient powder and shot at the post to throw the attacking forces back, and the Dutch retired to Fort Nassau with moderate losses. Before they left São Jorge, however, the village of Elmina was put to the torch. The Dutch had planned to rush the gates of the fortress if the governor opened them to let the stragglers from the village inside. But the Portuguese were not deceived by this tactic and the gates remained closed.[71]

Despite hardships suffered in recent months, Governor Silva decided upon a bold move. He would retaliate against the Dutch attacks with a surprise raid upon Fort Nassau and Moure. A handful of Portuguese soldiers, assisted by several hundred Elminan blacks, attacked the village of Moure and burned it to the ground. In addition, not only were large quantities of tradegoods captured in the course of the raid, but a Portuguese galley entered the harbor at Moure and made off with two merchant vessels anchored there.[72] The galleys were still a force to be reckoned with. Early the following year (1616), both Portuguese galleys attacked a lone Dutch merchant vessel as it returned to Fort Nassau from coastal trading. The post physician, Samuel Brun, who witnessed the fight and treated the survivors, reported that eleven Dutch seamen were killed before the ship reached safety under Fort Nassau's guns.[73] The situation seemed to be a standoff. The Dutch controlled the bulk of the coastal traffic, but thus far they had been unsuccessful in every attempt to dislodge the Portuguese from their entrenched positions at São Jorge and Axem.

By 1615 it was apparent that the Portuguese crown alone could not continue indefinitely to meet the needs of the Mina stations. Funds for overseas enterprises were extremely scarce and what little money was available in Portugal was being used to defend more productive areas of the empire—Brazil, Angola, and India. By this time also, the contract system in Mina had terminated. The last contract, that of Giovanni Baptista Rovelasco, had ended prematurely in 1607–9.[74] After that, the crown reassumed the burden of keeping Mina stations functioning. Then in 1615, following months of correspondence between Lisbon and Madrid, a new set of regulations for the Mina trade was promulgated. It was a radical departure from past crown efforts to restrict trade with this area; by a royal decree of 20 March 1615, all trade with the region of Mina was opened to crown subjects. Goods sent to Mina were to be registered in the Lisbon India House before leaving Portugal. These goods then could be transported to São Jorge accompanied by a copy of the cargo manifest issued by the India House, and at the Portuguese station a flat rate duty of twenty percent in kind was levied. Once this was paid, the trading vessels could sail wherever they liked and secure commerce. All the gold, ivory, and other items acquired were then to be registered with the factor of São Jorge before returning to Portugal, where a further five percent duty was imposed at the fortress. New within the *regimento* was a proviso permitting the capture and enslavement of Negroes in the coastal region beyond a distance of ten leagues from São Jorge.[75] The only limitations imposed upon private trade with Mina was the prohibition of individual voyages between São Tomé and the Portuguese mainland stations. It was reasoned by the crown that such an island commerce would lead to attempts to circumvent the paying of royal duties. Such commerce would be impossible to regulate. The proviso forbidding trade with São Tomé is not spelled out in the 1615 document save in its insistence that all goods must first be registered in the India House in Lisbon. Such a prohibition becomes apparent by 1622, when the inhabitants of the island persisted in their appeals to secure the opening of free commerce with Mina.[76]

The Portuguese viceroy expected that this new departure in trade with Mina would stimulate Portuguese voyages to the area. In this way the Portuguese stations' problems of supply would be alleviated. A further benefit would be an active competition with the Dutch for the coastal gold trade. Neither hope was to be realized. Few ships chose to take advantage of the new regulations. In fact, prices of tradegoods on the Mina coast were so depressed by

Dutch imports by this time that reasonable profits were no longer possible.[77] The burden of maintaining Portugal's Mina stations continued undiminished in the crown's hands, the annual cost for upkeep of São Jorge and Axem during the seventeenth century averaging about 20,000 *cruzados*. Receipts from gold fell far short of this figure. For instance, during the last year of Pero da Silva's governorship, revenues from the newly-freed trade amounted to 7.35 million *réis*, or 18,372 *cruzados*.[78] This left a deficit for the year of about 1,628 *cruzados*. Ahead for the Portuguese at Mina lay one brief period of respite when Manuel da Cunha would exercise a strong positive control. Ahead also lay a final Portuguese military victory in 1625. But the decline was already well established, and the ultimate collapse was in sight.

7

Ordeal with the Dutch: The Final Phase, 1615-37

Despite the freeing of the Mina trade in 1615, there were no significant changes in the commercial relations between Portugal and that region. When the new governor, Manuel da Cunha e Teive, arrived at his post in 1617, his correspondence with Lisbon continued to play traditional themes—shortages of men, munitions, provisions, low morale, and loss of trade to the Dutch. Yet despite all the setbacks the Portuguese had endured at Mina in the previous two decades, they still remained in control of the two most formidable stations on the entire coast. Portuguese land defenses had been assaulted without success; in each attack on São Jorge da Mina, the Dutch had been repulsed by the Portuguese garrison and their African auxiliaries. If sufficient reinforcements came from Portugal, then the Portuguese might even mount an offensive against the Dutch redoubt at Fort Nassau. There was still a slim chance for Portugal to recover the Mina gold trade. However, few Portuguese held great expectations that Mina would ever return to a profitable venture.

At least for a few years after 1615, the vigorous pursuit of Portuguese interests at Mina by Governor Cunha gave hope of recovering the lost gold trade. These aspirations were dashed by the late 1620s, when new elements in the Luso-Dutch struggle destroyed the tenuous balance of power on the coast. After 1630 there was a rapid withering away of African support for the Portuguese cause; the establishment by the Dutch of a West India Company in 1621 fostered new trade in Africa and America; attacks on the Portuguese empire in Brazil and the Orient drew support away from faltering Mina; finally, a further deterioration occurred in the military power of São Jorge and the garrison there from lack of supplies.

Early in the summer of 1617 Manuel da Cunha reached São Jorge with the largest squadron accompanying a new governor to that post since 1608: two caravels and a large supply ship. Cunha brought with him desperately-needed supplies for São Jorge and Axem: grain, powder, muskets, iron, lead, and a miscellany of other essential items.[1] Equally important were new personnel which came to the station. Sailing to Mina with Cunha were thirty-five soldiers, two stonemasons, new chief factors for both São Jorge and Axem, and the governor's personal staff of ten. The stonemasons were especially needed to repair the damage caused by the earthquake of 1615. Both new factors were men of experience. Both had served previous tours at Mina and were experienced soldiers. Francisco Soares, the new factor of São Jorge, had commanded the galley *Capitanea* during the governorships of Duarte de Lima and João de Castro and had captured several Dutch prizes. At Axem, Manuel de Lemos, the new factor, had served in Mina for more than fourteen years, from 1597 to 1611. Lemos had particularly distinguished himself for valorous conduct during attacks on Dutch ships and in the Portuguese surprise assault on Moure in 1610.[2] In addition to regular replacements for the fortress, Cunha carried a favorite Negress with him from Portugal. The governor obtained special dispensation from the crown to have her accompany him to his new post.[3] Also, since Mina was now considered a hardship post, Cunha asked for and received a personal *comenda* or subsidy of 200,000 *réis* above his normal salary of 800,000 *réis*.[4]

Under the new trade regulations of 1615, Cunha possessed the authority to grant licenses of residence to any persons who wished to stay at São Jorge to trade. But few persons sought to take advantage of this new privilege. Reinforcements were sorely needed since a severe outbreak of malaria at the post had killed many of the former governor's staff. This sickness continued for several months after Governor Cunha's arrival. Within two months, thirty soldiers from among the new arrivees were dead. Of the two galleys lying idle in the harbor in 1617, there was only enough manpower to activate one of these ships for patrol duties.[5] The situation at Mina during the period of Cunha's governorship is best summarized by two accounts written from São Jorge. The first is a report by a Portuguese captain who sailed there in 1617. The other is an analytical report composed by Cunha himself in 1623 near the end of his tour of duty.

Gaspar da Rosa, a *cavaleiro fidalgo* of Philip II of Portugal, had begun his career in the armada of 1576. He served in India for nine years and later occupied minor offices in São Jorge and Axem. In 1617 Rosa commanded the second ship in the squadron transporting Cunha to Mina. When this fleet returned to Portugal, Rosa prepared a lengthy report on the conditions he observed at Mina along with his recommendations for reforming the situation. Rosa stated that there was still a great volume of gold coming to the coast from the interior gold fields. In fact, the amount seemed to exceed the volume of previous decades. The problem was that most of this gold now fell into Dutch hands. The Portuguese governor was sending a few white troops from the garrison in the company of Elminan warriors to interdict shipping whenever possible, but this was not enough. Rosa suggested that reforms in Mina should be directed toward three goals. First, the governor of São Jorge should be awarded full powers to punish all private illicit traders within the garrison who sought to circumvent the payment of royal duties. Second, prices on trade merchandise offered at São Jorge and Axem should be cut drastically to compete with the similar commodities offered by Dutch merchants. If possible, Portuguese prices should be set even lower than those of their competitor. Even if such a reduction should involve a temporary loss, this policy would attract the African traders away from the Dutch factory. Once this was achieved, the old price structure could be reintroduced gradually and unnoticed. Finally, Rosa recommended that the king send a heavily-armed squadron of at least six warships to Mina to scatter Dutch naval units. Part of the regular India fleet could be detached, used for several months in Mina, and then rejoin their flotilla before the latter left Lisbon for the East. In addition, extra galleys should be assigned to accompany this coastguard squadron. Rosa's objective seems to have been not to drive all the Dutch from the Mina area, which would be an impossible task in a few brief months of naval combat, but rather, the recommendations concentrated on winning the Africans from the Dutch traders. Rosa reported that there were even possibilities of expanding Portuguese influence to other areas along the coast aside from São Jorge and Axem. While conducting a diplomatic mission to Accra for Governor Cunha, Rosa had met with the paramount chief of Accra and had again been offered a building site and permission to erect a new fortress in that land. Rosa returned to Cunha excited by the new prospect of reestablishing trade with Accra.[6] A substantial portion of the gold trade out of the Akan lands in the interior reached the coast at Accra.

Captain Rosa's description offered many suggestions which had already been tried and failed. Regarding the dispatch of a new coastguard squadron, the Portuguese were no longer capable of mounting such a large scale operation. The squadron which had traveled to Mina in 1614 was the last armed patrol sent there; after that time, only supply transports sailed to Mina. In 1622/23 active preparations were undertaken in Madrid and Lisbon to equip eight warships and three supply caravels to relieve the Dutch pressure on São Jorge. Unfortunately, Portugal could not raise the requisite 70,000 *cruzados* necessary to finance this squadron. Even extraordinary funds, such as forced loans from Lisbon merchants, were unobtainable. Since 1619 Lisbon businessmen had contributed nearly one million *cruzados* to meet the crown's expenses. No further levies could be drawn from them for Mina.[7] Consequently, the planned expedition was dropped in late 1623. During the seven years in which Manuel da Cunha oversaw Portuguese affairs at Mina, only eight caravels and one large supply ship were sent to him from Lisbon, and this number included the two caravels and supply ship which accompanied the new governor to Mina in 1617. Every Portuguese vessel now had to fight with the Dutch to reach São Jorge and at least one was captured, in 1618.[8] For the most part, Portuguese soldiers in Mina subsisted from locally produced foodstuffs raised by the villagers of Elmina. A solitary caravel did succeed in reaching São Jorge in 1619, and two more came from Portugal the following year. From 1620 to 1622, either no ships were sent or else those that did sail were seized by the enemy. It was not until the end of 1622 that the first letter since 1619 finally arrived in Lisbon from the Mina governor. It traveled by way of São Tomé and was forwarded to Portugal. Governor Cunha complained bitterly over the lack of support from Portugal for over two

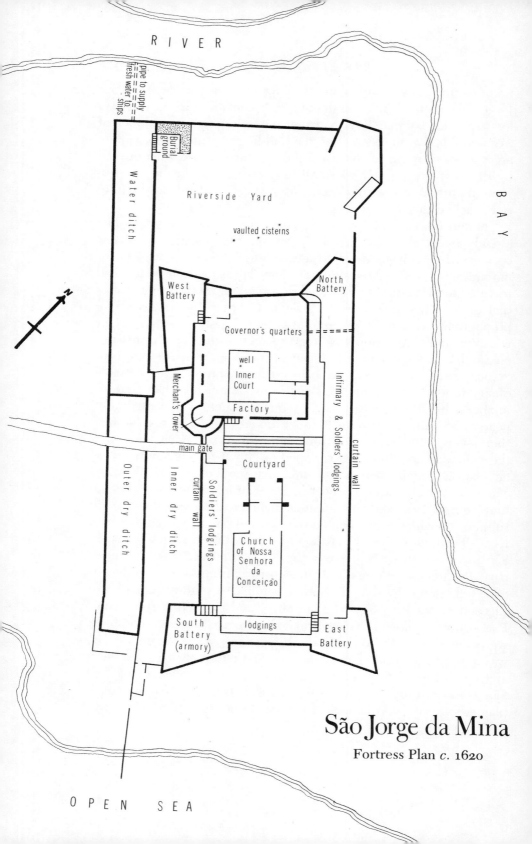

RIVER

pipe to supply
fresh water to
ships

Burial
ground

Water ditch

Riverside Yard

vaulted cisterns

BAY

N

West
Battery

North
Battery

Governor's quarters

Merchant's Tower

well
Inner
Court

Factory

Infirmary & Soldiers' lodgings

curtain wall

main gate

Outer dry ditch

Inner dry ditch

curtain wall

Soldiers' lodgings

Courtyard

Church
of Nossa
Senhora
da
Conceição

South
Battery
(armory)

lodgings

East
Battery

São Jorge da Mina

Fortress Plan *c.* 1620

OPEN SEA

years. The opening of the Mina trade to all crown subjects in 1615 had totally failed to relieve São Jorge's supply crisis. Not a single vessel had visited São Jorge since the last two supply caravels' arrival in 1620.[9]

Da Cunha was unaware of preparations underway in Portugal to organize a major coastguard and supply expedition to Mina. These efforts had begun since the last communiqués with São Jorge in 1620. But by April 1623 it was clear that the planned expedition would have to be aborted. The Portuguese viceroy decided instead to send a lone caravel to Mina with a small quantity of provisions and munitions.[10] However, its primary assignment was not to relieve São Jorge, but to gather intelligence on the overall disposition of Portuguese strength in the area. The captain of the vessel was instructed to secure from Governor Cunha a detailed report on his own position and Dutch strength. In the dispatches sent out to Cunha, several important questions were put to the governor: what was the state of the Portuguese posts; what was the number of Dutch forces and ships; where was the enemy trading and with which African rulers; which ports did the Dutch already control outright; were they well-received by the Africans; did they ever depart from the coast during bad weather; and several other queries. The report dated 15 May 1623 which Governor Cunha sent back to the viceroy, is one of the most enlightening accounts of the relative position of the Portuguese and Dutch in Mina during this time.[11] The dispatch comes from the pen of a man who already had six years' experience with the problems of the area. Cunha reported that São Jorge was in good physical condition. Fortifications damaged by the 1615 earthquake and by Dutch assaults had been repaired or replaced. The governor had under his command sixty Portuguese officials, craftsmen, and soldiers.[12] For defense, São Jorge boasted a respectable armament of twenty-one small bronze *falcons* and four large iron pieces of artillery. Over the past several years, a few bronze falcons had been taken from the fortress and had been mounted in the patrol galleys. Six cannon had been destroyed or lost at sea in encounters with the Dutch, and Cunha asked that these be replaced.[13] During calm periods in the Luso-Dutch struggle, the governor had set the garrison to work making up numbers of cartridges for the cannon and bullets for the few muskets at the post. Ship's carpenters sent there previously were now building two new galleys. A small galley of seven benches had already been completed, while another galley of twelve benches was nearing final construction. In the meanwhile, canoes were used to harass Dutch shipping. Only a few Portuguese troops remained on duty within the fortress walls. Cunha sent as many soldiers as possible on continual patrols by land and sea, warning blacks against trading with Dutch merchants. When the Dutch captured an unarmed Portuguese ship out of São Tomé which was forced into Fort Nassau's harbor from lack of water, Cunha retaliated immediately. Fourteen Portuguese soldiers sailed in two large war canoes and captured a Dutch vessel bound for Fort Nassau. The Dutch vessel's cargo was a windfall for the Portuguese. It included eleven cannon and tradegoods worth more than eight thousand *cruzados*. The cannon had been intended to arm the Dutch ramparts at Fort Nassau. Prisoners taken from the captured Dutch vessel were executed at São Jorge.[14]

Cunha's evaluation of Dutch forces was quite detailed. He described the Dutch station of Fort Nassau as a square enclosure about 210 feet on each side, with low ramparts and outer walls constructed of wood with earth fill packed between the inner and outer casings. Cunha remarked that following each rainy season on the coast the Dutch sent men into the forest for additional timber to shore up the walls. The ramparts especially were subject to frequent collapse because of the heavy cannon mounted there. A contemporary Dutch description of Fort Nassau by Samuel Brun confirms the accuracy of Cunha's report and notes how painfully slowly work was proceeding on the fortress during the 1620s.[15]

At Fort Nassau the Dutch had positioned thirteen pieces of iron cannon to defend the post. Eight were large-bore sixteen-pounders and faced the harbor. The Portuguese governor had learned from Negro spies set at Moure that ordinarily the Dutch garrison included only sixty men, counting both soldiers and officials. This number varied greatly since many visitors to the coastal regions of Mina died shortly after arriving. In fact during the spring of 1617 the garrison at Fort Nassau had been reduced to only forty men, most of these too ill to fight.[16] The death rate was much greater among the Dutch than among the Portuguese, most of whom were veterans of Mina service. However, Dutch forces constantly were replenished by a provision ship sent out each year. In addition to this large supply vessel, another thirty-odd smaller merchant ships remained on the coast almost year round. In the Dutch harbor, at least two or three large trading ships filled with wares remained anchored off shore.

The enemy's commerce was concentrated in three primary areas aside from Fort Nassau itself. These were at Cara (Accra), 35 leagues east of the Dutch fort; Cormantin, about 2 leagues from the Dutch station; and the tiny coastal settlement of Torto (Komenda?). This latter site was about 4 leagues west of São Jorge da Mina. Torto lay in territory under the rule of the king of Commany, who in previous years had been a friend of the Portuguese. He had even permitted members of the Portuguese garrison and their personal slaves to purchase food in the local African markets. However, Cunha reported that now one of the greatest problems facing the governor was the ill will of this king. Shortly before 1617, the king had become embroiled in a dispute with Cunha's predecessor, gathering his warriors and marching against Mina in a short war. The Commany were still attacking the Portuguese post sporadically when governor Cunha took over the post. The new governor moved quickly to resolve this critical situation by counterattacking some of the villages of Commany in the immediate vicinity of São Jorge da Mina. Local Commany chieftains captured by the Portuguese were summarily executed, and several distant coastal towns belonging to Commany were burned in a show of Portuguese military strength. Apparently, the ruler of Commany then came to terms. Cunha reported that the kingdom seemed peaceful now. Although the former friendship between the Portuguese and their African neighbors had been irrevocably destroyed, at least the Commany respected Portuguese cannon enough to remain neutral in the contest between the Dutch and the Portuguese.

On São Jorge's eastern flank, the activities of the ruler of Efutu and this chief's increasing contacts with Dutch traders raised the threat of a possible alliance between these two parties against the Portuguese. The Asebu, traditional allies of the Dutch since about 1595, were not considered a major threat to the Portuguese post.

During the 1620s Asebu was involved in a series of bloody conflicts with the eastern states of Cormantin and Fante. Few Asebu warriors could be spared to assist the Dutch in an attack on Portugal's posts.

The bulk of the gold traded on the coast came from forest Akan tribes in the interior. Merchants from inland towns like Assingrud still made their regular journeys to the coast to trade for European wares. Akan merchants now traded with the Dutch rather than the Portuguese because the Dutch commodities were plentiful and cheap. Akan merchants generally remained socially aloof from both European groups. The Akani were disdainful of all Europeans, no matter what their nationality; they looked to their own interests, seeking those white merchants who offered the greater bargains.

Governor Cunha's lengthy report ended with a recommendation that the king concentrate his energies on interdicting Dutch shipping to Mina. Because most Dutch vessels frequenting the coast were merchantmen and thus only lightly armed, two or three men-of-war sent from Portugal would suffice to drive the enemy from their coastal trade. Once this was accomplished, it would be easier to dislodge the Dutch from their land position at Fort Nassau. The increased share of the trade accruing to Portugal from such a policy would more than defray the expenses involved. But no squadron was sent. The first relief ships did not arrive until Cunha's successor, Francisco Sotomaior, cast anchor at São Jorge in mid-1624 with three vessels hauling much-needed supplies and troop replacements. It seemed as if Portugal had all but abandoned Mina. Precautions had been taken to ensure that, should Sotomaior find his predecessor dead, the proper steps could be taken to restore order. However, when the new governor arrived Cunha was still in office, the organization of the Mina staff was intact and operating, but the situation described the year before by Cunha had not changed significantly.[17] Governor Sotomaior assumed charge of a Portuguese outpost which was still a contender in the power struggle on the Mina coast.[18] Through the efforts of his predecessor, the neighboring tribes of Efutu and Commany had been neutralized, and by 1624 Commany was even opening its weekly markets to São Jorge's garrison for provision purchases. However, east of the state of Efutu Portuguese power and influence had been completely supplanted by the Dutch. Asebu was a staunch ally of the enemy. In 1624 the Dutch signed a trade agreement with the Fante nation whereby exclusive trade rights were ceded by that tribe to the Dutch. The Fante swore to undertake to cause the Portuguese every possible injury on land and sea whenever they met them.[19]

All the assistance Sotomaior could muster would soon be needed. The Dutch had begun to mount a new assault designed to destroy Portuguese power. The success of Cunha's governorship can be measured by the strong reaction of the Dutch following his departure. Seizures of Dutch merchant ships and constant patrols and raids from the galleys had earned a healthy respect for Portuguese strength from the Dutch. A mounting list of complaints against the Portuguese filtered to the Netherlands during the years of Cunha's administration. The Dutch West India Company, chartered in 1621 following the expiration of the truce between Spain and Holland, had committed itself to the destruction of Spain and Portugal's colonial dominions. Squadrons of Dutch warships were making ready to sail to New England, Brazil, and Mina. With their military preparation for conquering Brazil proceeding according to schedule, the Dutch West India Company saw new possibilities of profit in Mina. Not only could their share of the coastal gold trade be enhanced by the capture of São Jorge, but control of the station would serve as an admirable entrepôt for the collection of slaves to supply labor needs in Dutch Brazil. In September 1623 a new Dutch high commissioner, Adrien Jacobssen van Amersfort, sailed for Mina with 1,000 soldiers, thirteen warships, and orders to conquer São Jorge and Axem.[20] The major Dutch squadron proceeded first to Bahia in the New World and attacked this port. Then twelve ships from the fleet sailed east to rendezvous with Amersfort's transport ships sailing from Holland. On 26 July 1625 elements from Admiral Veron's Brazilian squadron joined up with Amersfort and the West India Company contingent. Command of the combined fleet was given to Admiral Jan Dirickszon Lam who had sailed from Holland with the three company troop transports.[21] When the Dutch fleet reached the Mina coast, it proceeded immediately to a prearranged landing site at Ampeni. This little village had been chosen because it lay west of São Jorge between the Portuguese post and the trading center of Torto and was far enough removed from the Portuguese station to allow an unhindered landing. The fleet anchored at Ampeni and was joined by Dutch military units from Fort Nassau. General van Amersfort had sailed ahead to Fort Nassau and gathered what reserves of black allies and Dutch soldiers he could muster. Altogether, the Dutch attack force included fifteen ships, 1,200 soldiers and sailors, and 150 Asebu warriors from Moure.

At São Jorge da Mina, Governor Sotomaior had only fifty-six men in the entire garrison and many of these were too ill to fight. On the other hand, allied with the Portuguese were three companies of black warriors from Elmina.[22] Sotomaior promised these African warriors tradegoods, wine, and even gold if they would fight on the Portuguese side in the impending battle. Runners were sent out to the capitals of Commany and Efutu. Sotomaior stripped São Jorge's coffers of all their gold and he took most of the tradegoods for gifts to lavish on the two rulers. Both chiefs agreed that they would not join the Dutch now marching on São Jorge. Without the neutralizing of Commany and Efutu, the situation at São Jorge would have been near hopeless. Now Sotomaior was pleased to learn that the king of Efutu had not only agreed to stand aside in the fight; he had even opened local markets to the Portuguese where they might procure additional provisions for a possible siege.

The battle for São Jorge opened on Saturday, 25 October 1625, with a heavy naval bombardment. The Dutch fleet blockaded the harbor to the Portuguese post. The same morning Dutch forces on land began marching from Ampeni along the coast road toward São Jorge. By 2:00 P.M. Portuguese lookouts sighted advance units in the column passing through a small clearing a half mile from the post. Confident in their numbers, no skirmishing lines had been set out nor were scouts patrolling the sides of the column. There was no need to fear only forty or fifty Portuguese soldiers. Surely the commander of São Jorge would not risk his few troops in an open fight outside the fortress. The Dutch learned too late that they had walked into a carefully-laid ambush. Three cannon shots were fired from the fort as soon as the main body of Dutch troops had reached a clearing near the fortress called *Pilicada*. Sotomaior had positioned most of his troops outside the walls in the brush on the side of the coast road. On the cannon signal the Elminan allies of the Portuguese burst into the clearing and charged the flank of the Dutch column. As the Dutch soldiers turned to fire, the Africans fell to the ground, and the first volley passed harmlessly overhead. Before the enemy could reload, the Elminans crashed down upon the formation, wielding axes and lances which the Portuguese had given them. Disorganized and confused by the unexpected assault, the enemy broke and ran toward Ampeni, pursued by Elminans and a few Portuguese archers. Stragglers were cut off from their line of retreat, driven into the surf and drowned. Other soldiers turned toward the interior, away from the beach. These also were caught and killed. The African warriors continued their attacks until darkness cut short the slaughter. The Elminans then returned to the site of their victory to recover the weapons and heads of the fallen enemy. Dutch heads were stuck on lances and carried in triumph to São Jorge to be redeemed for gold. Governor Sotomaior, who had organized the fight and had remained within São Jorge, exaggerated Dutch losses, reporting that all but 45 of the attacking forces were killed. The Dutch set their own losses at 441 killed or missing. By either estimate, the Pilicada ambush was an overwhelming Portuguese victory. Sotomaior's own losses in the fight consisted of 27 dead, including 11 whites from the garrison command. Fifteen Dutch company standards were captured, and more than a thousand muskets and lances were collected on the field of battle.

Ensuing encounters between Dutch forces and the Portuguese after the battle of Pilicada were anticlimactic. At dawn on 26 October Dutch ships outside the harbor at São Jorge were recalled to Ampeni by Admiral Lam. There they remained for eleven days, treating the wounded and trying to woo the rulers of Commany and Efutu from their neutral stand. When it became apparent that these two chiefs were not going to join the Dutch after such a disastrous defeat, the fleet sailed back to São Jorge. On 5 November the warships commenced a bombardment against the Portuguese fortress that continued from dawn to dusk for three days. More than a thousand heavy shot, some weighing upwards of eleven kilograms each, were hurled against the fortress and the village of

Elmina. Throughout the cannonade, however, the Portuguese lost only one man. The Dutch did not mention their own losses in the exchange; Portuguese gunners, however, reported several direct hits on the naval flotilla from the fort's large cannon. On the evening of November 7 the Dutch ships withdrew out of range of the fort's batteries and broke off the action. The blockade of the harbor continued until November 14, when Amersfort and Lam saw the futility of further action and withdrew all Dutch forces to Fort Nassau. The squadron which had come to Mina from Brazil and Holland finally departed for Europe on 29 November 1625.[23]

Although the Portuguese had won a great victory at Pilicada—so great that Sotomaior's account of the fight was printed and circulated in Lisbon in 1628—yet the final chapter of Portuguese decline in Mina had already begun. What the Dutch could not capture by force of arms was shortly to fall into their hands from attrition within the Portuguese ranks. São Jorge continued to survive from day to day. The main fare for the Portuguese soldiers was the produce purchased in the small market at Elmina. There were also a few cleared fields near the fortress which were tended by slaves or by the African wives of some members of the garrison. Widespread intermixing had taken place between the Portuguese and the Elminans over the previous century and a half. Although the Portuguese crown was disturbed by what clergy viewed as a serious spiritual void among the garrison, nonetheless it was this close association and intermingling with the local Elminan population that accounted for the longstanding, unflagging loyalty of the village.[24] Members of the garrison frequently took wives or mistresses from among the black villagers, and by the seventeenth century, São Jorge was filled with a melange of women, mulatto children, African allies, slaves, and prisoners of war.[25] In addition to the local produce, the Portuguese collected a tithe of the fish netted by the villagers of Elmina, who were among the most skilled fishermen along the entire stretch of Mina coast. Occasionally, the Portuguese were able to collect a tithe of the fish brought to Shama, but this depended largely on the current state of friendship between the Portuguese and this village. And there had been considerable animosity from the Shamans in recent years. Occasionally, too, grain and other staples were purchased from tribal markets within

Commany and Efutu whenever the two states opened their borders to Portuguese visitors. After the mid-1620s even these local sources of provisions began to disappear. The reason was quite simple: there were no more tradegoods with which the Portuguese could barter. In 1625, on the occasion of the Dutch attack, Governor Sotomaior stripped the fortress bare to ensure the neutrality of the states of Commany and Efutu. In future encounters with the Dutch, this neutrality could no longer be secured through gifts. At about the same time, the Dutch altered their tactics. Instead of attacking São Jorge da Mina again immediately after the 1625 defeat, the governor general at Fort Nassau enlisted as many African states as he could to assist in this undertaking. A great deal of the blame for the Dutch failure in 1625 was due to lack of preparation. The Dutch had not considered the Africans as a force with which they had to reckon.

Efforts in the Portuguese capital to collect supplies for beleaguered São Jorge and Axem were thwarted by depredations of Dutch fleets in Brazil and elsewhere throughout the empire. Spain could furnish no assistance. The limited naval resources which Portugal could muster to meet the Dutch were utilized in protecting Brazilian ports and returning carracks from the East. For instance, in 1625 every available vessel in Lisbon and all military reserves were sent to Brazil to help recapture Bahia. The relief of São Jorge during the following year consisted of one caravel. The next supply ship to that post did not come until two years later, in 1628. While Philip III of Portugal was sending this lone relief ship, his entire silver fleet from the Spanish New World was being captured by Dutch forces under the command of Piet Heyn.[26]

The resupply time for Portuguese Mina lengthened more and more. In 1632 the last known relief squadron for São Jorge arrived from Lisbon. Three caravels carried 180 soldiers, replacements for various offices, and a new governor, Pedro Mascarenhas.[27] In addition to the reinforcements, Governor Mascarenhas carried special orders for the vicar at the post. Two years before, Vicar Duarte Borges had written seeking special dispensation for the Mina church. Because it was now isolated even from the mother episcopate at São Tomé, Borges pleaded for the same concessions accorded to the discalced Carmelites by the Council of Trent. This would permit the vicar to bless and consecrate the host rather than depending on the Holy Eucharist's coming from outside.[28] After considerable debate by the Congregazione di Propaganda Fide in Rome, these privileges were conceded, and Mascarenhas carried the Church's official reply.[29] Also of religious note among the items in the governor's company were three statues sent to adorn the Mina church. They were figures of the Holy Virgin, St. Francis of Assisi, and St. Anthony of Padua. When these wooden figures reached São Jorge, they created an excitement among the superstitious Christian blacks there. After a few days in the humid climate, the pigment on the hands and face of St. Francis began to change color from white to black. Mascarenhas offered a prophetic explanation to the astonished villagers by claiming that St. Francis was revealing himself in a miracle as the patron saint of the Africans. This created rumors of other miracles performed by the figures. The statues were held in great reverence by the black Christian community even after the Portuguese had left.[30] Altogether, by the 1630s the village of Elmina boasted about four hundred Christians among its total population of perhaps eight hundred. But it was not uncommon even for these converts to participate in traditional fetish ceremonies or to consult the local shaman. Piromancy and sorcery were still very strongly rooted among converted blacks and the Christianity practiced by missionaries from São Jorge da Mina had done no more than impose a superficial veneer of the new religion over the black population.[31]

In 1632 the new Portuguese governor literally had to fight his way to his post to assume command. As soon as Governor General Amersfort learned of Mascarenhas's arrival, he sent a small force from Fort Nassau to test the station's defenses. Mascarenhas succeeded in repulsing the attack, but not before suffering heavy casualties; a number of African *caboceers* from Elmina perished in the fighting around the walls of the Portuguese fortress. In 1633 Mascarenhas dispatched the small caravel which was normally used to communicate with Axem on a voyage to São Tomé seeking assistance. But the Portuguese there were just as hard pressed by the Dutch as at the Mina posts. On the vessel's return to São Jorge, it fell into a fight with an unarmed French merchant ship which had ventured onto the coast in search of gold and the Portuguese ship

succeeded in capturing her. It was hauled back to São Jorge as a
prize and its cargo was unloaded. Part of the goods went to its captors while the remainder was used by the governor to replenish
the depleted stores of the fortress. The letters which the governor
had sent to São Tomé were forwarded to Lisbon in March 1634.
Mascarenhas spoke of the hopelessness pervading the São Jorge
garrison. In a letter from Duarte Borges accompanying Mascarenhas's dispatch, Borges reported that everything on the coast save
for the two Portuguese stations and their immediate environs was
now in Dutch control.[32] Borges's assessment was confirmed by a
Dutch memorandum dated 16 June 1633 which reported on the
status of the West India Company's trade and estimated that five
tons of gold annually were being extracted from the trade along
the coast.[33] During the first thirteen years of its existence, the
Dutch West India Company secured 40,461 marks in gold and
1,137,430 pounds of ivory from Mina valued at 17,733,899 and
1,178,688 florins, respectively.[34] It was estimated that up until
about 1630 most of the gold used by the Dutch for their coinage
originated from the Mina trade.[35]

On the Portuguese side, Governor Mascarenhas continued in his
report that almost all provisions in the post had been consumed.
The only item for which there was no urgent need was powder and
shot; a plentiful supply of armaments existed for the time being.
Worst of all were the first disturbing reports by the governor of
rebellion among the garrison soldiery, which had gone unpaid for
over two years.[36]

While Mascarenhas was composing his bleak letters to send to
Lisbon, aid was already on its way. In early May 1634 the Portuguese governor received word by canoe from Axem that a Portuguese relief vessel had been sighted making for São Jorge. The
blacks who carried this heartening news also reported that the ship
had been set upon by two Dutch ships about seven leagues from
São Jorge. To protect the much-needed supplies, a war canoe was
quickly loaded with twenty soldiers and sent to assist in the defense
of the provision ship. The Portuguese rendezvoused with the vessel and were able to keep the Dutch from closing on the ship until
it could slip away at dusk. It reached the protective cover of São
Jorge's main gun batteries with only superficial damage.[37]

Much to his surprise, Mascarenhas learned that the vessel which he had defended so stoutly was not Portuguese, but English. Yet she was flying the royal standard of Portugal. Her captain, Romão de Bocette (?), had contracted in Lisbon to haul three months' provisions and a handful of soldiers to the Mina post. The ship and its crew were forced to remain in the harbor of São Jorge for almost three months before departing because their sailing was blocked by seven Dutch warships on station opposite the Portuguese post. Two of the largest enemy vessels mounted thirty guns each, and they were under orders from the governor general of Fort Nassau to prevent further supplies from reaching the Portuguese.

During the months following the arrival of the English vessel, the situation in São Jorge deteriorated rapidly. Governor Mascarenhas, who had been suffering from fever even before the relief arrived, died on 27 June 1634, and like so many of his predecessors was buried in the small plot in the riverside yard. According to the regulations in the post, he was succeeded by the vicar. Normally, the commander of a relief squadron would have been in line for the governorship. But since the relief vessel was English, the vicar assumed authority. Duarte Borges, the new governor-vicar of São Jorge, had come to that post fifteen years before as chaplain, and it had only been after serving several years in the station that he had advanced to the headship of the church.[38] At the time he assumed the governorship, Borges also was in very poor health. For months he had been crippled and confined to his bed. Governor Borges served for less than four months. He too died, in early October 1634, leaving no second in command. The clerks and factor had all died previously. The *alcaide-mór* of São Jorge, André da Rocha Magalhães, then came forward to assume the headship. Rocha Magalhães had come to Mina in the company of Mascarenhas in 1632 as an ordinary soldier and had advanced into the office of *alcaide-mór* by an appointment from the former governor in recognition of his services.[39]

Rocha Magalhães immediately ordered an accounting of all provisions and tradegoods in post storehouses to determine the exact status of his new command. There was only food enough to sustain the garrison for a month, perhaps two, by strict rationing. When a second English ship paused at São Jorge in late 1634 to take on water, the Dutch blockade had lifted and the ship entered the Portuguese harbor with no difficulty. Governor Rocha Magalhães sent one of the soldiers from the post, Manuel de Bairros, to sail with the English vessel when it departed, for he feared that the first English ship, which had left months before, had been unable to deliver the dispatches sent to São Tomé. The new ship leaving from São Jorge was also bound for São Tomé, in search of a cargo of sugar. So Bairros was sent along in late 1634 with letters to the king which were quite brief. Rocha Magalhães reported on the recent misfortunes at the post, including the deaths of two governors within four months. At the time São Jorge was defended by thirty-five soldiers and officials. All were in relatively good health since they had all passed beyond the critical first few months of residence on the coast. The most essential items needed were cloth and other tradegoods with which to pay the soldiers and retain the wavering loyalty of the Elminan warriors. The Dutch infested every inlet on the coast by that time, and Portuguese galleys no longer went on patrol.[40] Bairros reached Lisbon with his report early in 1635. On the strength of the dispatches and his personal testimony, two caravels were ordered made ready immediately to carry a lengthy inventory of supplies to the beleaguered fortress.[41]

Despite the ambitious plan of officials in Lisbon for bolstering São Jorge's defenses, as usual neither funds nor even the two vessels in which to transport them were available anywhere in Portugal. All troops and funds were committed to the fleet of six galleons and 3,000 men being mustered to relieve Bahia.[42] The Council of Finance estimated the cost of sending two relief ships to Mina would be about 50,000 *cruzados*, not including the *roupas pretas* and other tradegoods which would be sent in the shipment.[43]

Preparation for the expedition dragged on through the fall of 1635 and throughout the following year. Reports came from the storehouses of the king in Lisbon that there were neither ships nor weapons nor powder to spare.[44] Meanwhile Princess Margarita, the viceroy, was trying desperately to find 460,000 *cruzados* to pay for relief squadrons ordered by the king to sail to Brazil, Angola, and Mina. But Mina had been of secondary importance for half a century now and the Portuguese had no choice but to defend the more productive parts of their empire. Mina would have to fend for itself.[45]

Opposition to Rocha Magalhães's assumption of the headship of São Jorge had sprung up almost as soon as he took over in late 1634. The majority of the soldiers in the garrison refused to recognize his authority.[46] By 1636 the opposition to the governor flared into open rebellion. Midway in the year, the governor managed to get letters out of the post reporting a further setback for the Portuguese station. The small garrison had revolted and demanded their back pay for the past two years. Rocha Magalhães had been seized and thrown in the post dungeon. In these bleak surroundings the captive governor sent his final report from São Jorge da Mina. The leaders of the coup d'etat were not named, except that the head of the rebellion was a person of foreign extraction (persona de nacion estrangera). Perhaps he was one of the English captains who frequently paused at the Portuguese station to take on stores of fresh water. There is no way to determine for certain. The important point was Rocha Magalhães's remark that most of the warriors of Elmina refused to obey the orders of this new commander and the inhabitants of the adjoining village began to leave the area in large numbers. Some went to Axem where legally-appointed Portuguese officials welcomed them.[47]

Rocha Magalhães's letter was the last Portuguese correspondence from São Jorge before the fall of the fort into Dutch hands. Plans were set in motion by the Dutch in 1636 for a renewal of the the attacks on São Jorge and its eventual capture. The military commander of Fort Nassau, Nicholas Van Ypren, had been busy winning support among the coastal African states for their assistance in crushing the Portuguese and their Elminan allies. Large gifts of trade goods were expended by the Dutch in this effort. Thus far he had scrupulously avoided any confrontation with the coastal states which might drive the Africans into an alliance with the Portuguese. In 1634, for instance, Van Ypren would have liked to have lent military assistance to Asebu in that kingdom's quarrel with Fante; to avoid pushing the Fante in the Portuguese camp, however, the Dutch governor mediated the dispute.[48] At the time there was little the Portuguese in São Jorge could do save watch and wait for a relief vessel. Whether or not the thirty or so rebels who had seized Governor Rocha Magalhães and imprisoned him were still in control is uncertain.

Van Ypren began to discuss a massive assault on the Portuguese in his correspondence with the Dutch West India Company directors in 1636. The Dutch campaign in Brazil was going well and Van Ypren proposed that Elmina and the Portuguese fort would make a valuable entrepôt for the slave trade which would be so badly needed once the Dutch settled in their New World conquests. He argued that there was little chance for reprisals by the Spanish and Portuguese, since the monarch of those two countries was already preoccupied with the defense of his American possessions.

Van Ypren's suggestions were well received in Holland. It was true that the Dutch were making great progress in the conquest of the northeast sector of Brazil during the past year (1635/36). In the latter part of 1636 a new governor general of the company's holdings in Brazil had been sent with reinforcements to complete the conquest of the former Portuguese possessions. Maurice of Nassau arrived in Brazil in January 1637 with a fleet of thirty-two ships and 2,700 troops. Shortly after his arrival, instructions from Holland reached him to assist in the conquest of São Jorge on the west African coast. In March 1637 nine men-of-war and 800 soldiers were detached and sent eastward toward Mina, with the command of the military forces placed in the hands of Colonel Hans Coine.

The fleet arrived off the Ivory Coast in late June 1637, and dispatches were sent ahead to the governor general in Fort Nassau informing him of the squadron's schedule and asking that a suitable site be chosen for disembarking the troops near São Jorge. It was hoped that the Portuguese would have no advance warning of the planned attack and would not have time to build up reserves and defenses. The fleet moved cautiously along the coast waiting for the governor's response before venturing too near the Portuguese post at Axem. It was early August before Van Ypren finally replied. He asked that the Brazilian fleet meet with forces from Fort Nassau at Kommenda. The Africans at that point on the coast had been won over to the idea of attacking the Portuguese and would lend their assistance. The two naval contingents met at Kommenda and sailed without further delay for the final site of disembarkation at Cabo Corso. Early in the morning of 26 August the main Dutch force went ashore and grouped together for the short march to São Jorge. Altogether their forces numbered about 800 soldiers, in addition to more than 400 sailors who remained with the fleet. African allies from Kommenda and Asebu composed another 1,000 to 1,400 men. The Dutch force was divided into three columns of march, and an advance unit was sent ahead to warn of any ambush. The Dutch did not intend to be caught as their fellow countrymen had been at Ampeni in 1625. The strategy of attack had been altered from the previous forays against São Jorge. Instead of attacking by way of the peninsula connecting the fortress with the mainland, Coine sought to gain the commanding heights of Santiago Hill on the opposite side of the river from the Portuguese post.

The Portuguese had not been idle. Word had reached them that the Dutch force was moving along the coast and probably intended to launch an attack on the Portuguese soon. The Portuguese governor (Rocha Magalhães?) realized that it was essential at all cost to retain control of the hill site of Santiago. The hill itself was thickly overgrown with brush and trees, and the only trail to the summit led up from the river on the Portuguese side. This narrow path could be covered by the fortress cannon. On the other hand, the main batteries of the fort faced seaward. The heaviest guns, therefore, were useless against any enemy which might become entrenched on the summit. The smaller falcons of the fortress did not have sufficient range to reach the hilltop. The governor mustered his available Elminan allies and ordered them to defend the foot of Santiago from the approaching Dutch divisions. The enemy were coming from the side opposite from the fortress and the fort could offer no assistance. A small redoubt was hurriedly re-constructed on the summit and manned by a handful of Portuguese soldiers and a few cannon of small caliber.

When Commander Coine learned of the Portuguese strategy, he decided to test the strength of the Elminan defenses. Four companies of Dutch troops were sent against the massed Elminan warriors at the foot of Santiago Hill, but in heavy fighting the Dutch were thrown back with the loss of one company commander and about fifty soldiers. The Elminans, thinking the battle won, decapitated the fallen enemy and returned to their village on the peninsula to celebrate their victory. A second Dutch unit, advancing quickly, captured the approaches to the hill, and two counterattacks launched by the Elminans failed to regain their lost positions. The Portuguese allies were driven back toward their village. Dutch troops made their way through the undergrowth to the summit of Santiago and attacked the outnumbered Portuguese there. The few Portuguese on the hilltop surrendered.

Colonel Coine then cleared a broad path to the summit of the hill, and up this trail were hauled two cannon and a large mortar. This Dutch battery was then aimed against São Jorge. Accurate fire from this great a distance was impossible; moreover, the strengthened walls of the Portuguese station easily withstood the Dutch cannonade. On the other hand, the Portuguese bronze cannon inflicted no damage to the Dutch atop the adjoining summit. A stalemate had been reached. The Dutch commanded the surroundings. The African allies of the Dutch had attacked and sacked Elmina, and most of the Elminans had fled within the fortress or into the bush. But the Dutch could not remain forever. The area was unhealthy for European troops which had just come from a grueling sea voyage. Many were already falling ill. Therefore Coine sent a message under a flag of truce to São Jorge demanding that the Portuguese surrender immediately or face execution once the fortress fell. The commander of the fortress put him off, asking for three days to consider this proposal. Dutch rations were low, and therefore Coine gave a single day. On the following morning, August 29, a Dutch officer went to the gates of São Jorge under a flag of truce to demand the governor's answer. He found the drawbridge up and the fortress securely locked. Coine sent his main body of troops onto the peninsula and brought his batteries close to the fortress. At point blank range, the Dutch recommenced their bombardment of São Jorge. After a dozen or so volleys from the Dutch cannon, the Portuguese commander appeared at the gate of São Jorge and agreed to surrender the fortress.[49]

The Portuguese were allowed to leave with their wives and children. They could carry nothing with them, neither standards nor arms. All merchandise, gold, and slaves (save for twelve blacks which accompanied the Portuguese) were to be left behind in the fortress. Only church ornaments not made of silver and gold could be removed. Finally, the surrendering garrison would be transported to São Tomé on a Dutch warship and turned over to Portuguese officials on that island. By that afternoon, Saturday, 29 August 1637, all formalities were complete and the keys to the fortress were turned over to Dutch hands. The Portuguese left São Jorge da Mina after a continuous occupation of 155 years. When this last garrison reached São Tomé, they were imprisoned by royal officials on that island.[50] Behind them they left a fortress virtually intact. Some damage had been inflicted by the Dutch bombardments, but no major structural faults were evident save one, a crack in the wall facing the harbor. Even this was due most likely not to Dutch cannon but to a violent earthquake in December 1636.

The Dutch had specified in the surrender agreement that all merchandise and gold be left behind by the withdrawing Portuguese. When the victors entered the castle for the first time they searched it thoroughly, but found no gold or merchandise of any sort. Instead, the Portuguese left behind them an impressive array of armaments: 30 bronze cannon, 9,000 pounds of powder and material with which to make powder, 800 cannonballs, 10 casks of musketballs, 300 packages of flints, and a mixed assortment of axes, pikes, crossbows, muskets, and personal weaponry. São Jorge had not fallen to Dutch control from want of fortifications or armament. The garrison simply had been drained of its ability to resist an assault. No provisions were left and the prospect of a prolonged siege with no hope of relief made the Portuguese commander elect to surrender. Maurice of Nassau was deeply impressed by the post's extensive defenses. In a letter to the directors of the West India Company he described the strong fortifications of the post and attributed the Dutch victory to divine providence.[51] A garrison of 175 men under the command of Captain Walraeven van Malburgh was left at the new Dutch station. Within several months the headquarters of all of Holland's Mina trade had been shifted from Fort Nassau to the former Portuguese post. The Dutch fortress, rather than continuing under its Portuguese name, was called simply "Elmina," a corruption of the Spanish version of its name. When arrangements for the garrisoning of São Jorge were complete, a small detachment of Dutch soldiers was sent to Shama to take possession of the Portuguese tower at that site, but the squad found only the ruins of the former fortress. During the 1600s, until 1637, only one official had been left in charge of this Portuguese lookout station. When the fighting began in 1637 he apparently abandoned his post and returned to São Jorge or Axem.

Portuguese occupation of São Jorge da Mina for over a century and a half left behind a mixed legacy. A patois Portuguese continued to be used by merchants in trade with Europeans in this area well into the eighteenth century. Many modern geographical terms (e.g., the Rivers Volta and Ancobra) owe their origin to Portuguese terminology. A veneer of Roman Catholicism also was introduced by the sporadic missionary activities of the various orders which served at São Jorge. However, the religious conversions were never more than superficial in their impact, and the inroads of Protestant missionaries from Holland and England soon erased most of the Catholicism from the area. Those Christian practices which survived became mingled with the fetishism of local religions and became virtually unrecognizable.

A positive contribution of the Portuguese was the introduction of new crops and plants to the region around São Jorge. In addition to citrus fruits (oranges and lemons) which were raised on the grounds around the fortress, the Portuguese introduced the prickly pear, sugarcane, bananas, cotton, and a plethora of other commodities. Economically, São Jorge's loss was of little consequence to Portugal. If anything, events at Mina in 1636 removed a financial burden from the Portuguese crown. The period when Mina had rendered a profit—any profit—for Portugal had ended forty years before. In reality, the great years of the gold trade at its height were but a century-old memory when the Dutch conquered São Jorge. The Portuguese ability to survive for so long on the end of a decaying line of supply was a remarkable accomplishment.

What the Portuguese defeat at São Jorge did symbolize, however, was the ultimate failure of the outmoded *feitoria* system upon which Mina trade had been premised. When Portugal lost its capability to provide her far-flung outposts with trade commodities, ships, and provisions, the fate of Mina and similar Portuguese posts was sealed.

8

Aftermath:
Santo António de Axem (1637-42) and Fort St. Francis Xavier (1679-82)

The news of the loss of São Jorge da Mina did not reach Lisbon until 13 February 1638, when a letter from the governor of São Tomé giving an account of the events surrounding the setback on the mainland was relayed to Philip III.[1] The news from Mina put an end to the projected relief expedition which had been in the planning stages for more than two years.[2] Although the dispatch occasioned surprise that such a strong redoubt could have fallen to Dutch hands, there was no special action undertaken to recover this lost fortress. The same messenger who carried the dispatches from São Tomé also brought disturbing news of fresh Dutch assaults on Portuguese towns in Brazil.[3] By February 1638 Mina had been pushed to the background while Portugal strained every nerve and resource in a massive effort to stem the enemy's advances in Pernambuco. All available ships (41) and soldiers (5,000) were in the final stages preparatory to departure for the New World. Even this large a force was considered insufficient by its commanders.[4] Not even the smallest contingent could be released from this expedition to recover São Jorge at that moment. Consequently, it was decided to wait until the situation improved in Brazil before undertaking the recovery of the lost fortress in Mina.

With the seizure of São Jorge, only the small redoubt of Santo António de Axem, located on a high bluff at the western edge of the Mina coast, remained under Portuguese control. Axem offered few of the advantages which the Portuguese had enjoyed at São Jorge. The harbor and fortress location possessed only minimal facilities. Access to the tiny bay in front of the fortress was possible only by means of a narrow inlet from the ocean beset with strong tidal currents. Once a ship was safely inside the harbor, the landing site below the walls of Axem was small and surrounded by heavy forest growth.[5] The fortress itself was limited in size by the steep bluff. The outcropping rock on which it was built, while serving as a formidable defense, made it impossible to expand the fortifications. Defended by only ten small bronze cannon, Axem was so small, in fact, that the garrison of a half-dozen men were forced to live outside the walls. Soldiers and officials had quarters in straw huts adjacent to the station. Yet all its drawbacks so far as space and convenience were concerned worked to the Portuguese advantage. No Dutch squadron of any size could approach close enough to the fortress walls to lay down a naval bombardment. Furthermore, access to the fortress from the landward site was possible only by a single forest path leading down the coast.[6]

The largest Portuguese garrison at Axem was there in 1608, when there were eighteen soldiers and officials altogether.[7] When Pieter de Marees had first seen this Portuguese station in 1602, he described it as "a little fortress . . . very ill defended."[8] When Portuguese power at São Jorge collapsed in 1637, there were eight Portuguese manning Axem. They were assisted by about one hundred and fifty African warriors in an adjoining village who had been enlisted as allies. As mentioned previously, such a minuscule Portuguese garrison was not unusual. Axem had always been considered as a satellite station to São Jorge da Mina; it had been supplied, administered, and controlled by the mother fortress. In the beginning the *raison d'être* for Axem's construction had been to tap the rich gold-bearing area behind Cape Threepoints, but because of closed roads merchants from this area and kingdoms farther east on the Ivory coast found it difficult to make their way to São Jorge. Therefore Axem performed an important function as a secondary trading station.

Axem, like São Jorge, had suffered considerably during the early seventeenth century from food shortages and lack of other provisions. However, after August 1637 the Dutch made no attempt to capture this station as a followup to their victory at São Jorge. Van Ypren felt that in time the post would simply fall into Dutch hands by default. Therefore the Dutch governor general concentrated his energies in relocating the headquarters of Dutch trading at São Jorge and in repairing and improving the fortifications of this new post.

At Axem, the Portuguese commander was Pascual de Almeida, a man with long experience with Mina's problems. Almeida had first come to Axem as factor and captain in 1628 and had remained ever since.[9] Supplies for his garrison had not come since 1634. Almeida had given what few tradegoods remained in the station warehouses to the *caboceers* of the village to preserve their allegiance.[10] Without African help, Axem too would succumb to the Dutch. Immediately following the capture of São Jorge, Nicholas Van Ypren sent representatives to Almeida at Axem demanding the surrender of his command, but the Portuguese captain defiantly refused and challenged the Dutch to try to drive him out. Almeida swore to fight to the last man before deserting his post. In late 1637 the valiant Portuguese commander was bolstered by a Portuguese caravel which arrived from São Tomé with provisions for the garrison. The captain of this relief vessel, José Martins, returned to São Tomé with a full report of the status of Axem and the necessities of the post. Among other things, Almeida asked that the following be sent immediately from Portugal: 200 bars of iron; 4,000 brass *manilhas;* 4,000 *varas* of *almafegas;* 40 lots of *chaudeis* and *manteses;* 6 capes for the *caboceer* chieftains; powder, shot, matches; a cleric, an apothecary, and ten soldiers; 100 dozen large knives; biscuits, flour, oil, wine; and, finally, brandy to serve as gifts to the Negro *caboceers.*[11]

When Almeida's report reached Lisbon in 1638, discussion began at once in the Council of State as to whether to succor the remaining Mina station, and if so, how. Philip III placed the final decision in the hands of Manuel da Cunha, a member of his privy council. As a veteran of seven years' service governing São Jorge da Mina, Cunha's recommendations carried formidable weight in the discussions. Cunha pointed out that Axem definitely should be defended. It would afford a future outpost from which to reconquer São Jorge when the opportunity presented itself. If Axem were lost, any reconquest would be forced to utilize the distant island of São Tomé as an operational base. São Tomé lay downwind from the Mina stations and a laborious three to four weeks of tack-ing was required to reach westward to the Mina coast. By contrast, Axem was at the western gateway to Mina. Ships could sail there directly from Lisbon almost as rapidly as the same vessels could make the journey from São Tomé.

Cunha disagreed with those advisors who thought that the provisioning of Axem should be handled through São Tomé. This proposal to use the island as a base of supply had first been put forth by the governor of the island, Lourenço Pires de Tavora. Cunha diplomatically pointed out to the governor that during his administration of São Jorge, between 1617 and 1624, vessels from São Tomé all too frequently had misjudged the strong eastward current along the coast and the ships had made a landfall on the coast somewhere between São Jorge and Fort Nassau. Some of these ships were picked off by Dutch corsairs as they sought to tack westward to São Jorge. Manuel da Cunha proposed that Axem's provisioning could be carried out from Portugal. Despite the lack of Portuguese ships, English vessels could be enlisted to carry goods to Mina. Every year for several decades, English ships had sailed under royal licenses to and from São Tomé carrying cargoes of sugar to Lisbon. Axem lay directly in the outward path of their route from Lisbon. Moreover, English ships usually made the voyage to Guinea with ballast only. Therefore, the English captains could probably be interested in carrying provisions. The English were at peace with the Dutch and thus English vessels were not subject to seizure, as was the case if Portuguese ships tried to use the São Tomé-Axem route.[12]

Philip III agreed with Cunha's basic recommendations. In June 1639 the *St. Mary Magdalene*, captained by Felix de Olanda and owned by William Rawles, sailed for Axem and São Tomé. In her hold were provisions for both of these Portuguese outposts. A new governor for the island was on board, as were a cleric, an apothecary, and forty soldiers.[13] At least twenty of the soldiers were men condemned to galley services because of criminal convictions in Portugal.[14] Everyone except the governor was assigned to duty in Axem. Captain Almeida had been given almost all the items he had requested, but some of the quantities had been trimmed, e.g. 200 bars of pig iron, 4,000 *manilhas*, 2,000 *varas* of *almafegas*, 40 lots of *chaudeis*, 3 capes, 12 *almudes* of flour, and 15 pipes of wine.[15] Cunha had examined the requests of the Axem captain meticulously, and the ex-governor carefully winnowed out what he deemed unnecessary items. Rawles arrived safely at Axem and the provisions were unloaded. Before sending José Martins to Portugal in 1638 in search of assistance, Almeida had worked out a recognition system by which he would know if a ship, of whatever nationality, came in peace bringing supplies.[16] The utilization of this English vessel proved so successful that it was decided to use the method a second time. In 1640 Nicholas Philip sailed with the ship *Sarah* bearing provisions for Axem. Unfortunately, the *Sarah* overshot Axem, and rather than tack westward, her captain sailed to São Tomé with the supplies. The provisions were unloaded and remained until December 1640 awaiting a ship which would haul them to Axem.[17] At that time Captain Rawles again appeared on the scene. He had come in search of a sugar cargo, and in return for a concession to transport such a cargo, he offered to haul the relief supplies to Axem. The municipal council and the governor accepted the offer.[18] However, Almeida reported from Axem in late 1641 that no new provisions had come to that station since the 1639 relief ship. Either Rawles never reached Axem or else his offer had been turned down after reconsideration by the governor.

In late 1641 Almeida wrote that Axem now needed munitions most urgently. At least the following minimum in arms should be sent at once: 20 quintals of powder, 50 muskets with cartridges, 6 quintals of lead, and a suitable quantity of crossbow bolts and cannonballs.[19] Without these the fortress could not resist an impending Dutch assault.

In the Iberian peninsula important events were occurring during the years 1638–42 which eventually accelerated the decline and ultimate collapse of Axem into Dutch hands. In Spain, discontent within the eastern provinces of Catalonia and Aragon had grown into open rebellion by the end of 1640. The Catalan revolt in turn had repercussions in Portugal. On 1 December 1640 Portuguese conspirators overthrew Spanish authority in Lisbon. Palace guards were disarmed and Princess Margaret, governor of Portugal, was escorted to the Spanish frontier. Portugal once more asserted its independence from Spain. During the next several years the new monarch, John of Braganza, subordinated all else toward protecting Portugal from a counterassault by Spain and recovering Brazilian territory lost to the Dutch.

By 1640 the issue of tiny Axem was put aside indefinitely because of the series of losses suffered by Portugal. The previous year the Dutch had inflicted a heavy defeat on a Portuguese armada off Pernambuco. Then in January 1641 Dutch forces captured Malaca, and by August of the same year the enemy held Maranhão in Brazil and Luanda in Angola. Moreover, the conquest of Ceylon was nearly complete. Portugal had little choice but to make peace, and on 12 June 1641 Portuguese diplomats in Holland concluded a ten-year truce with the Dutch. It was stipulated that the treaty would not take effect overseas for one year. In return for the right to recruit troops and buy munitions in the Netherlands, the Portuguese granted important economic concessions to the Dutch. The question of Brazil and the status of São Jorge da Mina was discussed by those who drew up this new agreement; however, the Dutch would agree to no clauses pertaining to transfers of Brazilian or African territory in the present 1641 treaty.[20]

The 1641 agreements between Portugal and Holland did little to stem the growing power of the latter in Mina. Governor Van Ypren died that year, and he was replaced by a new military figure, Captain Jacob Ruychaver. Ruychaver declared that one of his prime missions as governor general in Mina would be to take Santo António de Axem from the Portuguese as soon as possible. By February of the following year, he was prepared for the final assault on the Portuguese post. On 9 February 1642 a Dutch squadron consisting of seven warships and several hundred soldiers, along with some African allies, approached Axem. Before the ships came into the narrow harbor, Ruychaver sent a boat with six men and a trumpeter to approach the castle demanding the surrender of the post. Almeida responded to the messengers with a cannon blast. After Dutch ships had picked their way through the shallows at the mouth of the bay and arranged themselves in a half-moon formation, broadside after broadside was hurled against the defenders of Axem from the collected ships. One Dutch participant of the encounter estimated that in four hours of firing, the ship which he was on expended nearly a thousand pounds of powder from its twenty-eight guns.[21] When the firing fell off, the Dutch commander sent a company of troops ashore. However, when they landed, Dutch soldiers found themselves on the narrow beach below the fort, with Portuguese gunners pouring a withering fire from behind the protection of the fortress walls. The Portuguese defenders more than compensated for their diminutive number by the advantage they held. Axem was situated on high ground and the Dutch were at a severe disadvantage trying to storm these heights.

The battle was decided on the following day. The Dutch had temporarily withdrawn from land to assess the situation. On the next morning a company of fifty soldiers was sent ashore to set up a small battery on a rocky islet at the harbor entrance and within firing range to bombard Axem. When Almeida and his defenders saw that the Dutch intended to stay and that a siege was perhaps in the offing, the final decision had to be made to abandon the post. Axem had not been designed to withstand a prolonged siege. There was no cistern and water which was available was brought to the post from a nearby stream and stored in earthen jars. By now many of the Africans in the neighboring village had seen the strength of the Dutch, and the blacks' loyalty for the Portuguese cause waned. On the night of 8 February 1642 Almeida carefully lit the lamps of the fortress. Then, with a few African warriors he silently led his small company of Portuguese soldiers out of Axem and struck inland. The Dutch found the main gate open and the post empty the following morning.[22] Almeida hoped to make his way along the coast eastward and contact an English trading vessel along the coast. Almeida may have sought refuge at Cormantin, about forty-five miles' journey by the forest path and east of Fort Nassau. There the English had established a small trading post in 1632 and had converted it into a fort around 1638. Almeida's former association with English captains would have made this post a logical choice for safety. However, it is not known whether the small Portuguese band survived the trek. There is no record of either Almeida or any of his soldiers in archival documents after February, 1642. The only account we possess of the fall of Axem is the Dutch summary of the battle written by a witness to the encounter.

On 17 February 1642 the Dutch signed a formal accord with the military captains or *caboceers* of Axem who had not fled with the Portuguese garrison. The two *caboceers* placing their mark on the

Dutch document promised to serve their new allies in the same fashion as they had assisted the Portuguese, and Axem became a satellite post to the main Dutch fortress at Elmina. All Portuguese and mulattos of Portuguese descent were to be taken prisoner whenever they were found on the coast and carried to the Dutch for trial.[23]

In the aftermath of Portugal's losses in 1637 and 1642 organized Portuguese trade with Mina ceased for nearly three decades. Occasional ships sailed from São Tomé to the mainland to trade, but there were no more expeditions sent out from Lisbon. The records of the royal mint in the Portuguese capital do not note any shipments of Mina gold during the period 1642–79. However, if Mina lay neglected by the crown, Portugal's claims to the area were not forgotten entirely. Various plans designed to recover the lost patrimony of Mina were put forth during these years. Perhaps the most ambitious was a scheme proposed to Afonso VI in 1657 by Francisco de Brito Freire. Brito Freire was a man of considerable influence in the circles around the new king. He was one of the heroes of the recapture of Pernambuco in 1654, and he had been promoted to the rank of admiral as the result of his Brazilian victories. Brito Freire proposed the organization of a major naval squadron to sail to Mina and recapture the lost Portuguese fortresses and the gold trade. With ten warships and four galleys, he declared that he could sweep the seas around Mina clear of all foreign shipping. Once deprived of their naval strength, the Dutch garrisons in Mina would be no match for the soldiers which the Portuguese squadron would carry. A division of 1,200 soldiers would be required. Brito Freire proposed that armed ships of the Brazil Company (Companhia do Comércio) and royal galleons be joined into one massive effort to recover the fortresses. The rich harvest in gold which the Portuguese would gather in Mina would more than compensate for the expenses of such an undertaking. Besides, the recapture of São Jorge and Axem would deprive the Dutch of a valuable source of wealth. Brito Freire was among those who believed that the Dutch were able to wage war against Portugal and her colonies so effectively only because of such lucrative enterprises as the Mina gold commerce. After the ouster of the Portuguese from the coast, Dutch trade had grown until about six hundred thousand *cruzados* or nearly ten thousand marks in gold were being taken annually from Mina. This was only the major share of the trade, for smaller portions fell into English and Danish hands.[24]

Brito Freire's proposals were considered, but they were never put into operation. The last chapter in Portuguese occupation of a trading station in Mina did not occur until twenty-two years later, in 1679. The Portuguese force which then secured itself a position on the Mina mainland did not come from Portugal or Brazil, but from São Tomé. This time the Dutch were not the main target; the Portuguese chose instead to challenge the Danes at Accra.

By the 1670s there were European powers near the site of the ruined Portuguese fortress which had stood at Accra in 1578. In 1642 the Dutch erected a lodge at Little Accra and later converted it into an armed fortress called Fort Crévecoeur. In 1661 the Danes purchased a parcel of land from the paramount chief of Accra and constructed Fort Christiansborg.[25] Finally, in 1673 an English company built an armed fortress just to the west of the Dutch post. Christiansborg, the Portuguese objective, was the best of the three stations. It was located on a rock cliff at the edge of the beach, and the buildings and fortifications of the Danish post were more expansive than those of its neighbors. The Danish fort was square, seventy-five feet on each side, with projecting bastions at each corner.[26] However, landing facilities left much to be desired, since the harbor was shallow and choked with rocks.

The relationship between the European trading nations at Accra and the African merchants was undergoing drastic alterations during the late 1670s. The kingdom of Accra was being pressured by new waves of migration from the north. The Akan Akwamu were being pushed onto the coastal plain by more distant peoples in the forest belt. The Akwamu then began to clash with the Accra state. Finally, in 1680, the last of the Accra on that portion of the coast were subdued by the new invaders and fell under their sovereignty.[27]

While the fighting was continuing between the Accra and Akwamu nations, most of the paths of trade from the coast to the interior were blocked. Thus the gold trade temporarily came to a virtual standstill. The nadir of power for the Danes in Fort Christiansborg came in 1679 when the commander, Johan Ulrich, was

murdered by African assassins under the direction of one of Ulrich's subordinates, a Greek named Bolt. Bolt, Ulrich's successor,
was in charge of the post on 2 December 1680, when a Portuguese
vessel hove to anchor off the fortress. On board was Julião de Campos Barreto, former governor of São Tomé, accompanied by two
score soldiers and sailors. Campos Barreto already had a distinguished military career behind him. He had served as captain of
infantry and horse cavalry in the Portuguese struggle with the
Spanish along the Luso-Spanish frontier between 1657 and 1672.
Thrice wounded in battle in the peninsula, he had been rewarded
with the São Tomé governorship in 1672 for a term of three
years.[28] He had remained on the island after his term of office and
had made friends with the current governor, Jacinto de Figueiredo
de Abreu (1679–82). Together, these two men conspired to seize
one of the small fortified posts on the Mina mainland. The opportunity came when they learned of the plight of Fort Christiansborg.

Danish sources report that when Governor Bolt saw the inten-
tions of Campos Barreto and considered his own position, he
decided it politic to rid himself of his burdensome charge with at
least some profit. Bolt was said to have sold Fort Christiansborg to
the Portuguese in return for 36 pounds of gold.[29] Campos Barreto
immediately took possession of the post, renamed it São Francisco
Xavier, and remained as the fort's self-appointed commander and
chief factor with an initial garrison of 25 soldiers.[30] The Portuguese enlarged the post and at one time maintained a garrison of
nearly seventy soldiers and officials. Defenses were increased with
large shipments of munitions from São Tomé. The post account
books show Campos Barreto as receiving 148 muskets, 15,338 bullets with powder, and 166 swords in only 21 months of his occupation. This was in addition to a miscellany of other arms and
provisions for the post.[31]

Unfortunately, the lavish expenditures in physical improvements, an abnormally large garrison, and substantial arms shipments were not offset by a corresponding increase in the gold
trade. Campos Barreto was plagued by the same disruptions which
had caused the decline of Danish trade. The situation among the
African tribes had still not subsided sufficiently to permit the re-

opening of trade routes with the interior. In addition, the Portuguese alienated many Africans by using a nearby sacred lake as a salt pond. A paltry 33 marks, 4 oz., 12 grains of gold was the grand total of all gold traded by the Portuguese during their period of occupation.[32] When Jean Barbot visited the station in the spring of 1682 he reported that the post was in a chaotic state. Campos Barreto had been unable to control his soldiers. During the early months of 1682 the garrison had risen against its commander and imprisoned him in the large central tower of the fortress.[33]

On 3 May 1682 the Danish government lodged a strong protest with the Portuguese king through the Danish ambassador to Madrid. Probably because of the unprofitable nature of the trade thus far, or because the Portuguese feared armed Danish reprisals against maritime shipping, Pedro II, Portugal's new monarch, agreed to return the post to its former owners.[34] Orders were sent out from Lisbon to give São Francisco Xavier back to the Danes. When the dispatches reached the Mina station, rather than wait for the Dutch to occupy the post officially from nearby Fort Frederiksberg, the Portuguese chose simply to leave the station quietly. The garrison slipped out and left the gates to the fortress open on 29 August 1682. It had been exactly forty-five years to the day since the fall of São Jorge da Mina. Akwamu blacks quickly occupied the deserted fortress and were not dislodged until February of the following year when the Danes finally retook the station.

Conclusion

Portuguese rule over Mina represented a significant episode in the age of expansion for Europe. São Jorge da Mina was the first permanent trading station erected in the tropics by any European power, and for more than a century it stood as the keystone to Portuguese hegemony in the south Atlantic area. Equally important, the *feitoria* or "trading outpost" concept on which Mina's administration was based became the model for all subsequent stations erected by Portugal in Africa, Asia, and America until the commencement of colonization efforts in the 1530s in Brazil. Portugal structured her first overseas empire upon trading stations and the economic monopoly they created, and Mina was the forerunner of this new empire.

São Jorge da Mina symbolized the total commitment of the crown to the maintenance of an overseas empire, and by the reign of Manuel I (1495–1521) the Portuguese state had been transformed into a thalassocracy. After 1481 Portugal's expansive drive was turned southward into the south Atlantic, not to cease until footholds in Japan and China were attained three-quarters of a century later.

In retrospect, Portugal's fatal flaw in her overlordship of Mina was the absence of a colonization program for the area. Still, the crown should not be faulted for choosing to create a *feitoria* in Mina instead of a colony. A combination of inhospitable climate, dense local population, and the desire of the crown to maintain a strict monopoly over the trade in gold all precluded massive emigration there by the Portuguese. In 1481 John II elected instead to establish São Jorge with a diminutive, royally-appointed staff and to supply it from Portugal. His successors maintained this status for Mina and profited greatly from the arrangement until the 1560s, when a contract system for provisioning the outpost became necessary. Colonization projects were discussed late in the sixteenth century, but by this time Portugal had neither the facilities, nor sufficient population, nor the inclination to effect such a radical change for administering Mina. As the seventeenth century dawned the factory system, premised upon strategically-located, well-fortified coastal outposts, was proving incapable of withstanding the assaults made upon it by the English, French, and particularly the Dutch. The fault for Portugal's loss of stations like São Jorge lay not in the basic premise of the *feitoria* system—for later European nations successfully maintained outposts like the Portuguese stations—but rather with the Portuguese inability to support these stations from the mother country. The seventeenth century witnessed a number of trading posts erected along the Mina coast by competing European powers. Even before the collapse of Portuguese power, the English and Dutch maintained stations there, soon to be followed in the latter part of the century by the French, Danes, and Brandenburgers.

The Dutch acquisition of São Jorge in 1637 was mirrored by similar Dutch successes at Portugal's expense in the East. In rapid succession, Portugal lost Ceylon (1638–58), Malacca (1641), Malabar (1661–63), Cranganore and Cochin (1662), and a host of lesser trading posts and fortresses to Dutch assaults. Within twenty-five years Portugal's trading empire in west Africa and the Indian Ocean had been reduced to a fraction of its previous dimensions. The Lisbon government, faced with the dilemma of attacks on all fronts, chose reluctantly to surrender Mina and Asia and to concentrate recovery efforts in Brazil and Angola. By the mid-seventeenth century the most promising part of the Portuguese empire lay in America, where white settlement had spread over the Brazilian coast and profits from sugar promised to replace losses of Mina gold and Asian spices.

It would be too simple merely to term the Portuguese episode in Mina as a failure. A balanced assessment of Portugal's commercial empire in Mina from 1482 to 1637 should also take into account the remarkable achievements of the trading centers which Portugal maintained there. São Jorge da Mina and her satellite post of Santo António de Axem more than accomplished the mission set out for them by John II. For half a century, until the 1530s, a handful of men had supplied Portugal with the most significant gold treasure that Europe had ever known. Almost overnight, gold from Mina doubled public revenues during the reign of John II. The *cruzado* of Mina gold and, during Manuel I's reign, the *português*, worth ten *cruzados,* made the name of the Portuguese king synonymous with wealth throughout the breadth of the European continent. African gold was also important to Portugal's own economy since emissions of gold from Mina made possible the purchase of German silver and the stabilization of an economy which had been in serious financial straits during the early part of the fifteenth century. It is no mere accident that the period of greatest financial stability for Portugal's currency, 1489–1539, corresponds closely with the years of greatest productivity of her Mina holdings. During the half century preceding the establishment of Portuguese rule over Mina, the currency had undergone a 150% devaluation. In the next half century, thanks in large part to Mina revenues, the coin of the realm suffered only a 9% devaluation.

The first great economic cycle which Portugal experienced as a result of her overseas discoveries was the outpouring of gold from Mina between approximately 1475 and 1540. Although Asian trade increased in economic importance quite rapidly after 1510, the age of pepper and spices had to await the latter part of the sixteenth century. Mina gold was the key to Portugal's political and economic successes of the early sixteenth century. The African gold passed from Lisbon to European commercial centers to cover purchases of tradegoods needed in Portugal's world commerce. In Bruges in the late fifteenth century and later in Antwerp in the sixteenth century, gold *cruzados* secured purchases of silver, copper, fabrics, grain, and munitions unavailable in Portugal itself. Although the general economic philosophy of European monarchs in the fourteenth and fifteenth centuries had been to restrict the export of precious metals, especially gold, Portugal now found herself in the enviable position of having a vast surplus of this treasure with which to buy needed material and luxuries. Even during the centuries before the great Mina treasure, there had been allowances made for the export of gold in exchange for essential commodities, but the Portuguese now went far beyond such necessary purchases to include many other items. In the beginning, gold from Mina was exchanged for other mintable metals, particularly silver. It was also utilized to secure grain in times of famine and to feed the growing Lisbon populace. Gold purchased both arms and soldiers to fight in the wars of Afonso V and his successors. The sources that Portugal drew upon included not only the northern European centers, but Mediterranean states as well: shipments of grain could be bought in Sicily as well as France, and from Milan and Naples came thousands of arms to equip Portugal's army and navy.

Monarchs like Manuel I (nicknamed "The Fortunate" by his contemporaries) soon found new uses for the continuing outflow of treasure from Mina. In addition to securing basic necessities of tradegoods to resupply Mina (and for a time, the Asian trade), Manuel quickly surrounded himself with magnificent trappings of his wealth. The court of the Fortunate Monarch glittered with ostentatious display, and everywhere were reminders of his golden treasure: a solid gold table service, candelabras, gold basins of every size and use, brocaded gold in the wall tapestries, gold threads in the rugs underfoot, necklaces, rings, brocaded silks on the monarch himself, all these and more shouted out the value of Manuel's royal monopoly in Mina. All this display was designed to dazzle ambassadors and visitors to the royal presence, and it more than succeeded. It is little wonder, then, that when Manuel found himself short of funds in the late years of his reign and sought to strike a bargain with German merchants to exchange Asian spices for copper and silver, the Germans refused, preferring payment in gold.

By the latter part of Manuel's reign, the great age of golden opulence was past. The monarch's expenditures had exceeded the capacity of Mina to produce gold. India's trade was growing stronger every year and had surpassed in value the output of São Jorge da Mina. Although gold emissions from Mina would continue to be significant until the early 1530s, the relative value of Mina had begun to slip badly. Magalhães Godinho calculated annual Portuguese imperial revenues (excluding the Atlantic islands) for 1506 and again for 1518/19, in *réis* as follows:

	1506	*1518/9*
India and the East	51,300,000	114,000,000
Mina	43,776,000	51,072,000
Slaves and malagueta pepper from Guinea	4,180,000	?
Dyewood from Brazil	1,900,000	?

These figures, which are hardly more than rough estimates, illustrate clearly the importance of the Mina trade in the overall trade pattern of the empire. Aside from Asia, Mina was the most productive of Portugal's far-flung commercial enterprises. Yet these same figures reveal the beginning of Mina's relative decline. The peak of trade in absolute terms for Mina was reached during the early 1520s. In fact, commerce at Mina had been operating at full capacity for some decades, hampered only by the availability of trade-goods. Between 1506 and 1518 Eastern incomes grew by 123%, while Mina revenues increased only 16.6%. In the remainder of the sixteenth century, even absolute volume of trade began to decline for São Jorge da Mina and the other trading stations. This slippage is nowhere more pronounced than in the figures calculated by João de Andrade Corvo, and reproduced by T. Bentley Duncan, for the end of the century:

India and the East	697,810,000 *réis*
Brazil	63,000,000 "
Cape Verdes	27,400,000 "
Mina	24,000,000 "
Angola	22,000,000 "
São Tomé	9,500,000 "

By the end of the century Mina had dropped to a poor fourth place and accounted for only 2.8% of imperial revenues, compared with the former 45%. Income from slave-trading ventures in Angola was soon to surpass Mina also.

Much of the credit for maintaining Mina in the face of declining profits and increasing enemy attacks must go to the governor and his tiny garrison. Unlike Brazil and São Tomé, Mina was not a dumping ground for the criminal elements or political *degredados* condemned to overseas service for their crimes. The few convicts sent to Mina came late in her history and were never a part of the regular garrison; rather, they served alongside black slaves and foreign prisoners as rowers in the galleys. Indeed, the chancery books abound with petitions of men seeking appointments to Mina. The high number of such requests persists down into the 1620s, despite the declining fortunes of the Portuguese in the region. What moved men to seek royal service in such an inhospitable outpost, where fever, poor rations, and an oppressive climate took a heavy toll upon the garrison? Clearly the answer was the desire for monetary gain. Very modest salaries and poor living conditions were ameliorated by the opportunity to engage in private trade. Although the crown sought to limit tours of service in Mina, some officials succeeded in extending their service in Mina for more than a decade before returning home with their privately-acquired fortunes. Both contemporary and modern historians saw such corruption as playing a decisive role in contributing to or even determining the breakdown of Portugal's position in Mina, as well as in other parts of the empire. But the reader must not lean too heavily upon such a thesis in the case of Mina. Historical evidence does not seem to corroborate such a point of view. There was no more corruption among Mina officials than in, say, Brazil or Portugal itself or in any other colonial empire of the same period. Though the crown ringed officials in Mina with an elaborate set of strict regulations and prohibitions to prevent smuggling and illicit traffic, the crown also realized that the abundance of gold in Mina and the remoteness of the post made it virtually impossible to maintain absolute authority over all trading. The system of regulations and restrictions given was the system prescribed, not the actual policy practiced. The total prevention of private trading was impossible. A man could serve at Mina for three or four years and, if he were skillful in the use of his basic salary, he could return to Portugal with a respectable fortune. Only when the amounts of privately-acquired gold became excessive were the regulations enforced with vigor. Finally, in 1509 it was decided that no official would be permitted to acquire a sum of private gold in excess of his own salary. This rough measure apparently became the standard for the remainder of the Portuguese period at Mina.

The factors responsible for Mina's dramatic financial collapse are not to be found solely in a simple competition thesis. It is true that São Jorge da Mina had the threat of interlopers and later of European fortresses which sought to divert the trade from Portuguese hands. Yet Portugal, with its preeminent position on the Gold Coast, its already-established trade contacts with the interior, and a complex administrative establishment maintaining the outposts, might easily have parried these threats. Rather, Mina's loss is an excellent example of how the policies and problems affecting one part of the empire in the sixteenth century had repercussions in the other. Economically, Mina's success or failure was linked to the two major tradegoods which she offered black merchants, *manilhas* and cloth. Though Portugal shipped massive quantities of both these commodities to Mina, she did not provide them from herself. Instead the Portuguese crown was heavily dependent upon foreign suppliers in Flanders and north Africa for both these items. Any decision affecting Portugal's relations with these two areas ultimately had an impact upon the conduct of the Mina trade. Safi's abandonment in 1541 removed the primary source of Maghribine fabrics from the trade offerings of São Jorge. The closure of Portugal's Flanders factory later in the same decade dealt a serious blow to both the copper trade and the traffic in fabrics which had been funneled to Mina through the post. Attempts to overcome basic supply deficiencies were undertaken during the latter third of the century, beginning with the institution of a leasing system in 1567; however, this proved a failure and had to be abandoned shortly after 1600. When faced with the first serious challenge to her authority in Mina from the Dutch, Portugal found herself incapable of providing the necessary shipping and goods with which to compete.

Appendix A

Sale of metal hardware at São Jorge da Mina and Axem,
1504–31 (numbers of manilhas *per year)*

Years	Manilhas	Basins expressed as multiples of *manilhas* by weight; average yearly total	Combined average yearly totals
1504–7	120,720	15,929	136,649
1511–13	no data	38,664	?
1513–14	138,840	24,756	163,596
1517–19	128,652	46,384	175,036
1519–22	151,500	31,166	182,802
1529–31	97,800	31,302	129,102

Appendix B

Governors and factors of São Jorge da Mina

GOVERNORS

1482–84	Diogo de Azambuja
1485–86	Alvaro Vaz Pestana
1487–89?	João Fogaça
1489– ?	Alvaro Mascarenhas
? –1493	Dr. Fernando Pereira
1495–99	Lopo Soares de Albergaria
1499–1502	Fernão Lopes Correia
1502?	Nuno Vaz de Castelo Branco
1503–4	Diogo Lopes de Sequeira
1504–5	António de Miranda de Azevedo
1505– ?	D. Martinho da Silva
1508?–9	Bobadilha
1509–11?	Manuel de Goios
1511?–13	Afonso Caldeira
1514–16?	Nuno Vaz
1516–19	Fernão Lopes Correia
1519–22	Duarte Pacheco Pereira
1522–24	D. Afonso de Albuquerque
1524–25	Joao de Barros
1526–29	João Vaz de Almada
1529–32	Estevão da Gama
1532–36	António Lópes Pereira
1536–40	D. Manuel de Albuquerque
1540–43	António de Miranda
1543–45	António de Brito
1546–48	D. Martim de Castro
1548–50	Lopo de Sousa Coutinho
1550–52	Diogo Soares de Albergaria

1552–56	Rui de Melo
1556–58	Afonso Gonçalves Botafogo
1558–62	Ruy Gomes de Azevedo
1562–64	Manuel Mesquita de Perestrello
1564–67	Martim Afonso
1567–70	Francisco de Barros de Paiva
1570–73	António de Sá
1573?	Martim Afonso
1574?	Mendo da Mota
1574–79	?
1579–83	Vasco Fernandes Pimentel
1583–86	João Rodrigues Peçanha
1586–94?	João Roiz Coutinho
1596–1608	D. Cristóvão de Melo
1608–13	D. Duarte de Lima
1613	João de Castro
1613–16	Pero da Silva
1616–23	Manuel da Cunha e Teive
1623–26?	D. Francisco Sotomaior
1626?–29	João da Sera de Morais
1630–31	governorship vacant
1632–34	D. Pedro de Mascarenhas
1634	Frei Duarte Borges
1634–37?	André da Rocha Magalhães

FACTORS

1482–91?	———
1491?–95	Gil Velho
1495–99	Gil Matoso
1499– ?	João Fernandes
1504–7	Estevão de Barradas
1507–11	———
1511–13	Afonso Mexia
1513–14	Paulo da Mota
1514–17	Alvaro Salgado
1517–19	Manuel de Sande
1519–22	João de Figueiredo
1522–25?	Diogo Godinho

1526– ?	Paio Rodrigues
? –31	Gonçalo de Campos
1531–34	Lopo de Pina
1534–36	Sebastião Pestana
1536–38	Fernão Gomes
1538–39	João Vaz
1539	António Lopes
1540	Jorge Velho
1540–41	Barnabe Henriques
1541–43	João Leitão
1543– ?	Estevão Limpo
? –48	Ambrosio Roiz
1548–51	Jorge da Costa
1551	Estevão Limpo
? –57	Simão Roiz
1557–80	———
1580–85	Lourenço Carvalho
1585–90	João Marques da Costa
1590–93	Mateus Gonçalves
1593–96?	Gaspar da Rosa de Meira
1596–1603	———
1603–8	Afonso Martins Albernás
1608–16	———
1616–23?	Francisco Soares
1623–26	———
1626–28	Pero Sardinha
1628–37	———

Appendix C

Annual gold receipts of São Jorge and Axem, 1482–1560

The loss of São Jorge da Mina's original receipt ledgers has necessitated a reliance upon contemporary secondary sources of the gold trade. The chief figures on Mina's gold traffic are entries of gold received by the Casa da Moeda in Lisbon. The mint's registry books cover twenty-seven years of the period from 1517 to 1561. However, the mint's records reflect only those treasure shipments which reached Portugal safely. Whenever gold shipments are confirmed as having departed from Mina with no note of their arrival at the mint, they are presumed to have been lost through shipwreck or piracy. Therefore, the figures in brackets take these losses, whenever known, into account.

Prior to 1517, few statistics are available for the Mina gold trade. The quittances issued to factors of São Jorge da Mina from 1504 onward yield yearly average estimates of trade. Little in the way of concrete evidence is available for the period prior to 1501.

Similarly, the record of Mina gold receipts declines sharply after 1561. Aside from an isolated entry in a registry book at the mint for 1571, there are only two other notices of gold receipts at Mina for the years 1561–1604. The 1571 mint record shows the receipt of 146 marks, 1 dram, 36 grains; in 1577 a large transport ship carrying approximately 1800 marks of Mina gold was waylaid by French pirates from La Rochelle and the treasure removed. The following year, between 4,000 and 5,000 marks of gold from Mina safely reached Lisbon on board two returning transports. Finally, in 1604, when mint records again become available (the years 1570–1603 are missing except for scattered sheets), the amount of Mina gold is negligible.

The following table reflects the known gold receipts from Mina, expressed in a weight of marks, ounces, drams, and grains for each year. Unless otherwise noted, the source is Vitorino Magalhães Godinho's tables (pp. 228–43) in *L'économie de l'empire portugais aux XVe et XVIe siècles*. However, the original registry books of the *Casa da Moeda* were consulted to confirm the accuracy of these statistics. The amounts of gold reported can only be regarded as minimal amounts, since they do not take into account a great volume of private trading and the inevitable contraband trade. Therefore, the total amount of gold extraction from Mina would probably add another ten to twenty percent to the official figures:

	marks	ounces	drams	grains	
1482–86	no available data				
1487	982	0	0	0	(estimate)[1]
1488	982	0	0	0	(est.)[2]
1489	982	0	0	0	(est.)[3]
1490–93					n.a.
1494	2820	0	0	0	(est.)[4]
1495	2820	0	0	0	(est.)[5]
1496	2820	0	0	0	(est.)[6]
1497	1617	0	0	0	(est.)[7]
1498	1617	0	0	0	(est.)[8]
1499	1617	0	0	0	(est.)[9]
1500	1617	0	0	0	(est.)
1501	1220	5	0	0	(est.)[10]
1502–3					n.a.
1504	1910	3	0	0	(average)[11]
1505	1910	3	0	0	(avg.)[12]
1506	1910	3	0	0	(avg.)[13]
1507–10					n.a.
1511	1400	0	0	0	(avg.)[14]
1512	2255	4	2	?[15]	
1513	1805	6	0	0	(avg.)[16]
1514	1761	5	0	0	(avg.)[17]
1515–16					n.a.
1517	1846	2	4	4	
1518	1868	5	0	44	
1519	2001	5	0	0[18]	
1520	2025	0	5	37[19]	
1521	1867	5	7	9	[2187 5 7 8][20]
1522					n.a.
1523	1308	4	7	19	[1760 0 0 0][21]
1524	1237	3	3	53	[1310 0 0 0][21]
1525	897	0	0	0	
1526	1079	1	4	37	[1310 0 0 0][21]

1527					n.a.
1528	971	3	1	33	
1529	921	4	0	7	
1530	654	4	1	69	[1405 3 1 45][22]
1531	925	7	1	47	
1532	2960	7	7	35	
1533	1580	0	0	0	(est.)[23]
1534	1184	2	3	47	
1535–39					n.a.
1540	1447	7	2	56	
1541–42					n.a.
1543	1520	6	7	32	
1544	616	7	7	30	
1545	1671	2	7	11	(est.)[24]
1546–48					n.a.
1549	733	1	0	59	
1550	674	6	3	28	
1551	922	0	6	64	
1552	537	4	2	26	
1553	414	5	7	15	
1554					n.a.
1555	1645	1	7	30	
1556	1056	3	1	60	
1557–59					n.a.
1560	625	7	0	46	
1561	630	1	3	24	
1562–71					n.a.
1572 (incomplete)	146	0	1	36	

Notes to Appendix C

1. ATT-Chancelaria de D. Manuel, livro 17, fol. 20; Extremadura, livro 2, fol. 97v.
2. Ibid.
3. Ibid.
4. ATT-Chancelaria de D. Manuel, livro 17, fol. 20; Extremadura, livro 2, fol. 98.
5. Ibid.
6. Ibid.

7. ATT, Núcleo Antigo, livro 867, fols. 1–18v.

8. Ibid., fols. 1–18v.

9. Ibid., fols. 1–18v.

10. ATT-Chancelaria de D. Manuel, livro 6, fol. 39; Livro de Extras, fol. 26.

11. ATT-Chancelaria de D. Manuel, livro 3, fol. 9v.; Livro das Ilhas, fol. 180v.; Núcleo Antigo, livro 799, fols. 1ff.

12. Ibid.

13. Ibid.

14. ATT-Chancelaria de D. Manuel, livro 35, fol. 127; Livro das Ilhas, fol. 222v.; Corpo cronológico, part 2, m. 30, doc. 137.

15. Ibid.

16. ATT-Chancelaria de D. Manuel, livro 9, fol. 27; Livro das Ilhas, vol. 36, fols. 205–6.

17. Ibid.

18. 1519 figure was obtained by subtracting 1517 and 1518 totals, less 590 marks received before May 1517, from total gold recorded in quittance: ATT-Chancelaria de D. Manuel, livro 35, fol. 127; Livro das Ilhas, vol. 36, fols. 222v.–223.

19. ATT-Chancelaria de D. João 3, Doações, livro 4, fol. 22v.

20. ATT-CC, part 2, m. 97, doc. 15; m. 98, doc. 77.

21. In 1525 the *cortês* of Torres Novas complained of the damage which the Mina gold trade had suffered, citing that less than 300 kilograms (about 1310 marks) of gold had been received in 1524 and 1526, and 400 kilograms (about 1760 marks) in 1523. Cf. Magalhães Godinho, *Os descobrimentos* 1: 376.

22. São Jorge da Mina's receipt ledger for 1530 shows sales of goods valued at 1405 3 1 45. This is considerably in divergence with the 654 4 1 69 entered into the Lisbon mint that year. There is a strong likelihood that the governor held back considerable gold in 1530 and again in 1531 until he returned to Portugal in 1532. Also not to be discounted is the possibility of piracy of the gold ships for these years.

23. ATT-Chancelaria de D. João 3, livro 22, fol. 133.

24. ATT-Privilegios de D. João 3, livro 1, fol. 220v.

Appendix D

Gold weights and measures used in Mina
and their equivalencies in Portuguese currency, 1489–1537

WEIGHTS AND MONIES OF ACCOUNT

marco (mark) = 8 *onças* (ounces) = 230.4 grams metric = 24,320 *réis* (1514–37) = 60.8 *cruzados* (1514–37)
onça = 8 *oitavas* (drams)
oitava = 72 *grãos* (grains)
peso (weight of account) = 500 *réis*

COINAGE

cruzado = 380 *réis* (1489–1496); 390 *réis* (1496–1514); 400 *réis* (1514–37). During the period 1514–37 the *cruzado* was computed at 72 grains of gold, 23¾ carats fine.
justo = 600 *réis* (1489)
dobra = 460 *réis* (1514–37)

Notes

Chapter 1

1. E. W. Bovill, *The Golden Trade of the Moors*, pp. 67, 235.

2. Charles de la Roncière, *La découverte de l'Afrique au moyen âge*, plate xi.

3. John Vogt, "Crusading and Commercial Elements in the Portuguese Capture of Ceuta (1415)," *The Muslim World* 59 (1969): 287–99.

4. Ibn Battuta, *Travels in Asia and Africa, 1325–54; Book of the Knowledge of All the Kingdoms, Lands and Lordships That Are in the World.*

5. Jaime Cortesão, "Los portugueses," in Ballesteros, *História de América y de los pueblos americanos* 3: 497–766, and esp. 511–12, where Cortesão summarizes the positions of these scholars.

6. *Book of the Knowledge*, p. 28.

7. Armando Cortesão, *Cartografia e cartógrafos portugueses dos séculos XV e XVI* 1: 44.

8. Henrique Quirino da Fonseca, *A caravela portuguesa e a prioridade técnica das navegações henriquinas* offers the most complete study of the evolution of this type of sailing craft.

9. *Book of the Knowledge*, p. 28.

10. Rinaldo Caddeo, *Le navigazioni atlantiche di Alvise da Cá da Mosto, Antonietto Usodimare e Niccoloso da Recco*, p. 188.

11. ATT-Chancelaria de D. Afonso V, livro 33, fol. 147v.; Duarte Leite, *História dos descobrimentos* (Lisbon, 1958–1960) 1: 237; A. Fontoura da Costa, "Fernão Gomes e o monopólio do resgate da Guiné," *Boletim da Sociedade de Geografia de Lisboa* 56 (1938): 189–94.

12. Jaime Cortesão, *Os descobrimentos portugueses*, 2: 416.

13. A. Fontoura da Costa, *Uma carta náutica portuguesa, anónima, de circa 1471*, esp. pp. 11, 19.

14. Merrick Posnansky, "Ghana and the Origins of West African Trade," *Africa Quarterly* 11 (1971): 110–25.

15. Fontoura da Costa, "Fernão Gomes," pp. 189–94.

16. ATT-Gavetas 7, m. 11, doc. 3; Joaquim Bensaude, *L'astronomie nautique au Portugal à l'époque des grandes découvertes*, pp. 271–73.

17. Alonso de Palencia, *Cronica de Enrique IV* 4: 378–79.

18. F. M. da Costa Lobo, *A acção diplomática dos portugueses nos séculos XV e XVI, destinada à realização de descobertas e conquistas*, p. 106.

19. Bensaude, *L'astronomie nautique au Portugal*, pp. 273–76.

20. Duarte Pacheco Pereira, *Esmeraldo de situ orbis*, pp. 112–13; Palencia, *Cronica* 4: 127.

21. Ibid., p. 213.

22. Cortesão, *Os descobrimentos portugueses* 1: 472.

23. Ibid., pp. 473–74.

24. ATT-Gavetas 17, m. 6, doc. 16.

25. Raymond Mauny, ed., "Eustache de la Fosse-Voyage à la côte occidentale d'Afrique (1479–1480)," *Boletim Cultural da Guiné Portuguesa* 4 (1949): 181–95, and esp. 187–88.

26. Suárez Fernandez, Luis, ed., *Política internacional de Isabel la Católica: estudio y documentos*, p. 216.

27. For the king's order, see Academia das sciencias de Lisboa. *Alguns documentos do Archivo nacional da Torre do Tombo, acerca das navegações e conquistas portuguezas*, p. 45; Mauny, "Eustache de la Fosse," p. 194.

28. Ruy de Pina, "Chronica d'El Rey D. João II," 2: 11–17. Pina received a commission as royal chronicler to Manuel I of Portugal.

29. Jaime Cortesão, "Los portugueses," in Ballesteros, *História de América* 3: 540–41.

Chapter 2

1. The most convenient collection of sources surrounding the decision to erect a fortress in Mina and the subsequent fleet which was sent there in 1481 can be consulted in Alberto Iria's "Da fundação e governo do castelo ou fortaleza de São Jorge da Mina pelos portugueses," *Studia* 1 (1958): 24–69.

2. Ibid.

3. ATT-Bulas, m. 35, doc. 1.

4. Pina, "Chronica d'El Rey D. João II," 2: 11; G. R. Crone, *Voyages of Cadamosto and Other Documents on Western Africa in the Second Half of the Fifteenth Century*, p. 103.

5. Translated in Freda Wolfson, *Pageant of Ghana*, pp. 39–40.

6. Ibid., pp. 42–43.

7. The map of Mina by João Teixeira in 1630 confirms the amplitude of the sheltered harbor with the inscription: "Porto da Mina emq̃ podē ētrar Gales e navios de 300 toneladas." Cf. plate b.

8. The following description of São Jorge is derived primarily from A. W. Lawrence's important study on Gold Coast architecture, *Fortified Trade-posts: The English in West Africa, 1645–1822*, pp. 97–121.

9. W. J. Varley, "The Forts and Castles of the Gold Coast," *Transactions of the Gold Coast and Togoland Historical Society* 1 (1952): 1–15; Carlos de Azevedo, *Arte cristã na India portuguesa*, pp. 61–87; idem, *Algumas considerações sobre o estudo da arquitectura militar no ultramar*, pp. 5–11.

10. AHU-São Tomé, cx. 1, doc. 111 (10. x. 1634). These naval pieces were also sometimes called *berços*. The breech of such cannon was removable and the guns could be fired rapidly by keeping several loaded breech housings primed with powder and shot. Examples of *falconetes* or *berços* from the sixteenth century may still be seen in the Tower of Belém and the Museu de Marinha in Lisbon.

11. Damião Peres, *Regimento das Cazas das Indias e Mina*, p. 25.

12. Ibid., p. 23.

13. Inter alia, cf. ATT-Chancelaria de D. Manuel, livro 3, fol. 9v. (Livro das Ilhas, vol. 36, fol. 180v.); livro 5, fol. 20 (Livro das Ilhas, vol. 36, fol. 175); livro 9, fol. 27 (Livro das Ilhas, vol. 36, fols. 205–6); livro 35, fol. 127 (Livro das Ilhas, vol. 36, fols. 222v.–3); livro 44, fol. 46 (Livro das Ilhas, vol. 36, fol. 215v.).

14. ATT-CC, part 1, m. 8, doc. 45.

15. ATT-Chancelaria de D. Manuel, livro 31, fol. 84; Cortesão, *Os descobrimentos portugueses* 2: 67–68.

16. ATT-CC, part 1, m. 8, doc. 45.

17. Peres, *Regimento*, p. 12.

18. ATT-CC, part 1, m. 8, doc. 45; m. 19, doc. 49; ATT-Gavetas, 15, m. 1, doc. 15.

19. Cf., inter alia, ATT-Miscelanias Manuscritas, cx. 19, vol. 2E, fols. 281–84.

20. ATT-CC, part 1, m. 8, doc. 72; part 2, m. 202, doc. 133; part 3, m. 12, doc. 84.

21. ATT-Gavetas, 15, m. 1, doc. 15; CC, part 2, m. 200, doc. 127.

22. Peres, *Regimento*, p. 10.

23. Cortesão, *Cartografia e cartógrafos portugueses* 1: 149.

24. Vitorino Magalhães Godinho, *L'économie de l'empire portugais aux XVᵉ et XVIᵉ siècles*, p. 175.

25. ATT-Chancelaria de D. Manuel, livro 6, fol. 39 (Livro de Extras, fol. 26).

26. Magalhães Godinho, L'économie, pp. 228–43.

27. João de Barros, Da Asia de João de Barros e de Diogo de Couto 1: 279–80.

28. Magalhães Godinho, L'économie, pp. 228–43.

29. Ibid., pp. 230, 238.

30. ATT-Cartas Missivas, m. 3, doc. 175.

31. ATT-Núcleo Antigo, no. 928. This undated assay of Mina gold, written in a clerical hand from the early sixteenth century, sets the value of a mark of Mina gold at 23,145 réis. Pacheco Pereira, Esmeraldo, pp. 118, 122.

32. The only known exception to this rule occurred in 1610, when Gaspar de Souza, a mulato, was appointed gatekeeper (porteiro) of the satellite station of Axem. Souza had carried dispatches from Mina to Lisbon and had given a good account of his responsibilities. Therefore, the viceroy of Portugal assigned him to the position "despite his being a native of the region." ATT-Chancelaria de Felipe II, livro 21, fol. 142v.

33. Jorge Faro, "Estevão da Gama, capitão de S. Jorge da Mina e a sua organização administrativa em 1529," Boletim Cultural da Guiné Portuguesa 12 (1957): 391; BSGL-Res. Prat. A, codex 55, fol. 2v.

34. ATT-Cartas Missivas, m. 4, doc. 151.

35. ATT-CC, part 1, m. 103, doc. 57.

36. The work composed at São Jorge was published first in Lisbon in 1564 in the offices of João de Barreira under the title Relação summaria da viagem que fez Fernão d'Alvares Cabral, desde que partio deste Reyno por Capitão mór da Armada que foy no anno de 1553 ás partes da India athé que se perdeo no Cabo de Boa Esperança no anno de 1554. Reproduced in Bernardo Gomes de Brito (ed.), Historia tragico-maritima 1: 38–168. A brief analysis of the life of Perestrello is in James Duffy, Shipwreck and Empire, p. 28.

37. ATT-Chancelaria de D. Sebastião e D. Henrique, Perdões, livro 10, fol. 135.

38. Grande enciclopédia portuguesa e brasileira 15: 445–46. Prior to his appointment to São Jorge, Lopes de Sequeira had served as the head of the Lisbon alfândega with the title of almoxarife from 1499 to 1503: ATT-Chancelaria de D. Manuel, livro 14, fol. 87v. In 1519 he was chosen governor of India by Manuel I: Elaine Sanceau, The Reign of the Fortunate King, 1495–1521, p. 158.

39. Garcia de Resende, Chronica dos valerosos, e insignes feytos del

Rey Dom Ioam II, pp. 77–78; ATT-Chancelaria de D. Manuel, livro 28, fol. 98.

40. For a modern treatment of the political intrigue surrounding this Indian appointment, see Sanceau, *Reign of the Fortunate King*, pp. 109–14.

41. Diogo Barbosa Machado, *Bibliotheca Lusitana historica, critica, e chronologica* 3: 18–20. Sousa Coutinho had gone to the East in 1538 as a young man of eighteen in the company of Pedro de Castelo Branco. There he served as a soldier and rose to the rank of military captain. Coutinho distinguished himself in the siege of Diu and was first mentioned as a choice for commander of São Jorge da Mina on 29. x. 1541. However, the post was filled at that time and Coutinho's final letter of appointment was not signed until 17. iv. 1548. ATT-Chancelaria de D. João III, livro 70, fols. 42ff.

42. Lopez Correa's quittance as steward is to be found in A. Braamcamp Freire, "A feitoria de Flandres," *Archivo historico portuguez* 2: 238–39. His dates of service in his first tour at São Jorge are cited in ATT-Núcleo Antigo, no. 867, and also in ATT-CC, part 2, m. 85, doc. 8. The records of the Casa da Moeda for 1520 report Correa's final return from his Mina command aboard the caravel *Santa Maria da Ajuda* on 9 January of that year. Cf. Magalhães Godinho, *L'économie*, p. 230.

43. BAL-Ms. 51–viii–25, fols. 119–30. Also cited in Jorge Faro, "Estevão da Gama," *Boletim Cultural de Guiné Portuguesa* 12 (1957): 389–90.

44. Faro, "Estevão da Gama," p. 102.

45. BAL-Ms. 51–viii–25, fols. 119–30.

46. ATT-Núcleo Antigo, no. 867, fols. 1–17.

47. ATT-CC, part 1, m. 8, doc. 116.

48. ATT-CC, part 1, m. 71, doc. 37.

49. ATT-Chancelaria de D. João III, livro 66, fol. 269.

50. Frédéric Mauro, *Le Portugal et l'Atlantique au XVIIe siècle, 1570–1670*, p. lvi.

51. ATT-CC, part 1, m. 13, doc. 48.

52. Joaquim Pedro Oliveira Martins, *Os filhos de D. João I*, p. 240 n. 1; António Caetano de Sousa, *História genealógica da casa real portuguesa* 1: 442; F. Miranda da Costa Lobo, *A acção diplomática dos portugueses*, p. 105.

53. P. António Brásio, S. J. (ed.), *Monumenta missionaria africana* [hereafter cited as MMA] 2: 9, 35–36.

54. Ibid., pp. 16–18, 22–34.

55. Barros, *Asia* 1: 169–170.

56. J.D.M. Ford, *Letters of John III, King of Portugal, 1521–1557*, pp. 3–4.

57. ATT-CC, part 1, m. 4, doc. 32.

58. ATT-Inquisição de Lixboa, process no. 11,041.

59. ATT-Chancelaria de D. Sebastião e D. Henrique, Perdões, livro 10, fol. 135.

60. AGS-Secretarias provinciales, Portugal, libro 1476, fols. 136–36v., 284–84v.

61. John Vogt, "The Early São Tomé-Príncipe Slave Trade with Mina, 1500–1540," *International Journal of African Historical Studies* 6 (1973): 453–67.

62. ATT-CC, part 2, m. 138, doc. 32; m. 200, doc. 127.

63. ATT-CC, part 1, m. 42, doc. 90.

64. Inter alia, see the ship log for the *São Cristovão* and its sailing to São Jorge in February–March 1535: ATT-CC, part 2, m. 202, doc. 133.

65. ATT-CC, part 3, m. 12, doc. 103.

66. ATT-CC, part 2, m. 181, doc. 78.

Chapter 3

1. BSGL, Res. Prat. A, codex 55, fol. 36.

2. ATT-CC, part 1, m. 4, doc. 42.

3. ATT-Núcleo Antigo, no. 722, fols. 32 passim.

4. Ibid., fols. 94–102.

5. ATT-Misticos, livro 5, fol. 28.

6. Ford, *Letters of John III*, pp. 3–4. See also ATT-Cartas Missivas, m. 1, doc. 55.

7. ATT-Chancelaria de D. Manuel, livro 44, fol. 46 (Livro das Ilhas, fol. 215v.).

8. BSGL, Res. Prat. A, codex 55, fols. 28v.–29.

9. Ibid., fols. 39–39v.

10. ATT-CC, part 1, m. 4, doc. 32. Also transcribed in Brásio, MMA-1, 190–93.

11. ATT-Núcleo Antigo, no. 722, fols. 23v. passim.

12. In 1503, Diogo de Alvarenga reported that the *feitoria da roupa velha* had obtained an additional six per cent in gold during sales transactions. During the nine and a half months prior to 15 August 1503, 5,300 *dobras* (about 71.4 marks) had been received, 5,000 from the sale of mer-

chandise, and 300 from the reweighing of gold: ATT-CC, part 1, m. 4, doc. 32.

13. This practice was first begun in 1529 in an attempt to curb illicit trading. In the *regimento* issued to Estevão da Gama, the king ordered that "eu hei per bem, per alguns respeitos, que me a isto movem, que todos os offiçiães que hora estão na dita Mina e Axem, vencão e ajão . . . os ordenados . . . e assim hum per çento que lhes era ordenado." Cf. BSGL, Res. Prat. A, codex 55, fol. 57v.

14. Peres, *Regimento*, p. 22.

15. ATT-Leis e Regimentos de D. Manuel, fol. 104.

16. Magalhães Godinho, *L'économie*, pp. 228–43.

17. Ford, *Letters of John III*, pp. 275–76.

18. J. W. Blake, *Europeans in West Africa, 1450–1560* 1: 97; Pacheco Pereira, *Esmeraldo*, p. 117; ATT-Chancelaria de D. Manuel, livro 3, fol. 9v. Regarding the acquisition of *aljaravias* and *lambens* from Oran and Mazouna, see Robert Ricard, *Etudes sur l'histoire des portugais au Maroc* pp. 194–96.

19. ATT-Chancelaria de D. Manuel, livro 35, fol. 127; Chancelaria de D. João III, livro 1, fol. 34v; BAL-Ms. 51–viii–48, fol. 175.

20. AHU-São Tomé, docs. 116 (10. iii. 1635), 171 (16. x. 1638), 176 (4. vi. 1639), 177 (24. v. 1639).

21. AHU-São Tomé, docs. 48 (18. iii. 1617), 116 (10. iii. 1635), 171 (16. x. 1638), 177 (24. v. 1639), 250 (3. xi. 1641).

22. ATT-CC, part 2, m. 66, doc. 79.

23. Ricard, *Etudes*, pp. 198–99.

24. J. D. Fage, "Some Remarks on Beads and Trade in Lower Guinea in the Sixteenth and Seventeenth Centuries," *Journal of African History* 3 (1967): 343–47. Fage presents a summation of recent scholarship on this subject.

25. Magalhães Godinho, *L'économie*, p. 382.

26. Marion Johnson, "The Cowrie Currencies of West Africa," *Journal of African History* 11 (1970): 17–49.

27. Alan Ryder, *Benin and the Europeans, 1485–1897*, p. 61.

28. ATT-CC, part 2, m. 85, doc. 75.

29. ATT-CC, part 1, m. 3, doc. 125.

30. ATT-Cartas Missivas, m. 3, doc. 79; CC, part 1, m. 8, doc. 45.

31. Pacheco Pereira, *Esmeraldo*, p. 120; BAL-Ms. 51–viii–25, fols. 115–16v.

32. ATT-CC, part 1, m. 8, doc. 45.

33. ATT-Chancelaria de D. Sebastião, livro 2, fol. 443v.

34. ATT-Cartas Missivas, m. 3, doc. 180.

35. Vogt, "Slave Trade," 453–67; ATT-Núcleo Antigo, fols. 23–27v; Ford, *Letters of John III*, p. 266. Hans W. Debrunner, *A History of Christianity in Ghana*, p. 20, suggests that about 1525 the Mina slave traffic was forbidden by John III on religious grounds. Debrunner's source is Crone's *Voyages of Cadamosto*, p. 125, where that author in turn cites a remark by Barros in the *Asia*. However, contemporary ledger books for São Jorge da Mina in 1529–31 and receipts for slaves carried to that post throughout the period of 1514–55 clearly refute this claim. Vitorino Magalhães Godinho, *Os descobrimentos e a economia mundial*, 1: 188, expresses similar skepticism regarding the accuracy of this supposed interdiction of the Mina slave traffic.

36. ATT-Chancelaria de D. Manuel, livro 36, fol. 24v; Misticos, livro 6, fol. 70. For Loronha's wine contract, see ATT-CC, part 1, m. 4, doc. 42.

37. ATT-CC, part 2, m. 73, doc. 135; m. 77, doc. 134; m. 85, doc. 44.

38. ATT-CC, part 2, m. 93, doc. 75.

39. ATT-Núcleo Antigo, no. 722, fol. 23 passim.

40. Ford, *Letters of John III*, pp. 84–85.

41. ATT-CC, part 3, m. 17, doc. 41.

42. H. P. Bigger, *A Collection of Documents Relating to Jacques Cartier and the Sieur de Roberval*, pp. 172–73.

43. ATT-CC, part 1, m. 18, doc. 10.

44. Magalhães Godinho, *L'économie*, p. 373.

45. Ibid.

46. BSGL, Res. Prat. A, codex 55, fols. 32v.–33v.

47. Ricard, *Etudes*, pp. 194–96.

48. ATT-Chancelaria de D. Manuel, livro 17, fol. 20.

49. A partial listing of some major hardware items sold at Mina during the period 1503–34 has been assembled and may be consulted in Appendix A. Records for the later decades of John III's reign and thereafter are too sketchy to afford any accurate data. The accounts and ledgers for the Philippine era (1580–1640) have been scattered or lost.

50. Pacheco Pereira later was exonerated of the charges. It was discovered that the majority of the complaints leveled against him by other garrison officials were false or misleading.

51. Ford, *Letters of John III*, pp. 4–5.

52. Cf. Appendix B.

53. Pacheco Pereira, *Esmeraldo*, p. 118.

54. ATT-Livro da Estremadura, livro 2, fol. 26v.

55. Cortesão, *Os descobrimentos portugueses* 1: 494; João Martins da

Silva Marques, *Descobrimentos portugueses: documentos para a sua história* 2: 538.

56. ATT-Cartas Missivas, m. 3, doc. 180.

57. ATT-Chancelaria de D. Manuel, livro 6, fol. 39; Livro de Extras, fol. 26.

58. ATT-CC, part 1, m. 8, docs. 72, 116; m. 9, doc. 61; Fragmentos, m. 20.

59. This ledger is number 722 of the Núcleo Antigo collection in ATT.

60. ATT-Núcleo Antigo, no. 722, fols. 27v.–38v. Also consult Appendix D for a detailed analysis of the individual trade items in this ledger.

61. Ibid., fols. 26, 37v–38v.

62. Barros, *Asia* 1: 169.

63. A detailed study of this point may be consulted in K. Y. Daaku, *Trade and Politics on the Gold Coast, 1600–1720* (1970), pp. 146–47.

64. ATT-CC, part 1, m. 13, doc. 48.

65. Ibid.

66. ATT-CC, part 2, m. 72, doc. 26.

67. ATT-CC, part 2, m. 83, docs. 1, 130.

68. Inter alia, cf. ATT-CC, part 2, m. 89, doc. 82.

69. ATT-CC, part 2, m. 77, docs. 31, 85, 132.

70. ATT-CC, part 2, m. 86, docs. 80, 115, 137.

71. ATT-CC, part 2, m. 89, docs. 79, 80.

72. ATT-CC, part 2, m. 92, doc. 91.

73. ATT-Cartas Missivas, m. 3, doc. 180.

74. ATT-CC, part 1, m. 3, docs. 119, 125.

75. ATT-CC, part 1, m. 16, doc. 30.

76. Pacheco Pereira, *Esmeraldo*, p. 122.

77. ATT-CC, part 2, m. 86, doc. 138.

78. ATT-CC, part 2, m. 92, doc. 93.

79. ATT-CC, part 2, m. 73, doc. 112; m. 85, docs. 8, 9; m. 88, doc. 137.

80. ATT-Núcleo Antigo, no. 722, fol. 23 passim.

81. Magalhães Godinho, *L'économie*, p. 236.

82. It would appear that John III was indeed impressed with the accomplishments of da Gama at São Jorge. In 1534 the former Mina captain general was appointed head of the captaincy of Malaca, and six years later, in 1540, Estevão da Gama became Governor of India. Cf. Faro, "Estevão da Gama," pp. 393–94.

83. Magalhães Godinho, *L'économie*, pp. 829–30.

84. Anselmo Braamcamp Freire, "A feitoria de Flandres," *Archivo histórico Portuguez* 6 (1908): 394.

85. Between 1516 and 1519, the crown's contract for Mina slaves specified that the contractor, Antonio Carneiro, would receive two thirds of the price obtained for the slaves sold at Mina. After 1519 a fixed sum of between 5,000 and 6,000 réis per slave was paid by the crown to the Mina slave contractors who delivered their cargoes to São Tomé for transshipment to São Jorge. Cf. ATT-CC, part 1, m. 4, doc. 102; m. 20, doc. 127.

86. Pacheco Pereira, Esmeraldo, p. 121.

87. Barros, Asia 2: 24.

88. Girolamo Priuli, I Diarii di Girolamo Priuli (1494–1512) 2: 227.

89. ATT-Chancelaria de D. Manuel, livro 16, fol. 46; Livro de Extras, fol. 7v.

90. Marino Sanuto, I Diarii di Marino Sanuto (MCCCXCVI–MDXXXIII) 51: 212.

91. Ford, Letters of John III, pp. 228–29, 315–16, 341.

92. John W. Blake, European Beginnings in West Africa, 1454–1578, p. 107.

93. Ibid., p. 83; Marques, Descobrimentos portugueses 2: 472–73.

Chapter 4

1. Barros, Asia 1: 264; translation from Crone, Voyages of Cadamosto, p. 147.

2. D. W. Waters, The Art of Navigation, p. 47; Jaime Cortesão, "Influencia dos descobrimentos dos portugueses na história da civilização," in História de Portugal, ed. Damião Peres 4: 219.

3. Waters, Art of Navigation, p. 575.

4. Ibid., p. 79.

5. ATT-Gavetas, 20, m. 1, doc. 49.

6. Ford, Letters of John III, pp. 153–58, 211–12.

7. Edouard Gosselin, Documents authentiques et inédits pour servir à l'histoire de la marine normande et du commerce rouennais pendant les XVIe et XVIIe siècles, pp. 144–45.

8. Robillard de Beaurepaire, "La marine normande sur les côtes de Guinée," Bulletin de la Société de l'Histoire de Normandie, p. 255.

9. ATT-CC, part 2, m. 234, doc. 86.

10. ATT-CC, part 2, m. 235, doc. 6.

11. ATT-CC, part 1, m. 73, doc. 62.

12. Ibid.

13. ATT-CC, part 2, m. 237, doc. 78; part 3, m. 17, doc. 4.

14. ATT-CC, part 1, m. 80, doc. 74.

15. Ford, *Letters of John III*, pp. 376, 394.

16. ATT-CC, part 1, m. 101, doc. 25.

17. ATT-CC, part 2, m. 217, doc. 119; m. 226, doc. 4.

18. ATT-CC, part 2, m. 227, docs. 29, 118; m. 229, doc. 56.

19. ATT-CC, part 2, m. 231, doc. 36; m. 232, doc. 24; m. 233, doc. 49.

20. ATT-CC, part 2, m. 234, docs. 110, 175.

21. Lawrence, *Fortified Trade-posts*, pp. 62, 108.

22. ATT-Chancelaria de D. Sebastião, Doações, livro 6, fol. 186.

23. ATT-CC, part 3, m. 17, doc. 6.

24. ATT-Cartas Missivas, m. 4, doc. 151.

25. ATT-CC, part 1, m. 89, doc. 120.

26. Thomas Astley, ed., *A New General Collection of Voyages and Travels* 1: 142.

27. ATT-CC, part 1, m. 94, doc. 28.

28. Martín Fernández de Navarrete, *Colección de documentos y manuscriptos compilados por Fernández de Navarrete* 28: 523–25.

29. ATT-Livraria. Collecção de São Vicente, livro 5, fols. 164–69.

30. Richard Hakluyt, *The Principal Navigations, Voyages, Traffiques, and Discoveries of the English Nation* 6: 216–30. Hakluyt is the primary source for the three expeditions of Towrson to Guinea.

31. ATT-CC, part 1, m. 98, doc. 42.

32. ATT-Gavetas, 2, m. 6, doc. 1.

33. Hakluyt, *Navigations* 6: 212, 216.

34. Ibid., pp. 221–22.

35. Ibid., p. 226.

36. ATT-CC, part 1, m. 101, doc. 18.

37. ATT-Núcleo Antigo, no. 722, fol. 31v.

38. ATT-CC, part 1, m. 101, docs. 24, 25.

39. AGS-Secretarias provinciales, Portugal, codex 1467, fols. 325–29.

40. AHU-São Tomé, cx. 1, doc. 86, 3. iii. 1625.

41. This expedition departed from England on 25. ii. 1562; it included the *Minion*, *Primrose*, and several unnamed merchant vessels. The English squadron arrived on the Mina coast on 21. iv. 1562 and was promptly driven off by Portuguese galleys on 28. iv. 1562. Cf. Hakluyt, *Principal Navigations* 6: 253–54.

42. ATT-CC, part 1, m. 106, doc. 11.

43. Gt. Britain, P.R.O., Calendar of State Papers, Foreign, Elizabeth, vol. 95, fol. 247b.

44. ATT-CC, part 1, m. 107, doc. 4.

45. Beaurepaire, "La marine normande," pp. 256–57. The survivors

made their way in this longboat westward toward Brazil. They encountered extreme hardships and privations before finally being picked out of the water by a passing French vessel.

46. ATT-CC, part 1, m. 112, doc. 3.

47. BNL-Fundo Geral, Ms. 8457, fols. 100v–102v.

48. Ibid.

49. BM-Cottoniana, Nero B-1, fols. 88v–89v.

50. John Roche Dasent, ed., *Acts of the Privy Council of England* 16: 294.

51. BM-Cottoniana, Nero B-1, fols. 154–54v.

52. Leon Bourdon, "Deux aventuriers portugais: Gaspar Caldeira et Antão Luis (1564–1568)," *Bulletin des études portugaises* 18: 5–56.

53. BM-Landsdowne, Ms. 171, fols. 143–47b.

54. J. M. de Queiroz Velloso, *D. Sebastião, 1554–78*, p. 76.

55. BM-Cottoniana, Nero B-1, fol. 141.

56. Ibid., fols. 154–54v.

57. Diogo Barbosa Machado, *Memorias para a história de Portugal que comprehendem o governo delrey D. Sebastião* 2: 730.

58. Ibid., p. 735.

59. Manuel Francisco de Barros, visconde de Santarém, ed., *Quadro elementar das relações politicas e diplomaticas de Portugal com as diversas potencias do mundo* 15: 232.

60. BM-Cottoniana, Nero B-1, fol. 173.

61. M. L'Abbé Douais [Marie Jean Célestin], ed., *Dépêches de M. de Fourquevaux, 1565–1572*, pp. 288, 301.

62. BNL-Fundo Geral, Ms. 8457, fol. 104. The names of the first Mina contractors have not survived in the archival records.

63. ATT-CC, part 1, m. 80, doc. 74. In a letter dated 14. iv. 1548, Gonçalo Toscano de Almeida, vicar of São Jorge, felt obliged to write the king to inform him of "shameful things" at the post. He stated that fifteen Negresses were being kept within the fortress and being used as prostitutes by the soldiers.

64. BNL-Fundo Geral, Ms. 8457, fols. 100v., 103–3v.

65. BNL-Fundo Geral, Ms. 3776, fols. 79–83; Ms. 8058, fols. 107–11; Ms. 8457, fols. 100v–110; Ms. 8920, fols. 76–78. Regarding da Silva, see also Queiroz Velloso, *D. Sebastião*, pp. 108, 351, 400, 409.

66. BNL-Fundo Geral, Ms. 8457, fol. 105.

67. Cf. da Silva's complete report on the Mina reforms, dated 22. viii. 1573, in BNL-Fundo Geral, Ms. 2422, fols. 145–48; Ms. 3776, fols. 79–83; Ms. 8058, fols. 107–11; Ms. 8920, fols. 76–78.

68. ASV-Nunziatura di Portogallo, vol. 2, fols. 124–24v., 130–30v.

69. ATT-Cartas Missivas, m. 1, doc. 434.

70. ASV-Nunziatura di Portogallo, vol. 2, fols. 124–24v., 130–30v. In the earlier dispatch, Caligari erroneously reports the Mina caravel's treasure shipment at 40,000 escudos ($\overset{m}{40}$ scudi); this figure is corrected in the second dispatch dated 26. ix. 1575 when the amounts are written out in full, i.e., 180,000 and 400,000 escudos.

71. Ibid., vol. 1, fols. 199–99v.

72. When the contractual system was inaugurated in 1567, the commanding officer at São Jorge took the title of governador in place of capitão-mór.

73. ATT-CC, part 1, m. 101, doc. 24.

74. Astley, A New General Collection of Voyages and Travels 2: 568.

Chapter 5

1. Pedro de Frias, Crónica del-Rei D. António, p. 92.

2. Beaurepaire, "La Marine normande," pp. 258–61.

3. Guido Battelli, ed., "Filipo Terzi, architetto e ingegnere militare in Portogallo (1577–97): Documenti inediti dell'archivio di stato di Firenze e della biblioteca Oliveriana di Pesaro," Documentos para o estudo das relações culturais entre Portugal e Italia 3: 19.

4. ATT-CC, part 1, m. 111, doc. 98.

5. Beaurepaire, "La Marine normande," pp. 260, 262.

6. Frias, Crónica, p. 192.

7. ATT-CC, part 1, m. 111, doc. 98.

8. Frias, Crónica, p. 210.

9. Gt. Britain, P.R.O., Calendar of State Papers, Foreign Series, of the Reign of Elizabeth, January–June 1583 and addenda, ed. A. J. Butler and S. C. Lomas (London: n.p., 1913), no. 142, p. 157.

10. Frias, Crónica, p. 373.

11. Beaurepaire, "La Marine normande," p. 263.

12. Frias, Crónica, pp. 364–65; Beaurepaire, "La Marine normande," p. 263.

13. AGS-Secretarias provinciales, Portugal, codex 1455, fols. 28v., 39, 43.

14. Beaurepaire, "La Marine normande," p. 263; Frias, Crónica, p. 365.

15. By 11. v. 1583, the news of Philip's fleet and its departure had reached Paris. This information was relayed in English dispatches directly to Walsingham on that date. Cf. Calendar of State Papers, Foreign Series, January–June 1583, and addenda no. 309, pp. 339–42.

16. Frias, *Crónica*, pp. 364–65.

17. Azevedo, *Arte cristã*, pp. 75–76.

18. Lawrence, *Fortified Trade-posts*, pp. 108, 116.

19. ASV-Nunziatura di Portogallo, vol. 1, fols. 409, 425–26.

20. ATT-CC; part 1, m. 111, doc. 119.

21. ATT-CC, part 1, m. 112, doc. 3.

22. Astley, *Voyages and Travels* 2: 570.

23. ASV-Nunziatura di Portogallo, vol. 1, fol. 388v.

24. Magalhães Godinho, *Os descobrimentos* 1: 386.

25. ASV-Nunziatura di Portogallo, vol. 1, fol. 409v.

26. ATT-Chancelaria de Felipe I, livro 10, fol. 188v.

27. AGS-Secretarias provinciales, Portugal, codex 1550, fols. 33–34v, 506–12v.

28. Frédéric Mauro, *Le Portugal et l'Atlantique au XVIIe siècle*, pp. 465–67.

29. AGS-Secretarias provinciales, Portugal, codex 1550, fols. 567, 589.

30. Ibid., codex 1550, fols. 673–81v.

31. ATT-Chancelaria de Felipe I, Doações, livro 15, fols. 287–87v.

32. Ibid., fols. 287–87v.

33. Battelli, "Filipo Terzi," p. 50.

Chapter 6

1. J. H. Elliot, *Imperial Spain, 1469–1716*, p. 265.

2. AR-Admiraliteit in Zeeland, no. 2448, dated 22. viii. 1594; W. S. Unger, "Nieuwe gegevens betreffende het begin der vaart op Guinea," *Economisch-Historisch Jaarboek* 21 (1940): 194–217.

3. J.K.J. de Jonge, *De Oorsprong van Neerland's Bezittingen op de Kust van Guinea*, pp. 8–9.

4. BNM-Estado, libro 76, fol. 363. In a letter from François d'Aerssen to Jacques Valcke, dated 4. v. 1600, the former noted "J'ai apprins d'un Portugais peu affectioné à nos prosperites que le reste de vostre flotte se seroit saisi du Château de la Mine; je crains toutefois que vos forces naient pas assez de reins pour tel exploit." J. Nouillac, ed., *Lettres inédites de François d'Aerssen à Jacques Valcke, trésorier de Zélande (1599–1603)*, p. 74.

5. Cf. Herman van der Wee, *The Growth of the Antwerp Market and the European Economy*.

6. Edmundo Correia Lopes, *A escravatura: subsídios para a sua história*, pp. 78–79.

7. Ibid., pp. 68–69.

8. Awnsham Churchill, comp., *A Collection of Voyages and Travels* 3: 474.

9. AR-Archieven van de Staaten van Holland en West Friesland, resolutien van de Staaten, no. 367, fols. 365v., 373–73v.

10. AR-Archieven van de Staaten van Holland en West Friesland, raedpensionarissen, C. Oldenbarnevelt, no. 2608x, docs. b, c.

11. Georg Michael Asher, *A Bibliographical and Historical Essay on the Dutch Books and Pamphlets Relating to New Netherland and to the Dutch West-India Company*, p. xvii.

12. AGS-Secretarias provinciales, Portugal, codex 1476, fols. 125–26v.

13. BAL-Ms. 51–viii–48, fols. 99–100.

14. AGS-Secretarias provinciales, Portugal, codex 1476, fols. 376–77v.

15. Ibid., codex 1467, fol. 268.

16. Luiz de Figueiredo Falcão, *Livro em que se contém toda a fazenda e real patrimonio dos reinos de Portugal, India e ilhas adjacentes e outras particularidades* [1607], p. 59.

17. Cf. Sir William Monson's naval tracts in Churchill's *Collection of Voyages* 3: 471–74.

18. Figueiredo Falcão, *Livro*, pp. 8, 23.

19. Ibid., p. 59.

20. AHU-São Tomé, cx. 1, doc. 3, 24. xi. 1600.

21. Faro's lengthy dispatch to the viceroy and the latter's reply are in ATT-Miscelania manuscritas do convento da Graça, cx. 19, vol. 2E, fols. 235–38.

22. AHU-Reino, m. 1, 26. iv. 1603. The document is in a very poor state of preservation.

23. The vessels were the *Nossa Senhora da Piedade*, which brought a cargo of 19 marks, 4 oz., 6 drams, 6 grains on 14. i. 1609; and the *São Vicente*, with 18 marks, 5 oz., 5 drams, 2 grains on 28. ii. 1609. Cf. Mauro, *Portugal et l'Atlantique*, p. 418.

24. AGS-Secretarias provinciales, Portugal, codex 1476, fols. 148–49v. On the return voyage to Portugal the *Nossa Senhora da Piedade* was set upon by Dutch privateers and captured. AHU-São Tomé, cx. 1, doc. 15, 16. vi. 1639.

25. ATT-Chancelaria de Felipe II, livro 6, fol. 330v.

26. BAL-Ms. 51–vii–7, fols. 22; José Justino de Andrade e Silva, *Collecção chronologica da legislação portugueza* 1: 104.

27. AHU-São Tomé, cx. 1, doc. 3, 24. xi. 1600; BAL-Ms. 51–vii–8, fols. 242–43v; Ms. 51–viii–40, fol. 60.

28. BAL-Ms. 51–vii–8, fols. 242–43v; Ms. 51–viii–40, fol. 60; AGS-Secretarias provinciales, Portugal, codex 1476, fols. 284–84v.

238 NOTES

29. AGS-Secretarias provinciales, Portugal, codex 1476, fols. 146–49v.
30. Ibid., codex 1476, fols. 376–77v.
31. Ibid., codex 1476, fol. 377v.
32. Ibid., codex 1476, fols. 382–83. João Gentil da Silva, *Stratégie des affaires à Lisbonne entre 1595 et 1607*, cites this information on the Dutch attacks on Mina as being included in Victor von Klarwill, *The Fugger News-Letters* 2, no. 745, p. 345. However, this particular report on p. 345, from Antwerp, dated 3. xii. 1604, concerns debates on the union of England and Scotland. A cursory search of both volumes of Klarwill's work has failed to turn up da Silva's reference.
33. AGS-Secretarias provinciales, Portugal, codex 1476, fols. 53–54. The candidates for governor and the number of votes received in the election held by the viceroy's advisory council were: M. Pereira, 4 votes; Duarte de Lima, 3 votes; C. de Noronha, 3 votes; and Manuel da Cunha, 3 votes.
34. Ibid., codex 1476, fols. 125–26v.; BAL-Ms. 51–viii–48, fols. 99–100.
35. AGS-Secretarias provinciales, Portugal, codex 1476, fols. 144–47v.
36. AHU-São Tomé, codex 1, doc. 9, 18. xi. 1606.
37. BAL-Ms. 51–viii–48, fol. 112v.
38. AHU-São Tomé, codex 1, doc. 10, 23. i. 1607.
39. AGS-Secretarias provinciales, Portugal, codex 1476, fols. 376–77v.
40. AHU-Codex 283, fol. 55, 15. viii. 1607; BAL-Ms. 51–viii–48, fol. 165.
41. AGS-Secretarias provinciales, Portugal, codex 1476, fols. 372–75v.
42. BAL-Ms. 51–viii–48, fol. 169.
43. AGS-Secretarias provinciales, Portugal, codex 1466, fol. 207.
44. Ibid., codex 1476, fols. 369–70v.
45. BAL-Ms. 51–viii–48, fol. 239.
46. De Jonge, *Oorsprong*, p. 13.
47. ATT-Chancelaria de Felipe II, livro 6, fol. 330v.
48. BNM-Ms. 9419, fols. 68–68v.
49. AGS-Secretarias provinciales, Portugal, codex 1498, fol. 70v.; Vertoog of remonstrantie van de Bewindhebbers der verschillende Compagnien, handelende op de Kust van Guinea . . . 1609–11, reproduced by de Jonge, *Oorsprong*, Appendix 2, pp. 33–39, esp. p. 36.
50. K. Ratelband, ed., *Reizen naar West-Afrika van Pieter van den Broecke*, pp. lxxxv, 42.
51. The galleys which arrived at Mina in the summer of 1609 were royal vessels built in Lisbon. They were not sent pursuant to stipulations in Rovelasco's contract. This particular contractor of Mina had surren-

dered his lease by 1609, begging forgiveness from Philip II because of his advanced age and paralytic state. Rovelasco had not complied with most of the contract requirements. Cf. AHU-São Tomé, codex 1, doc. 14, 17. iii. 1610.

52. Ratelband, *Reizen*, p. lxxxv.

53. De Jonge, *Oorsprong*, p. 37.

54. Ibid.

55. AHU-São Tomé, cx. 1, doc. 32, 26. ix. 1615; de Jonge, *Oorsprong*, p. 37.

56. AHU-São Tomé, cx. 1, docs. 27 (19. xi. 1614), and 32 (26. ix. 1615).

57. Jean Denucé, *L'Afrique au XVIe siècle et le commerce anversois*, p. 44.

58. AGS-Estado, Portugal, legajo 436, fols. 78–79.

59. BNM-Ms. 9419, fol. 69; AGS-Estado, Portugal, legajo 436, fols. 78–79.

60. AHU-São Tomé, codex 1, doc. 19, 7. xi. 1610; ATT-Chancelaria de Felipe II, livro 20, fol. 240; livro 21, fol. 151.

61. AR-Archief van het college ter admiraliteit te Amsterdam, vol. 1357, 25. viii. 1611.

62. De Jonge, *Oorsprong*, p. 64.

63. AGS-Estado, Portugal, legajo 436, fol. 57.

64. AR-Archief van het college ter admiraliteit te Amsterdam, vol. 1357, 10. xii. 1611.

65. S. P. L'Honoré Naber, ed., *Toortse der Zee-vaert door Dierick Ruiters (1623). Samuel Brun's Schiffarten (1624)*, p. 49; de Jonge, *Oorsprong*, p. 15.

66. AHU-Codex 1192, fols. 139–39v, 13. x. 1615.

67. Denucé, *L'Afrique au XVIe siècle et le commerce anversois*, p. 44.

68. BAL-Ms. 51–vii–6, fols. 168–69v.

69. L'Honoré Naber, *Toortse*, pp. 33, 43, 58, 63.

70. AGS-Secretarias provinciales, Portugal, codex 1512, fols. 104–4v.; AHU-Codex 1192, fols. 167–68, October 1615; AHU-São Tomé, cx. 1, doc. 33, 11. i. 1616.

71. AHU-Codex 1192, fols. 139–139v, 13. x. 1615.

72. Ibid.

73. L'Honoré Naber, *Toortse*, p. 55.

74. AHU-São Tomé, cx. 1, doc. 14, 17. iii. 1610.

75. ATT-Legislação, Leis, livro 3, fols. 30v.–33; José Justino de Andrade e Silva, *Collecção chronologica da legislação portugueza* 2: 119–21.

76. AHU-São Tomé, cx. 1, doc. 79, 18. ix. 1622.

77. ATT-Miscelanias manuscritas do convento da Nossa Senhora da Graça, vol. 6-D, fols. 192–94.
78. AHU-São Tomé, cx. 1, doc. 48, 18. iii. 1617.

Chapter 7

1. BAL-Ms. 51–viii–48, fol. 239; AGS-Secretarias provinciales, Portugal, codex 1468, fol. 29; AHU-São Tomé, cx. 1, doc. 69, 1623?
2. AHU-São Tomé, cx. 1, doc. 32, 26. ix. 1615.
3. ATT-Chancelaria de Felipe II, livro 36, fol. 121.
4. AHU-São Tomé, cx. 1, doc. 36, 23. vi. 1616.
5. Ibid., cx. 1, doc. 56, 14. i. 1619?
6. BAL-Ms. 51–viii–25, fols. 115–16v.
7. Mauro, *Le Portugal et l'Atlantique au XVIIe siècle*, pp. 468–69.
8. AHU-São Tomé, cx. 1, docs. 52 (1618), 58 (19. ii. 1619); codex 115, fol. 45, 16. ii. 1623.
9. AHU-São Tomé, cx. 1, doc. 63, 7. iii. 1622.
10. Ibid., cx. 1, doc. 72, 4. iii. 1623.
11. BM-Egerton, Ms. 1131, fols. 230–30v.
12. AHU-São Tomé, cx. 1, doc. 71, 21. ii. 1623. The most critical need within the garrison was for an apothecary and a priest. Both of these officials had died and their posts were vacant, and replacement of the former post was most urgently needed.
13. BM-Egerton, Ms. 1131, fol. 232.
14. AHU-São Tomé, cx. 1, doc. 84, 10. ii. 1624.
15. L'Honoré Naber, *Toortse*, p. 58.
16. Ibid., p. 62.
17. AHU-São Tomé, cx. 1, doc. 91, 10. vi. 1625; codex 35, fol. 52v., 23. ii. 1623.
18. AHU-São Tomé, cx. 1, doc. 89, 15. ii. 1624.
19. A full translation of this Dutch-Fante agreement is in Appendix II, p. 185, of Kwame Yeboa Daaku, *Trade and Politics on the Gold Coast*.
20. AR-Archief van de Eerste West Indische Compagnie, vol. 39, fols. 7, 10, 11v.; Navarrete, *Colección de documentos* 25: 697–99.
21. De Jonge, *Oorsprong*, p. 18; AR-Archief van de Eerste West Indische Compagnie, vol. 43, fol. 5v.
22. ASV-Nunziatura di Portogallo, vol. 16, fols. 238–41.
23. Ibid.
24. AHU-São Tomé, cx. 1, doc. 101, 31. iii. 1626.
25. AHU-codex 283, fol. 95, 30. x. 1607.

26. AHU-São Tomé, cx. 2, doc. 110, 13. iv. 1628; S. P. L'Honoré Naber and Irene A. Wright, eds., *Piet Heyn en de Zilvervloot*.

27. APF-Scritture Originali riferite nelle Congregazioni Generali, vol. 74, fols. 316–16v.; ATT-Ministerio do Reino, Livros Varios, livro 278, fol. 164v.

28. APF-Memoriali, vol. 391, fols. 36, 45v.

29. APF-Lettere Volgari, vol. 11, fols. 26v., 107–7v.; vol. 12, fols. 5, 15; Memoriali, vol. 391, fols. 36, 45v.

30. The description of this event as reported by a Capuchin father is worth noting. He described St. Francis's appearance as "the abominable color of the Negroes" [Negrorum tetrum induit colorem] APF-Scritture Originali riferite nelle Congregazioni Generali, vol. 83, fols. 386–88v.

31. Ibid., vol. 99, fols. 14–14v.

32. Ibid., vol. 103, fols. 83–84.

33. M. G. de Boer, ed., "Een Memorie over den Toestand der West Indische Compagnie in het Jaar 1633," *Bijdragen en Mededeelingen van het Historisch Genootschap* 22 (1901): 348.

34. Daaku, *Trade and Politics*, p. 14; K. Ratelband, *Vijf dagregisters van het kasteel São Jorge da Mina . . . 1645–1647*, p. lxxx; de Jonge, *Oorsprong*, p. 15.

35. Charles R. Boxer, *The Dutch in Brazil, 1624–1654*, p. 6.

36. BNM-codex 3014, fols. 279–79v.

37. AHU-São Tomé, cx. 1, doc. 105, 15. v. 1634.

38. ATT-Chancelaria de Ordem de Cristo, livro 22, fol. 166v.

39. AHU-São Tomé, cx. 1, doc. 112, 25. xi. 1634.

40. Ibid., cx. 1, doc. 111, 10. x. 1634.

41. Ibid., cx. 1, doc. 116, 10. iii. 1635. The items considered most necessary for the preservation of the post included the following:

> 100 soldiers
> *roupas* for the garrison and Africans worth 3000 *cruzados*
> provisions—2000 *cruzados*' worth
> 50 quintals powder
> 4 pieces of bronze artillery of 16 and 24 pounds (2 of each)
> 4000 cannonballs
> 6 experienced gunners
> 20 quintals cord
> 20 quintals of musketballs and crossbow bolts
> 100 muskets
> 100 pikes
> 50 half pikes

200 iron ingots
200 hoes
100 axes
20 liters saltpeter
1 man experienced in the art of refining gunpowder
2 locksmiths
2 blacksmiths
2 carpenters
forges in addition to 60 quintals of iron and 10 quintals of steel
1 military engineer for fortifications.

42. ASV-Nunziatura di Portogallo, vol. 23 (cipher), fol. 6v.

43. AHU-São Tomé, cx. 2, doc. 130, 12. xi. 1635. The estimate of 50,000 *cruzados* provided for reduced quantities of all the itemized list of provisions above.

44. AHU-Reino, Papeis avulsos, 1636.

45. AGS-Secretarias provinciales, Portugal, codex 1469, fols. 311–11v.

46. AHU-São Tomé, cx. 1, doc. 124, 17. iii. 1635.

47. AGS-Secretarias provinciales, Portugal, codex 1469, fols. 709–9v.

48. Daaku, *Trade and Politics*, p. 74.

49. De Jonge, *Oorsprong*, pp. 46–47.

50. AHU-São Tomé, cx. 1, doc. 169, 16. x. 1638.

51. When Maurice, Count of Nassau, was shown drawings of the fortress following its capture, he termed the Dutch success there as "une chose inouye et incroyable, quand un veut considerer la force de ceste place, ayant double fossé de quarante pieds de profondeur, taille dans un rocher. . . . Il n'y a point apparence d'approcher, ny de miner, tellement qu'il faut confesser que c'est le Dieu seul, qui a mis ceste place entre vos mains." De Jonge, *Oorsprong*, p. 47.

Chapter 8

1. AGS-Secretarias provinciales, Portugal, codex 1570, fol. 24v.

2. AHU-São Tomé, cx. 2, docs. 67 (12. xi. 1635), 138 (19. v. 1637).

3. AGS-Secretarias provinciales, Portugal, codex 1570, fol. 24v.

4. Charles R. Boxer, *Salvador de Sá and the Struggle for Brazil and Angola*, p. 116.

5. AHU-São Tomé, cx. 1, doc. 175, 4. vi. 1639.

6. Ibid., cx. 1, doc. 168, 1638.

7. Michael Hemmersam, "Reise nach Guinea und Brasilien, 1639–1645," *Reisebeschreibungen von Deutschen Beamten und Kriegsleuten im*

Dienst der Niederländischen West- und Ost-Indischen Kompagnien, 1602–1797, part 3, p. 24.

8. Pieter de Marees, *Beschrijvinghe ende historische Verhael van het Gout Koninckrijck van Guinea*, pp. 15, 81–82.

9. ATT-Chancelaria de D. Felipe III, livro 31, fol. 326.

10. AHU-São Tomé, cx. 1, doc. 163, 13. xi. 1638.

11. Ibid., cx. 1, docs. 165 (16. vi. 1639), 171 (16. x. 1638).

12. Ibid., cx. 1, doc. 175, 4. vi. 1639.

13. Ibid., cx. 2, doc. 154, 9. ix. 1640.

14. Ibid., cx. 1, doc. 157, 19. v. 1639.

15. Ibid., cx. 1, docs. 176 (4. vi. 1639), 179 (20. vi. 1639).

16. Ibid., cx. 1, doc. 170, 16. x. 1638.

17. Ibid., cx. 1, docs. 215 (27. xi. 1640), 250 (2. xi. 1641).

18. Ibid., cx. 1, doc. 214, 28. xi. 1640.

19. Ibid., cx. 1, doc. 250, 3. xi. 1641.

20. ATT-Gavetas, 18, m. 1, doc. 7.

21. Hemmersam, "Reise nach Guinea," p. 30.

22. Ibid., p. 31.

23. De Jonge, *Oorsprong*, pp. 48–49.

24. Frazão de Vasconcelos, "A fortaleza de S. Jorge da Mina," *O Mundo Português* 12 (1934): 5–14.

25. A mud-built lodge had been constructed on this site by the Swedes in 1652.

26. Lawrence, *Trade Castles and Forts*, p. 201.

27. Georg Nørregård, *Danish Settlements in West Africa, 1658–1850*, p. 45.

28. ATT-Chancelaria de D. Afonso VI, livro, fol. 269.

29. Nørregård, *Danish Settlements*, p. 45.

30. AHU-Codex 478, fols. 31v–33, 21. iii. 1682.

31. ATT-Chancelaria de D. Pedro II, livro 19, fol. 21.

32. Ibid.

33. Nørregård, *Danish Settlements*, p. 46.

34. ASV-Nunziatura di Portogallo, vol. 38, fols. 242–43v.

Sources Consulted

A. Archives

There exists no single major collection embodying the bulk of documentation relevant solely to São Jorge da Mina and the Portuguese administration of this region. Those Mina records housed in the *Casa da Mina* were destroyed in the earthquake and fire of November 1755 which reduced that building to rubble. The documents which survived had been transferred earlier to other collections between 1482 and 1755. Therefore, it would be fruitless to attempt a description of each collection within the various Portuguese archives as to the extant Mina material. After a careful search, I uncovered a total of about three thousand documents housed in Portugal and other European collections. The vast majority of the documents are now gathered within the *Corpo cronológico* of the Archives of Tôrre do Tombo, Lisbon, and the São Tomé collection of the Overseas Historical Archives, Lisbon. However, even in these cases, Mina documents constitute only about one percent of both collections combined. A similar scattered effect is evident in foreign archives outside Portugal. Therefore, I have chosen only to list the major collections in each respective archive by title where documentation was found. The individual documents may be consulted in footnote citations.

PORTUGAL

I. Arquivo Histórico Ultramarino, Lisbon (AHU).
   a. Angola
   b. Codices
   c. Reino
   d. São Tomé

   The first two *caixas* in this collection are still being processed. Since many letters contain two separate document numbers, the date has been added in footnote citations to the *caixa*'s and document's designations to avoid confusion.

II. Arquivo Nacional da Tôrre do Tombo, Lisbon (ATT).
   a. Bulas
   b. Cartas Missivas

    c. Chancelarias
    d. Colecção de São Vicente
    e. Corpo cronológico
    f. Gavetas
    g. Legislação
    h. Leitura Nova
    i. Livraria
    j. Miscelanias Manuscritas do Convento da Nossa Senhora da Graça
    k. Mesa da Consciencia e Ordens
    l. Ministerio do Reino
    m. Misticos
    n. Núcleo Antigo
III. Biblioteca da Ajuda, Lisbon (BAL).
    a. Codices
IV. Biblioteca Nacional, Lisbon (BNL).
    a. Fundo Geral

SPAIN

V. Archivo General de Simancas (AGS).
    a. Estado, Portugal
    b. Secretarias Provinciales, Portugal
VI. Biblioteca Nacional, Madrid (BNM).
    a. Codices

HOLLAND

VII. Algemeen Rijksarchief, The Hague (AR).
    a. Archieven der Admiraliteitscolleges
    b. Archief van de Eerste West Indische Compagnie
    c. Archieven van de Staaten van Holland en West Friesland
    d. Kaarten
VIII. Rijksarchief, Middelburg.
    a. Staten van Zeeland. Resolutiën

GREAT BRITAIN

IX. British Museum, London (BM).
    a. Cottoniana
    b. Egerton
    c. Landsdowne

ITALY

X. Archivio della Sacra Congregazione di Propaganda Fide, Rome (APF).
   a. Acta Sacrae Congregationis de Propaganda Fide
   b. Lettere Volgari
   c. Memoriali
   d. Scritture Originale riferite nelle Congregazioni Generali
XI. Archivio Segreto Vaticano, Rome (ASV).
   a. Nunziatura di Portogallo

B. Published Sources

Abendanon, J. H. "De Vlootaanval onder Bevel van Jhr. Pieter van der
    Does op de Canarische Eilanden en het Eiland Santo Thomé in 1599
    volgens Nederlandsche en Spaansche Bronnen." *Bijdragen voor Va-*
    derlandsche Geschiedenis en Oudheidkunde 8 (1921): 14–63.
Abreu e Brito, Domingos de. *Um inquérito à vida administrativa e eco-*
    nómica de Angola e do Brasil em fins do século XVI, segundo o manu-
    scrito inédito existente na Biblioteca Nacional de Lisboa. Coimbra:
    Imprensa da Universidade, 1931.
Academia das Sciencias de Lisboa. *Alguns documentos do Archivo nacio-*
    nal da Torre do Tombo, acerca das navegaçoës e conquistas portugue-
    zas. Lisbon: Imprensa nacional, 1892.
————. *Collecção de livros inéditos de história portugueza dos reinados*
    de D. João I, D. Duarte, D. Affonso V, e D. João II. Ed. José Francisco
    Correa da Serra et al. 5 vols. Lisbon: Imprensa nacional, 1790–1936.
Adams, Captain John. *Remarks on the Country Extending from Cape*
    Palmas to the River Congo. London: F. Cass, 1966.
Ahmad, Nafis. *Muslim Contribution to Geography.* Lahore: M. Ashraf,
    1943.
Algemeen Rijksarchief. *Inventaris der Archieven van de Staten van Hol-*
    land en West Friesland en van hun Gecommitterde Raden benevens van
    enige andere Collegien van bestuurder voormalige Provincie Holland.
    22 January 1795. Typed manuscript in AR, the Hague, 1957.
Almeida, Fortunato de. *História de Portugal.* 6 vols. Coimbra: F. de Al-
    meida, 1922–29.
Alvares d'Almada, André. *Tratado breve dos rios de Guiné do Cabo-*
    Verde. Ed. Diogo Köpke. Porto: Typographia Commercial Portuense,
    1841.
Alves, Padre Francisco Manuel. *Catálogo dos manuscritos de Simancas*

respeitantes à história portuguesa. Coimbra: Imprensa da Universidade, 1933.

Andrade e Silva, José Justino de. *Collecção chronologica da legislação portugueza.* 10 vols. Lisbon: J.J.A. Silva, 1854–59.

Andrews, Kenneth R. *Elizabethan Privateering: English Privateering during the Spanish War, 1585–1603.* Cambridge: Cambridge University Press, 1964.

Archivo historico portuguez. Edited by A. Braamcamp Freire et al. 11 vols. Lisbon: n.p., 1903–16.

Asher, Georg Michael. *A Bibliographical and Historical Essay on the Dutch Books and Pamphlets Relating to New Netherland and to the Dutch West-India Company and to Its Possessions in Brazil, Angola, etc.* Amsterdam: N. Israel, 1960.

Astley, Thomas, ed. *A New General Collection of Voyages and Travels.* 4 vols., London: n.p., 1743–47.

Aubigné, Théodore Agrippa d'. *Histoire universelle.* 10 vols. Paris: Librarie Renouard H. Laurens, 1886–1909.

Azevedo, Carlos de. *Algumas considerações sobre o estudo da arquitectura militar no ultramar.* Coimbra: Gráfica de Coimbra, 1966.

———. *Arte cristã na India portuguesa.* Lisbon: Junta de Investigações do Ultramar, 1959.

Azevedo, João Lúcio d'. *Epocas de Portugal económico.* Lisbon: Livraria Clássica, 1947.

———. *Novas Epanáforas.* Lisbon: A. M. Teixeira & Cia., 1932.

al-Bakri, Abu 'Ubayd. *Description de l'Afrique septentrionale.* Translated and edited by Mac Guckin de Slane. Algiers: Typographie A. Jourdan, 1913.

Ballesteros y Beretta, Antonio, ed. *História de América y de los pueblos americanos.* 10 vols. Barcelona: Salvat, 1918–41.

Bang, Nina Ellinger, ed. *Tabeller over skibsfart og varetransport gennem Øresund, 1497–1660.* Copenhagen: Nordisk forlag, 1906.

Barbosa Machado, Diogo. *Bibliotheca Lusitana historica, critica, e chronologica.* 4 vols. Lisbon: Officina de A. I. da Fonseca, 1741–59.

———. *Memorias para a história de Portugal, que comprehendem o governo delrey D. Sebastião.* 4 vols. Lisbon: Officina de J. A. da Sylva, 1736–51.

Barlowe, Roger. *A Brief Summe of Geographie* [ca. 1541]. Edited by E.G.R. Taylor. London: The Hakluyt Society, 1932.

Barros, João de. *Da Asia de João de Barros e de Diogo de Couto.* 13 vols. Lisbon: Regia Officina Typografica, 1777–88.

Battelli, Guido, ed. "Filipo Terzi, architetto e ingegnere militare in Portogallo (1577–97): Documenti inediti dell'archivio di stato di Firenze e della biblioteca Oliveriana di Pesaro." *Documentos para o estudo das relações culturais entre Portugal e Italia.* Vol. 3. Edited by S. E. Henrique Trinidade e Coelho and Guido Battelli. 4 vols. Florence: n.p., 1934–35.

Ibn Battúta. *Travels in Asia and Africa, 1325–54.* Translated by H.A.R. Gibb. London: G. Routledge & Sons, 1929.

Beaurepaire, Robillard de. "La Marine normande sur les côtes de Guinée." *Bulletin de la Société de l'Histoire de Normandie,* 1887–90, pp. 253–65.

Bensaude, Joaquim. *L'astronomie nautique au Portugal à l'époque des grandes découvertes.* Bern: M. Drechsel, 1912.

Benzoni, Girolamo. *Novae Novi orbis historiae.* Geneva: Eustathium Vignon, 1581.

Bigger, H. P. *A Collection of Documents Relating to Jacques Cartier and the Sieur de Roberval.* Ottawa: n.p., 1930.

Birmingham, David. "A Note on the Kingdom of Fetu." *Ghana Notes and Queries* 9 (1966): 30–33.

———. *The Portuguese Conquest of Angola.* London: Oxford University Press, 1965.

Blake, John W. *European Beginnings in West Africa, 1454–1578.* London: The Hakluyt Society, 1937.

———. *Europeans in West Africa, 1450–1560.* 2 vols. London: The Hakluyt Society, 1941–42.

———. "The Organization of Portuguese Trade with West Africa during the Sixteenth Century." *Congresso do Mundo Português* 5 (1940): 31–33.

Boer, M. G. de. "Een Memorie over den Toestand der West Indische Compagnie in het Jaar 1633." *Bijdragen en Mededeelingen van het Historisch Genootschap* 22 (1901): 343–62.

Book of the Knowledge of all the Kingdoms, Lands and Lordships That Are in the World. Translated and edited by Clements Markham. London: The Hakluyt Society, 1912.

Bourdon, Leon. "Deux aventuriers portugais: Gaspar Caldeira et Antão Luis (1564–1568)." *Bulletin des études portugaises* 18 (1954): 5–56.

Bovill, Edward William. *The Golden Trade of the Moors.* London: Oxford University Press, 1958.

Boxer, Charles R. *The Dutch in Brazil, 1624–1657.* Oxford: Clarendon Press, 1957.

————. "Portuguese and Dutch Colonial Rivalry, 1641–1661," *Studia* 2 (1958): 7–42.

————. *The Portuguese Seaborne Empire, 1415–1825.* New York: A. A. Knopf, 1969.

————. *Salvador de Sá and the Struggle for Brazil and Angola.* London: University of London, 1952.

Boxer, Charles R., and Carlos de Azevedo. *A fortaleza de Jesus e os portugueses em Mombaça, 1593–1729.* Lisbon: Centro de Estudos Históricos Ultramarinos, 1960.

Brásio, Antonio Duarte, ed. *Monumenta missionaria africana.* 10 vols. Lisbon: Agência Geral do Ultramar, 1952–.

Braun, Georg, and Franz Hogenberg. *Civitates Orbis Terrarum: Beschreibung und Contrafactur der vornembster Stat der Welt.* 6 vols. 1574–1618. Facsimile edition. Plochingen: Verlag Müller und Schindler, 1965–70.

Brun, Samuel. *Schiffarten in etliche newe Länder und Insulen.* Edited by Walter Hirschberg. Graz: Akademische Druck- u. Verlaganstalt, 1969.

Caddeo, Rinaldo, ed. *Le navigazioni atlantiche di Alvise da Cá da Mosto, Antonietto Usodimare e Niccoloso da Recco.* Milan: Edizioni "Alpes," 1928.

Cardinall, A. W., *A Bibliography of the Gold Coast.* Accra: Government printer, 1931.

Carvalho Dias, Luiz Fernandes de. "As ordenaçoës da India." *Garcia de Orta,* special number (1956), pp. 229–45.

Christensen, James B. *Double Descent among the Fanti.* New Haven: Human Relations Area Files, 1954.

Church, Ronald James Harrison. *West Africa.* 2nd ed. London: Longmans, 1960.

Churchill, Awnsham, and John Churchill, comps. *A Collection of Voyages and Travels.* 4 vols. London: Awnsham and J. Churchill, 1704.

Claridge, William Walton. *A History of the Gold Coast and Ashanti.* 2nd. ed. 2 vols. London: F. Cass, 1964.

Coelho, Possidonio Matheus Laranjo. *Cartas de el-rei D. João IV ao conde da Vidigueira (marquês de Niza) embaixador em França.* 2 vols. Lisbon: Editorial Atica, 1940–42.

Coolhaas, Willem Philippus. *A Critical Survey of Studies on Dutch Colonial History.* The Hague: Nijhoff, 1960.

Cordeiro, Luciano. *Questões histórico-coloniais.* 3 vols. Lisbon: Agência Geral das Colónias, 1935–36.

Correia Lopes, Edmundo. *A escravatura, subsídios para a sua história.* Lisbon: Agência Geral das Colónias, 1944.

Cortesão, Armando. *Cartografia e cartógrafos portugueses dos séculos XV e XVI: contribuïção para um estudo completo.* 2 vols. Lisbon: Edição da "Seara nova," 1935.

Cortesão, Armando, and Avelino Teixeira da Mota. *Portugaliae monumenta cartographica.* 6 vols. Lisbon: n.p., 1960–62.

Cortesão, Jaime. *Os descobrimentos portugueses.* 2 vols. Lisbon: Arcadia, n.d.

Crone, G. R., trans. and ed. *The Voyages of Cadamosto and Other Documents on Western Africa in the Second Half of the Fifteenth Century.* London: The Hakluyt Society, 1937.

Cunha Matos, Raymundo José da. *Chorographia histórica das ilhas de São Tomé e Príncipe, Anno Bom e Fernando Pó.* São Tomé: Typographia da Revisto, 1905.

Daaku, Kwame Yeboa. "The Basis of Dutch Relations with Axim." *Ghana Notes and Queries* 9 (1966): 19–20.

———. *Trade and Politics on the Gold Coast, 1600–1720.* London: Clarendon, 1970.

Daaku, Kwame Yeboa, and A. van Dantzig. "An Annotated Map of 1629."

Dapper, Olfert. *Naukerige Beschrijvinge der Afrikaensche Gewesten.* Amsterdam: J. van Meurs, 1676.

Dasent, John Roche, ed. *Acts of the Privy Council of England.* 48 vols. London: H. M. Stationery Office, 1890–1949.

Davenport, Frances Gardiner, ed. *European Treaties Bearing on the History of the United States and its Dependencies to 1648.* 4 vols. Washington: Carnegie Institution of Washington, 1917–37.

Debrunner, Hans W. *A History of Christianity in Ghana.* Accra: Waterville Publishing House, 1967.

Denucé, Jean. *L'Afrique au XVIe siècle et le commerce anversois.* Antwerp: De Sikkel, 1937.

———. *Privilèges commerciaux accordés par les rois de Portugal aux Flamands et aux Allemands (XVe et XVIe siècles).* Lisbon: n.p., 1909.

Dias, Manuel Nunes. *O capitalismo monárquico português (1415–1549): Contribuïção para o estudo das origens do capitalismo moderno.* 2 vols. Coimbra: Instituto de estudos historicos Dr. Antonio de Vasconcelos, 1963–64.

Douais, M. L'Abbé [Marie Jean Célestin], ed. *Dépêches de M. de Fourquevaux, 1565–1572.* Paris: E. Leroux, 1896.

Duffy, James. *Shipwreck and Empire: Being an Account of Portuguese Maritime Disasters in a Century of Decline.* Cambridge, Mass.: Harvard University Press, 1955.

Elliott, John Huxtable. *Imperial Spain, 1469–1716*. New York: St. Martin's Press, 1963.

Engelbrecht, W. A. "Esbôço das relações historicas entre Portugal e a Holanda." *Congresso do Mundo Português* 6 (1940): 414–35.

Ericeira, Luis de Menezes, conde da. *História de Portugal restaurado*. Edited by António Alvaro Dória. 4 vols. Porto: Livraria Civilização, 1945–46.

Fage, J. D. *Ghana: a Historical Interpretation*. Madison: University of Wisconsin Press, 1959.

———. *A History of West Africa*. London: Cambridge University Press, 1969.

———. "Some Remarks on Beads and Trade in Lower Guinea in the Sixteenth and Seventeenth Centuries." *Journal of African History* 3 (1967): 343–47.

Faro, Jorge. "A organização comercial de S. Jorge da Mina em 1529 e as suas relaçoẽs com a ilha de S. Tomé." *Boletim Cultural da Guiné Portuguesa* 13 (1958): 305–63.

———. "A organização fiscal de S. Jorge da Mina em 1529." *Boletim Cultural da Guiné Portuguesa* 13 (1958): 75–108.

———. "Estevão da Gama, capitão de S. Jorge da Mina e a sua organização administrativa em 1529." *Boletim Cultural da Guiné Portuguesa* 12 (1957): 385–442.

Feinberg, H. M. "Who are the Elmina?" *Ghana Notes and Queries* 11 (1970): 20–26.

Fernandes, Valentim. *Reportorio dos tempos, que contem o regimẽto da declinaçam do sol*. Lisbon: Valentim Fernandes, 1518.

Figanière, Frederico Francisco de la. *Catálogo dos manuscritos portuguezes existentes no Museu Britanico*. Lisbon: Imprensa nacional, 1853.

Figueiredo Falcão, Luiz de. *Livro em que se contém toda a fazenda e real patrimonio dos reinos de Portugal, India e ilhas adjacentes e outras particularidades* [1607]. Lisbon: Imprensa nacional, 1859.

Fitzler, Mathilde Auguste Hedwig. *A secção ultramarina da Biblioteca Nacional*. Edited and with notes by Ernesto Ennes. Lisbon: Oficinas gráficas da Biblioteca nacional, 1928.

Fontoura da Costa, Abel. "A actividade dos descobrimentos desde a morte de D. Henrique até ao advento de D. João II: Pero de Sintra, Diogo Afonso, Fernão Gomes, Soeiro da Costa, João de Santarém, Pero Escobar, Fernando Po e Rui Sequeira." *História da expansão portuguesa no mundo* 1 (1937): 357–61.

————. "Descobrimentos marítimos africanos dos portugueses com D. Henrique, D. Afonso V e D. João II." In *Congresso da história da expansão portuguesa no mundo—publicaçoēs, primeira secção*, pp. 3–78. Lisbon: n.p., 1938.

————. "Fernão Gomes e o monopólio do resgate da Guiné." *Boletim da Sociedade de Geografia de Lisboa* 56 (1938): 189–94.

————. *Roteiros portugueses inéditos da carreira da India do século XVI.* Lisbon: Agência Geral das Colónias, 1940.

————. *Uma carta náutica portuguesa, anónima, de circa 1471.* Lisbon: Agência Geral das Colónias, 1940.

Ford, J.D.M. *Letters of John III, King of Portugal, 1521–57.* Cambridge, Mass.: Harvard University Press, 1931.

Ford, J.D.M., and L. G. Moffatt. *Letters of the Court of John III, King of Portugal.* Cambridge, Mass.: Harvard University Press, 1933.

Frazão de Vasconcelos, José Augusto do Amaral. *Subsídios para a história da carreira da India no tempo dos Felipes.* Lisbon: Mundo do Livro, 1960.

Freire de Oliveira, Eduardo. *Elementos para a história do municipio de Lisboa.* 17 vols. Lisbon: Typographia universal, 1882–1911.

Frias, Pedro de. *Crónica del-Rei D. António.* Coimbra: Imprensa da Universidade, 1955.

Furley, John T. "Notes on Some Portuguese Governors of the Captaincy of Mina." *Transactions of the Historical Society of Ghana* 3 (1958): 194–214.

————. "Provisional List of Some Portuguese Governors of the Captaincy da Mina." *Transactions of the Historical Society of Ghana.* 2 (1956): 53–62.

Garfield, Robert. "A History of São Tomé Island, 1470–1655." Ph.D. dissertation, Northwestern University, 1971.

Gentil da Silva, João. *Marchands et finances: lettres de Lisbonne, 1563–78.* 3 vols. Paris: S.E.V.P.E.N., 1959–61.

————. *Stratégie des affaires à Lisbonne entre 1595 et 1607.* Paris: A. Colin, 1956.

Godard, Leon. "Les évêques de Maroc." *Revue africaine* 2 (1857): 124–29; 3 (1858): 1–8; 4 (1859); 259–73.

Goes, Damião de. *Chronica d'el-rei D. Manuel.* 12 vols. Lisbon: Escriptorio, 1909–12.

Gomes de Brito, Bernardo, comp. *Historia tragico-maritima.* 2nd ed. 3 vols. Lisbon: Editorial Sul, 1956–57.

Goris, Jan Albert. *Etude sur les colonies marchandes méridionales (por-*

tugaises, espagnoles, italiennes) à Anvers de 1488 a 1567. Contribution à l'histoire des débuts du capitalisme moderne. Louvain: Librarie universitaire, Uystpruyst, 1925.

Gosselin, Edouard Hippolyte. *Documents authentiques et inédits pour servir à l'histoire de la marine normande et du commerce rouennais pendant les XVIe et XVIIe siècles.* Rouen: Imprimerie de H. Boissel, 1876.

Gray, Richard, and David Chambers. *Materials for West African History in Italian Archives.* London: Athlone Press, 1965.

Great Britain, Public Record Office. *List of Volumes of State Papers, Foreign.* New York: Kraus Reprint Corporation, 1963.

Hakluyt, Richard. *The Principal Navigations, Voyages, Traffiques, and Discoveries of the English Nation.* 12 vols. Glasgow: James MacLehose and sons, 1903–5.

Haring, Clarence Henry. *Trade and Navigation between Spain and the Indies.* Cambridge, Mass.: Harvard University Press, 1918.

Hemmersam, Michael. "Reise nach Guinea und Brasilien, 1639–1645." *Reisebeschreibungen von Deutschen Beamten und Kriegsleuten im Dienst der Niederländischen West- und Ost-Indischen Kompagnien, 1602–1797.* Edited by S. P. L'Honoré Naber. The Hague: n.p., 1930.

Henige, David P. *Colonial Governors from the Fifteenth Century to the Present.* Madison: University of Wisconsin Press, 1970.

Hullu, J. de. *Algemeen Rijksarchief. De Archieven der Admiraliteits-colleges.* The Hague: Algemeene Landsdrukkerij, 1924.

Imamuddin, S. M. *Some Aspects of the Socio-Economic and Cultural History of Muslim Spain, 711–1492.* Leiden: E. J. Brill, 1965.

Iria, Alberto. "Da fundação e governo do castelo ou fortaleza de São Jorge da Mina pelos portugueses." *Studia* 1 (1958): 24–69.

Johnson, Marion. "The Cowrie Currencies of West Africa." *Journal of African History* 11 (1970): 17–49.

Jonge, J.K.J. de. *De Oorsprong van Neerland's Bezittingen op de Kust van Guinea.* The Hague: M. Nijhoff, 1871.

Kea, R. A. "Firearms and Warfare on the Gold and Slave Coasts from the Sixteenth to the Nineteenth Centuries." *Journal of African History* 12 (1971): 185–213.

Klarwill, Victor von, ed. *The Fugger News-Letters. Being a Selection of Unpublished Letters from the Correspondents of the House of Fugger during the Years 1568–1605.* Translated by Pauline de Chary. 2 vols. New York: Putnam, 1925–26.

Kramers, Johannes Hendrick. *Geography and Commerce in the Legacy of Islam.* Oxford: Oxford University Press, 1952.

Krueger, Hilmar C. "Genoese Trade with Northwest Africa in the Twelfth Century." *Speculum* 8 (1933): 377–95.

Kwamena-Poh, M. A. "The Emergence of Akuapem State: 1730–1850." *Ghana Notes and Queries* 11 (1970): 26–30.

Lang, John. *The Land of the Golden Trade.* London: Caxton Publishing Company, 1915.

La Roncière, Charles Germain Marie Bourel de. *La découverte de l'Afrique au moyen âge.* 3 vols. Cairo: Société royale de géographie d'Egypte, 1924–27.

———. *Histoire de la marine française.* 6 vols. Paris: Plon-Nourrit, 1909–32.

Lawrence, Arnold W. *Fortified Trade-posts: The English in West Africa, 1645–1822.* London: Cape, 1969.

———. *Trade Castles and Forts of West Africa.* Stanford: Stanford University Press, 1964.

Leite, Duarte. *História dos descobrimentos.* 2 vols. Lisbon: Edições Cosmos, 1958–60.

L'Honoré Naber, Samuel Pierre. *De Nederlanders in Guinee en Brazilië.* The Hague: M. Nijhoff, 1931.

———. *Toortse der Zee-vaert door Dierick Ruiters (1623). Samuel Brun's Schiffarten (1624).* The Hague: M. Nijhoff, 1913.

L'Honoré Naber, Samuel Pierre, and Irene A. Wright, eds. *Piet Heyn en de Zilvervloot.* Utrecht: Kemink & zoon, 1928.

Lopes de Castanheda, Fernão. *História do descobrimento e conquista da India pelos portugueses.* Edited by Pedro de Azevedo. 4 vols. Coimbra: Imprensa da Universidade, 1924–33.

Luz, Francisco Paulo Mendes da. *O Conselho da India.* Lisbon: Agência Geral do Ultramar, 1952.

MacDonald, George. *The Gold Coast Past and Present.* London: Longmans, Green, 1898.

Magalhães Godinho, Vitorino de. *Os descobrimentos e a economia mundial.* Lisbon: Editora Arcadia, 1963.

———. *L'économie de l'empire portugais aux XVᵉ et XVIᵉ siècles.* Paris: S.E.V.P.E.N., 1969.

Malvezzi, Virgilio. *Historia de los primeros años del reinado de Felipe IV.* Edited by D. L. Shaw. London: Tamesis Books, 1968.

Manoukian, Madeline. *Akan and Ga-Adangme Peoples of the Gold Coast.* London: Oxford University Press, 1950.

Marees, Pieter de. *Beschrijvinghe ende historische Verhael van het Gout Koninckrijck van Guinea.* Edited by S. P. L'Honoré Naber. The Hague: M. Nijhoff, 1912.

Marques, João Martins de Silva. *Descobrimentos portugueses: documentos para a sua história*. 2 vols. Lisbon: Instituto para a alta cultura, 1944.

Mas-Latrie, M. L. de. *Traités de paix et de commerce et documents divers concernant les relations des chrétiens avec les arabes de l'Afrique septentrionale au moyen âge*. 2 vols. New York: Burt Franklin, 1963.

Mauny, Raymond, ed. "Eustache de la Fosse-Voyage a la côte occidentale d'Afrique (1479–1480)." *Boletim Cultural da Guiné Portuguesa* 4 (1949): 181–95.

Mauro, Frédéric. *Le Portugal et l'Atlantique au XVIIᵉ siècle, 1570–1670*. Paris: S.E.V.P.E.N., 1960.

Mercado, Thomas de. *Tratos y contratos de mercaderes y tratantes*. Salamanca: M. Gast, 1569.

Miranda de Costa Lobo, Francisco. *A acção diplomática dos portugueses nos séculos XV e XVI, destinada à realização de descobertas e conquistas*. Lisbon: n.p., 1937.

Múrias, Manuel. "Os domínios ultramarinos portugueses e a administração Felipina." *Congresso do Mundo Português* 6 (1940): 495–513.

Navarrete, Martín Fernández de. *Colección de documentos y manuscriptos compilados por Fernández de Navarrete*. 32 vols. Nendeln, Liechtenstein: Kraus-Thomson, 1971.

Newberry Library, Chicago. *Catalogue of the Greenlee Collection*. 2 vols. Boston: G. K. Hall, 1970–71.

Nørregård, Georg. *Danish Settlements in West Africa, 1658–1850*. Translated by Sigurd Mammen. Boston: Boston University Press, 1966.

Nouaillac, J., ed. *Lettres inédites de François d'Aerssen à Jacques Valcke, trésorier de Zélande (1599–1603)*. Paris: Champion, 1908.

Nunes Costa, Mário Alberto. "Os arquivos del-rei D. António e de seus servidores." *Boletim da biblioteca da universidade de Coimbra* 22 (1955): 446–538.

Oliveira Martins, Joaquim Pedro. *Os filhos de D. João I*. 4th ed. Lisbon: Parceria A. M. Pereira, 1922.

Pacheco Pereira, Duarte. *Esmeraldo de situ orbis*. Translated and edited by George H. T. Kimble. London: The Hakluyt Society, 1937.

Palencia, Alfonso Fernández de. *Crónica de Enrique IV*. 5 vols. Madrid: Revista de archivos, 1904–9.

Pereira, Gonçalves. *India portuguesa*. Lisbon: n.p., 1953.

Peres, Damião, ed. *Diário da viagem de Vasco da Gama*. 2 vols. Porto: Livraria Civilização, 1945.

———. *História de Portugal*. 9 vols. Barcelos: Portucalense, 1928–65.

————. *Regimento das Cazas das Indias e Mina.* Coimbra: Fundo Sá Pinto, 1947.

Pérez Embid, Florentino. *Los descubrimientos en el Atlántico hasta el tratado de Tordesillas.* Seville: Escuela de Estudios Hispano-Americanos de Sevilla, 1948.

Pina, Ruy de. "Chronica d'El Rey D. João II." In Academica real das sciencas, *Collecção de livros inéditos de história portugueza,* . . . Edited by Jose Correa da Serra et al. 2 vols. Lisbon: Jose Correa da Serra, 1790–1936.

Porter, Philip W. *Benin to Bahia: A Chronicle of Portuguese Empire in the South Atlantic in the Fifteenth and Sixteenth Centuries, with Comments on a Chart of Jorge Reinel.* St. Paul: North Central Publishing Co., 1959.

Portugal, Centro de Estudos Históricos Ultramarinos. *Boletim da Filmoteca Ultramarina Portuguesa.* 10 vols. Lisbon: 1954–64.

Posnansky, Merrick. "Ghana and the Origins of West African Trade." *Africa Quarterly* 11 (1971): 100–25.

Priuli, Girolamo. *I Diarii di Girolamo Priuli (1494–1512).* Edited by Arturo Segre and Roberto Cessi. 2 vols. Bologna: Casa editrice S. Lapi, 1912–38.

Queiroz Velloso, José Maria de. *D. Sebastião, 1554–78.* Lisbon: Empresa Nacional de Publicidade, 1945.

Quirino da Fonseca, Henrique. *A caravela portuguesa e a prioridade técnica das navegações henriquinas.* Coimbra: Imprensa da Universidad, 1934.

Ratelband, K., ed. *Vijf dagregisters van het kasteel São Jorge da Mina* . . . *1645–1647.* The Hague: M. Nijhoff, 1953.

————. *Reizen naar West-Afrika van Pieter van den Broecke.* The Hague: M. Nijhoff, 1950.

Read, Conyers. *Mr. Secretary Walsingham and the Policy of Queen Elizabeth.* 3 vols. Oxford: The Clarendon Press, 1925.

Resende, Garcia de. *Chronica dos valerosos, e insignes feytos del Rey Dom Ioam II.* Lisbon: M. da Sylva, 1752.

Ribeiro, Freitas, and Visconde de Lagoa. *Grandes Viagens portuguesas de descobrimento e expansão.* Lisbon: Junta das Missões e de Investigações do Ultramar, 1951.

Ricard, Robert. *Etudes sur l'histoire des portugais au Maroc.* Coimbra: Imprensa da Universidade, 1955.

Rodrigues, José Honório. *Brazil and Africa.* Berkeley: University of California Press, 1965.

————. *Historiografia e bibliografia do domínio holandes no Brasil.* Rio de Janeiro: n.p., 1949.

Ryder, Alan. *Benin and the Europeans, 1485–1897.* New York: Humanities Press, 1969.

————. *Materials for West African History in Portuguese Archives.* London: Athlone Press, 1965.

Sanceau, Elaine. *The Reign of the Fortunate King, 1495–1521.* Hamden, Conn.: Archon Books, 1969.

Santarém, Manuel Francisco de Barros, 2nd Viscount of, ed. *Quadro elementar das relações politicas e diplomaticas de Portugal com as diversas potencias do mundo.* 18 vols. Paris: J. P. Aillaud, 1842–76.

Sanuto, Livio. *Geografia dell'Africa.* Venice: D. Zenaro, 1588.

Sanuto, Marino. *I Diarii di Marino Sanuto (MCCCXCVI–MDXXXIII).* 58 vols. Venice: F. Visentini, 1879–1903.

Saraiva, António José. *História da cultura em Portugal.* 3 vols. Lisbon: Jornal do Fôro, 1951–55.

Sarbah, John Mensah. *Fanti Customary Laws.* 2nd edition. London: W. Clowes and Sons, Ltd., 1904.

Serrao, Joaquim Verissimo. *Do Brasil filipino ao Brasil de 1640.* São Paulo: Cio. Ed. Nacional, 1968.

Severim da Faria, Manuel. *Discursos Varios Politicos.* Evora: M. Carvalho, 1624.

Shaw, C. T. "Bead-making with a Bow-drill in the Gold Coast." *Journal of the Royal Anthropological Institute of Great Britain and Ireland* 75 (1945): 45–50.

Sluiter, Engel. "Dutch Maritime Power and the Colonial Status Quo, 1585–1641." *Pacific Historical Review* 11 (1942): 29–41.

Sousa, António Caetano de. *História genealógica da casa real portuguesa.* 12 vols. Lisbon: J. A. da Silva, 1735–48.

Suárez Fernandez, Luís, ed. *Política internacional de Isabel la Católica: estudio y documentos.* Valladolid: Instituto "Isabel la Católica" de Historia Eclésiastica, 1965.

Taylor, Eva Germaine Rimington. *Tudor Geography, 1485–1583.* New York: Octagon Books, 1968.

Teixeira da Mota, Avelino. "Fernão Vaz, explorador ignorado do Golfo da Guiné." *Boletim Cultural da Guiné Portuguesa* 5 (1951): 379–84.

Tovar, Conde de. *Catálogo dos manuscritos portugueses ou relativos a Portugal existentes no Museu Britanico.* Lisbon: Academia das Ciências, 1932.

————. "Manuscritos Portugueses existentes no estrangeiro: Os arquivos do Vaticano." *Anais das bibliotecas e arquivos de Portugal* 9 (1931): 87–104; 10 (1932): 45–58.

Trocmé, Etienne, and Marcel Delafosse. *Le commerce rochelais de la fin du XVIIe siècle*. Paris: A. Colin, 1952.

Unger, W. S. "Nieuwe gegevens betreffende het begin der vaart op Guinea." *Economisch-Historisch Jaarboek* 21 (1940): 194–217.

Varley, W. J. "The Forts and Castles of the Gold Coast." *Transactions of the Gold Coast and Togoland Historical Society* 1 (1952): 1–15.

Vasconcelos, Frazão de. "A fortaleza de S. Jorge da Mina." *O Mundo Português* 12 (1934): 4–14.

Verlinden, Charles. *L'esclavage dans l'Europe médiévale*. Bruges: De Tempel, 1955.

Vogt, John L. "The Early São Tomé-Príncipe Slave Trade with Mina, 1500–1540." *International Journal of African Historical Studies* 6 (1973): 453–67.

Ward, William Ernest Frank. *A History of the Gold Coast*. London: G. Allen and Unwin, 1948.

Waters, David Watkin. *The Art of Navigation*. New Haven: Yale University Press, 1958.

Watjen, Hermann. "Zur Geschichte des Tauschhandels an der Goldküste um die Mitte des 17. Jahrhunderts. Nach holländischen Quellen." In *Forschungen und Versuche zur Geschichte des Mittelalters und der Neuzeit: Festschrift Dietrich Schäfer*. Jena: 1915.

Wee, Herman van der. *The Growth of the Antwerp Market and the European Economy*. 3 vols. The Hague: Nijhoff, 1963.

Wiltgen, Ralph M. *Gold Coast Mission History, 1471–1880*. Techny, Illinois: Divine Word Publications, 1956.

Wolfson, Freda. *Pageant of Ghana*. London: Oxford University Press, 1958.

Index